D0216968

Child's Garden

The Kindergarten Movement from Froebel to Dewey

Child's Garden

The Kindergarten Movement from Froebel to Dewey

Michael Steven Shapiro

The Pennsylvania State University Press
University Park and London

Library of Congress Cataloging in Publication Data

Shapiro, Michael Steven.
Child's garden.

Includes index.
1. Kindergartens—History. I. Title.
LB1199.S43 1983 372'.218'09 82-42774
ISBN 0-271-00350-2

Designed by Dolly Carr

Printed in the United States of America

For Susan

Contents

Preface

This book is the study of a nineteenth-century social-educational movement, a collective attempt to bring about change in American society by reforming its educational institutions. It is the story of the men and women who believed that they had special insight into the nature, development, and education of children age three to six. Having studied the ideas of the German reformer Friedrich Froebel, they attempted to bring to America a new institution, the kindergarten. Since their efforts met with strong initial resistance from a conservative society whose child-training notions derived from Evangelical Protestantism rather than Romantic poetry, the American Froebelians were forced to mount an organized campaign for the acceptance of the kindergarten. This investigation records their accomplishments and their failures, their contributions and their shortcomings.

Since the Froebelians themselves believed that the success of the kindergarten movement depended upon changing fundamental attitudes of Americans toward child training, this study is also an interpretation of American social and intellectual history. Initially, I had hoped to write a history that placed the kindergarten movement into the perspective of the new social history, particularly the contributions of childhood, family, women's, and urban history. My original intention is still apparent in many chapters of the book. Gradually, however, I became fascinated with the intellectual universe of the American kindergartners between the Civil War and World War I, an unusually fluid period in American social and educational life. I was impressed with the freedom with which these women (and their ideas) circulated within the seemingly rigid order of Victorian society. The family, the public school, social settlements, normal schools, and universities all provided temporary shelter for the kindergarten. I decided that a full exposition of the ideas and institutions of the American kindergartners would be most helpful.

Almost seventy-five years have elapsed since a similar story has been told. Nina Vandewalker's pioneering work, *The Kindergarten in American Education* (1908), was the progressive account of the victory of curriculum reform over orthodoxy, public kindergartens over private. As the history of a successful movement, Vandewalker's study quickly overshadowed Susan Blow's *Educational Issues in the Kindergarten* (1908), the gloomy tale of the defeat of nineteenth-century kindergarten idealism. Behind the long shadow of John Dewey, the American Froebelians fell into historical eclipse for almost six decades. Revisionist historians, most notably Marvin Lazerson, Selwyn Troen, and Dominick Cavallo, have resurrected the kindergarten movement in order to demonstrate the emergence of a professional, bureaucratic school system. The reputation of the Froebelians fared little better in the revisionist interpretation. Once viewed as educational reactionaries who were able to hold educational progressivism at bay for almost three decades, the Froebelians were now seen as pawns in a larger struggle to control public schooling. In the process the kindergarten movement was truncated, complex social-educational issues oversimplified, and the context of educational innovation ignored. My own point of view, frankly more sympathetic to the Froebelians, is a refinement of the revisionist perspective. I have not ignored their shortcomings—the pettiness of debate, the condescension toward immigrant groups, the willingness to surrender social-reform objectives for professional status. However, I have attempted to show how American kindergartners, in both words and actions, responded to the social and educational realities that confronted them, while working in a social-educational movement.

My interest in the kindergarten movement began when I was a doctoral candidate in the American Civilization Program of Brown University. I wish to record my appreciation for the advice, wisdom, and patience of my academic advisers, William G. McLoughlin, John L. Thomas, and Reginald D. Archambault. The manuscript also profited by the suggestions of my colleagues and students at the George Washington University. The comments of Professor Bernard Mergen and of Louis Kemp, a doctoral candidate in American Civilization, were especially helpful. Professors Daniel Calhoun of the University of California at Davis, Allen Davis of Temple University, and Paul Mattingly of New York University read the manuscript carefully and thoughtfully; I am most appreciative of their advice. A grant from the John Dewey Foundation helped to defray some of the costs associated with research, and a grant from the University Facilitating Fund offset the cost of retyping. I am grateful for the aid of library and archives staffs throughout the nation; a complete list appears at the end of the book. The staff of the American Association of Education International were particularly helpful and hospitable. Finally, I wish to thank my wife, Susan, whose efforts, advice, and encouragement made the labor lighter, the fruit sweeter.

1

An American Setting (1830–1860)

After 1830, most Americans were in general agreement about the aims of early childhood education. The primary objective of all American education was to provide for the spiritual salvation of the individual and for the continuity and moral order of society. The task for the individual was to build a foundation for later learning and useful citizenship by transmitting the social and moral rules of society. Americans had also come to believe that the process of education began early in life—between the ages of two and six—while the child was still in the nurture of the family. Here the child gained the discipline over self and will that would lead in school to reading, writing, and arithmetic. Such knowledge and skills prepared the child for the spiritual and worldly journey that lay ahead. Francis Wayland, a Baptist minister and author whose popular tracts on childrearing and education made him a spokesman for his generation, summarized the chief aims of this Evangelical Protestant theory of early childhood training. "The duty of the parents is to educate their children in such a manner as they believe will be most helpful for their future happiness, both temporal and eternal."[1]

Though Americans in the decades before the Civil War could agree about the aims of early education, there was no consensus about the concepts that defined its method and content. Wayland's brand of evangelical childrearing, while increasingly accepted by most Americans, failed to quiet the many voices in the new debate over child nurture as the older religious and social controls once associated with orthodox religion began to fade in antebellum America. While Americans agreed on the need for mental and moral discipline, preparation for spiritual conversion, and submission to authority in early child training, there was little accord on the role of family members, on the outward signs of conversion, and on the moral nature of the child. The evangelical consensus on childrearing was limited. "The danger is that our liberties will degenerate into licentiousness," wrote one particularly anxious advice writer in 1840, "and that the growing laxity of family government in this country will hasten on the fearful crisis."[2]

The basis of the evangelical consensus, or family government, had become clear long before 1830. A gradual but dramatic transformation of American attitudes toward childhood education helped to pave the way for the new consensus that arose after 1830. This intellectual reorientation was composed of at least three separate elements that defined the moral, psychological, and metaphysical assumptions of American early childhood education in the nineteenth century. First, the moral basis of American early childhood education was changing from Calvinist to Evangelical. Second, the associationalist psychology of Locke was giving way to faculty psychology as the basis of understanding the child's mind. Finally, Scottish Common Sense philosophy was supplanting Lockean rationalism as the underlying epistemology of child training. Together these intellectual changes fundamentally affected the way in which Americans perceived the mental and moral development of their children as well as the meanings they attached to that behavior. In order to understand both the initial resistance of the kindergarten in America and its gradual acceptance as well as the victories and defeats of the Froebelians, we must first understand the Calvinist and evangelical ideologies they challenged.

For almost two hundred years Calvinism had defined the underlying concepts that in turn influenced the method and content of early childhood education in America. The central tenet of Calvinism was that God's power was absolute and that man was totally depraved. Since mankind was born in sin, so Calvinists believed, depravity was innate and its presence could be traced to the earliest years of childhood. The child had simply inherited man's depravity. Just as God's sovereignty was infinite, man's ability to atone for sin was limited. God, however, had elected or predestined some children for salvation and drew them irresistibly toward him at the time when grace was freely offered. Though subject to endless interpretation, these five tenets of Calvinism—divine sovereignty, total depravity, limited atonement, predestination, and irresistible grace—continued until the mid-nineteenth century to determine the basic attitudes of American parents and teachers toward the nurture and early education of their children. As late as 1814, one advice writer reminded American parents: "The root and foundation of misconduct in children is human depravity; depravity in the parent and depravity in the child."[3]

To Puritan parents, who subscribed to Calvinism, the nature of the child was not only corrupt but also ignorant. "They are all born in ignorance," one Calvinist minister wrote in the middle of the seventeenth century, "and this ignorance layeth them open to Satan to lead them whither he will." Accordingly, most Puritan parents insisted upon the education of their children from the earliest years, but were careful not to confuse the role of early education with the Arminian notion that man could achieve salvation through free will and good works. Early education could not guarantee grace, which could be granted only freely from God, yet devotion to ignorance could surely block the path to salvation. The primacy of early education, then, was a simple matter for Puritan parents. To gain salvation, men must understand the doctrines of Christianity, and since children were born in ignorance, they had to be educated. Grace entered the child's soul through the understanding, and it was the child's understanding at which Calvinist education was aimed. As historian Edmund Morgan has suggested, the main business of Calvinist early education was to "prepare children for conversion by teaching them the doctrines and moral precepts of Christianity."[4]

One of the most important aspects of early education of the child was the discipline of the will. Puritan parents acted on the assumption that any expression of stubbornness was the outward expression of inner corruption. The educational implications were clear. Autonomy or self-assertiveness must be completely suppressed during the earliest years or the child would be damned for eternity. In this process of discipline, parents also assumed that their authority was unlimited. So strong was the Calvinist conviction that the will of the child should be broken early that an anonymous writer noted as late as 1814: "Here begin; here interpose your parental authority; accustom him to be denied, and to take it patiently; habituate him to submit *his* will to *yours,* and to take pleasure in gratifying *you,* as well as himself."[5]

The discipline of the will and early instruction worked together, for Calvinist clergymen and parents believed that education should be based on the most efficient transfer of the moral and social rules of the society. Since the rules were derived entirely from the Bible, Calvinists also agreed that Scripture should be the source of all content in early education. The catechetical method of instruction, a question-and-answer drill on doctrinal matters, was most frequently employed. The first obligation of the parent was to provide the child with the rudiments of instruction. Pious fathers paid close attention to the details of the moral instruction of their children, usually catechizing them twice per week. The method of catechizing was, then, the perfect expression of the Calvinist ideology of education, for it efficiently filled the inherently rational but evil minds of children with useful knowledge.[6]

Lockean psychology, introduced into America about 1750, was gaining in popularity because it seemed to provide a way out of the psychological cul-de-sac of the Calvinists. By steadfastly refusing to pit the reason against the emotions, however, the Calvinists had limited the usefulness and appeal of their child psychology, which by the mid-eighteenth century most Americans came to see as outmoded. By contrast, John Locke, in his widely read treatise *Some Thoughts Concerning Education* (1693), proposed that early education should be based upon the primacy of sensation in the formation of ideas and assumed that the child's mind was plastic during the earliest years. It was a mechanistic conception of the human mind, not unlike the Calvinist view, but the stylus of experience transcribed impressions on a blank tablet where previously the hand of God had written through pious parents. By stressing the need for early rational education, Locke had sidestepped the problem of the split between the emotions and understanding. Reading Isaac Watts's popularizations of Locke's treatise *Improvement of the Mind* (1741), Calvinists believed they had a new powerful ally in the fight against psychological dualism. As historian Daniel Calhoun has suggested, American parents welcomed not so much the celebrated notion of the *tabula rasa* as Locke's advice to begin the rigorous rational education of the child at an early age.[7]

Armed with this popular theory of psychology, Calvinist early education found new support among those who called for more restraint than freedom in the early years. These years of the child's development were considered too impressionable to be disregarded. "The great mistake I have observed in people's breeding of their children has been, that this has not been taken care enough in its due season," Locke noted, "that the mind has not been made obedient to discipline and pliant to reason, when at first it was most tender, most easy to be bowed." Locke had proposed not only the early acquisition of impressions and ideas, nothing more than "brain stuffing," but also the formation of character through regular habits of living. "The great Thing to be minded in Education is, what Habits you settle," Locke reminded parents. Not unlike the methods of Calvinist early education, discipline of the mind, the body, and the appetites were necessary steps to rational education. Calvinist parents even found in Lockean psychology a new justification for early spiritual instruction in the home, although Locke himself was silent on the question of the moral nature of the child. Using Locke, then, many American parents in the years 1750–

1830 found new authority to reassert parental control, strengthen family discipline, and demand submission at an early age. Family government, the dominant American theory of child training, to some seemed more entrenched than ever by the beginning of the nineteenth century.[8]

But by 1830 a growing number of detractors, mostly Evangelical Protestants, felt that Lockeanism failed to provide an adequate psychology of early childhood education. They ridiculed the underlying Calvinist tenets of original sin and regeneration as outdated theologically and psychologically. Evangelical parents and childrearing experts wanted Calvinist divines to pinpoint the exact location of the mental component of innate depravity in the child's brain. In the absence of an adequate psychological explanation of evil, evangelicals advanced their own theory that sin arose not from an innate disposition but rather from the circumstances that surround the child. They argued that sin originated in the child's actions and not in his mind or heart. The central issue for evangelicals was the perfectibility of the child. Though predisposed to evil, the nature of the child was perfectible, evangelicals explained.

The lack of an adequate explanation of the child's moral nature was especially troublesome for evangelical parents in New England, many of whom had rejected Calvinism by 1830. They did not like to think of themselves as Arminians though they could no longer accept the notion that their children could be damned at birth with no individual recourse to salvation. Lyman Beecher, a New England Congregational minister, recognized the depth of parental concern. Making the theological distinction between "infant damnation" and "innate depravity" or original sin, Beecher argued that children could be depraved at birth without being eternally damned. Beecher explained to anxious parents that punishments meted out to children at birth were not necessarily enforced in later life. Beecher's views, widely accepted by American parents, in some ways made matters worse. Without the doctrines of innate depravity and divine sovereignty, the parental responsibility to educate had increased without clear moral rules or guidelines for early education. Jacksonian parents, then, sought simple educational methods that would allow them to distinguish between good and evil and cultivate the former without committing the destiny of their offspring for eternity.[9]

By 1830 Scottish Common Sense philosophy was also beginning to attract attention among certain clergymen and educators who would provide some of the answers. It did so by providing a psychological middle ground between Calvin and Locke. For Calvin, the child's mind had contained only one innate disposition, depravity. Child psychology was of little interest to most Calvinist theologians, for childhood remained a brief, unimportant period before conversion and adult responsibilities. Locke, on the other hand, had also minimized the importance of the mental life of the child before age seven. The proponents of Scottish Common Sense, by contrast, advanced the notion that the consciousness of the child contained principles independent of experience and prior to reasoning which could sort out and place in context the manifold impressions received by the mind. Such principles were the furniture of the mind and made up, according to Scottish philosopher Thomas Reid (1764), "what is called the common sense of mankind."[10]

Faculty psychology, a loose-knit theory of the mind derived from Scottish Common Sense, gained a wide audience by the nineteenth century. The new theory of mind postulated the existence of separate mental components, which Locke had called embryonic but felt were less important than sensation in the early formation of ideas. Though Common Sense also viewed the faculties of the child as embryonic or immature, it did help to reverse Lockean assumptions about their importance. In theory, each human action was matched by a corresponding faculty, governing its use. Only the most important types of action, however—such as the conscience, the appetites, the feelings, the passions, and the emotions—were named. The higher spiritual faculties, according to Scottish Common Sense, governed the understanding, the reason, and the will. The number of faculties was limitless though only the spiritual faculties occupied the attention of teachers and parents. Francis Wayland offered perhaps the most comprehensive definition in his *Elements of Moral Science* in 1835, calling a faculty "any particular part of our constitution, by which we become affected by the various qualities and relations around us."[11]

The educational implications of faculty psychology were important, for only the relative immaturity of the child's faculties now distinguished the adult from the child. The child's faculties, like muscles, could be trained to grow through exercise; immaturity was simply a lack of early exercise, training, or education. Faculty psychology, moreover, provided the first rationale for training not only the child's understanding but also the other faculties. "It appears unaccountable that teachers have directed their instruction to the head," one advice writer noted, "with very little attention to the heart." Faculty psychology seemed to provide a means for achieving both spiritual conversion and social stability. The potential social significance of faculty psychology was major, for it now seemed possible to provide for the child's early education without the repression of Calvinism or the social dislocations of revivalism. So impressed were some American teachers, parents, and clergymen with the educational implications of Common Sense that one author called it "the plan of our Creator for giving access to the heart even in that period."[12]

God's plan was given specific educational content in the religious tracts of clergymen throughout the nineteenth century. Perhaps the first to elaborate the implications of Common Sense was the Presbyterian minister John Witherspoon in his "The Religious Education of Children" (1800). Witherspoon began his tract with the prevailing belief in the malleability of the child's mind. But to Witherspoon, sense impressions could not act alone to shape the child's development, for he believed that only when children connected the observed actions of parents with ideas did early education begin. By uniting ideas and actions, Witherspoon argued, the child "acquired many sentiments of good and evil, right and wrong, in that early period of life." The association of ideas by "union or frequent repetition," Witherspoon advised parents, could produce the "most lasting effects," for in the process the moral sense of the child could be trained. Advice writers now thought they could discern the path that led from sense impressions to ideas, to the moral sense, and ultimately to "national characters and national manners, and every characteristic distinction of age and place.[13]

Though the parent was advised to be tender and kind, indulgent but not lenient, authoritarian but not tyrannical, evangelical childrearing did provide for submission to parental authority. To advice writers influenced by faculty psychology, obedience was a habit that could be learned like any other lesson. The child was first taught to associate adult superiority with all actions; gradually the habit of compliance was formed out of association with other ideas. "The most important advantage of lessons—of regular, daily lessons in childhood is this," wrote Louisa Hoare in one popular guide, "that they afford us an excellent opportunity of enforcing habits of self-subjection, diligence and attention, and a taste for intellectual pursuits." As the emphasis of evangelical childrearing shifted toward habit formation, there was little room for lenience among parents. Advice writers like Wayland, Lydia Child, and Theodore Dwight, all influenced by Common Sense thought, were careful to point out the importance of establishing parental authority at an early age. "The authority ought to be absolute," wrote the Reverend John Witherspoon, "that it may not be severe." Francis Wayland was more blunt in his advice to parents when he wrote: "The right of the parents is to command—the duty of the child to obey. Authority belongs to the one, submission to the other."[14]

The cultivation of the child's moral sense became one of the most widely discussed issues in child training at mid-century. Under Calvinism parents could not hope for the salvation of their children without divine intervention. Family government, softened by Lockean psychology, continued to place greater emphasis on divine intervention than on parental influence. Both theories implied that the child was not a moral agent and could not be held responsible for his actions. Common Sense philosophy simply reversed this assumption. Advice writers influenced by Scottish thought proposed the new view that the child, born neither depraved nor innocent, rapidly became a moral agent. Though the path toward spiritual conversion was no longer marked by clear signs, anxious parents were at least assured that the moral sense of the child could be cultivated. It was a comforting notion that fitted the qualified optimism of the age.

The idea of the child's "moral sense" also provided a rationale for the shifting of the burden of education from divine sovereignty to parental responsibility. By isolating the appropriate faculty, evangelical parents could now take steps to correct the child's behavior after making judgments on the morality of any particular action. Since the child's moral sense provided the unique "supervisory authority" over all other faculties, Wayland advised parents that by creating a sense of pleasure or pain associated with specific behavior the child could be made to distinguish between right and wrong actions. It was a behavioristic theory of childhood education in which the moral authority of the parents was maintained over the child's growing faculties. For parents, the theory of the child's moral sense also carried grave responsibilities, for morality itself was defined by evangelical ministers as the use of the faculties as God had intended. "For this purpose, God gave you this faculty," Wayland warned parents; "if you do not use it, you are false to yourself, and inexcusable to God." It was to be the awesome responsibility of the parents, and ultimately the mother; for Common Sense philosophers argued that "there is no school, public or private, for teaching the art of cultivating the heart." The cultivation of the child's moral sense, evangelical advice writers noted, was the "mother's peculiar province" because only she was in possession of the "knowledge of human nature and the art of improving the heart."[15]

The advice literature on childrearing, then, helped to validate the transformation of the mother's role in the home, a social process already well under way by 1815. Formerly, women were principal actors in all of the productive aspects of the family, many functions of which had been displaced by industrialization. "Once her family had looked to her quite literally to clothe and feed them," wrote historian Ann Douglas. "Now they expected a complex blend of nurture and escape from 'voluntary' care." Not all change, however, implied loss. Though American women had always borne and reared children, motherhood prior to the nineteenth century had not assumed a transcendent value in American culture. It was the patriarch who kept a "stern fatherly eye" over the flock, subduing the will, educating, and guiding toward spiritual conversion, and preparing the child for a vocation. An industrializing economy was dramatically changing the division of labor within the household by the nineteenth century.

The household had become a place where the children stayed before they began school or work and where the husband rested after a day of labor. With the father absent from the home for long periods of time, the primary responsibility of childrearing and early instruction by 1830 was assigned to the mother. In the apt phrase of historian Louise Kuhn, the mother became the "gentle ruler" of the home entrusted with the physical, religious, and psychological custody of the children.[16]

With a virtual monopoly on her children's time, mothers were now responsible for both the instructional and recreational activities of the home. Discharging that duty was all the more difficult, for advice writers were sharply divided over the role of play in early education. Calvinists, though waning in influence, continued to take a harsh view of the children's desire for playthings as a sign of willfulness and inner depravity. "No sooner does a child begin to take notice of objects so as to be placed with them, than he covets them," wrote one writer, "and no sooner does he covet, than he endeavors, by all means in his power, to possess them, not by gentle methods, but by force." Calvinists counseled parents to remove all play material as part of the process of instructing self-denial. Other advice writers, like Lydia Child in *The Mother's Book* (1831), advocated a more lenient approach: "As soon as it is possible to convey instruction by toys, it is well to choose such as will be useful." Most parents were guardedly optimistic about the educational advantages of play. Theodore Dwight addressed this audience in his popular *The Father's Book* (1835): "The time may come when good men may devote due attention to the improvement of toys and games for children. There is room for the exercise of much ingenuity, talent and learning, which if well exerted would produce great effects."[17]

The Hartford Congregational minister Horace Bushnell addressed himself specifically to the leisure and recreation time of women and children, respectively. Like other advice writers of the period, Bushnell had come to replace the vision of the active, willful American child acting out inner passions with the view that outer calm reflected a more benign moral state. But Bushnell also shared the concerns of his prosperous congregants, who were disquieted by revivalism but at the same time feared for the spiritual salvation of their children. Bushnell, then, was understandably more interested in the social and religious aspects of Common Sense thought than in its psychological content. The minister, in fact, never fully developed a theory of child psychology and remained content with prevailing descriptions of the child's mind as easily molded, imitative, ductile, and waxlike. Bushnell noted only that the earliest "age of impression" gradually yielded to an "age of language," the threshold of religious education. The child's mental and moral state during this final period, a time Bushnell called the child's "sensitivity" to religion, was what most interested the New England theologian. "The great point is never to jar the child's sensitivity, never to disturb the infant soul," he advised his congregants, "which, like the needle of a compass, points unerringly and instinctively toward its maker."[18]

Sensitivity was not to be confused with passivity, for Bushnell assigned a new importance to the early activities of the child, including play. Bushnell first formulated his ideas on the subject by observing his own children. What impressed him was the muscular, uncontrolled, physical nature of the activity, but gradually he perceived more. "When a child goes to his play, it is no painstaking, no means to an end; it is itself rather both an end and joy." Reflection prompted Bushnell to contrast children's play with the adult's work, which by its very nature indicated a "defect or insufficiency." Reversing the prevailing Calvinist and Evangelical views on the subject, Bushnell concluded by calling play ". . . the highest complete state of man . . . the only perfect activity conceivable." Bushnell's view of play was, however, less radical than it appeared; for "caprice" and "fancy"—sure signs to conservative evangelicals of the inner corruption of the child—also had no place in Bushnell's thought. Since play was, in the end, "a free state of man," Bushnell argued that of necessity it also involved "moral choices" that should be made in the context of firm family government. "If so much depends on the soul's choices, it needs to be made wise that it may choose wisely," Bushnell preached, "and possibly to choose unwisely in order that it may be wise."[19]

In the context of Christian family life, Bushnell's apparently random observations on the role of play and on women and his reading in psychology and education gained meaning. More than other advice writers in antebellum America, Bushnell was able to integrate diverse social and intellectual currents into a coherent prescription for family-based early education. In *Views of Christian Nurture* (1848), Bushnell reassuringly argued that in the quiet nurture of the Christian home, guided by the mother toward Christianity from the first moments of play, the child could experience inward conversion often without the outward emotional signs. In a simple Christian formula, Bushnell attempted to answer some of the most painful social issues of the day. He counseled that the new leisure time of the American woman could best be employed through the supervision of the child's play. Presenting the "smiling" aspects of Christianity was crucial, for the earliest perception of the child often determined "his eventual love of God." At the proper moment, religious impressions "might be permanently and preservingly engraven" on the child's mind. His final reassuring message to anxious parents was that the "child is to grow up a Christian and never know himself as being otherwise."[20]

Not all Americans were willing to accept the limitations of Bushnell's use of Scottish Common Sense. While few parents wanted to return to the older concepts of Calvinism and family government, others thought that the Evangelical revolt against Lockeanism had not gone far enough. To some, the answer to the childrearing problem lay not in restraining the emotional side of the child but rather in probing even deeper into its mysterious, hidden nature. If the moral sense could be cultivated, could it not also be perfected? If depravity was not innate but learned, could not proper early education eliminate evil entirely? The questions attracted a handful of Romantic educational reformers, largely identified with the Transcendental movement. With an enthusiasm characteristic of antebellum Romantic reform, these educators set out to prove the total innocence of early childhood as a symbol of human potential.[21]

No one was more influential as a spokesman for American Romantic education before the Civil War than Amos Bronson Alcott. Alcott, a poor farm boy from Connecticut, entered a career as a country schoolmaster (1823–1828) and soon became a district school teacher in Connecticut, where he implemented several educational reforms. Hoping to make education a more pleasurable experience, Alcott improved classroom furniture, eliminated corporal punishment, and introduced songs and games into the classroom. The innovations, at first cautiously received, ultimately proved a success. What was unusual, however, was that Alcott began to think of himself as an educator-prophet, a person able to reform society through the education of children. His early experience as a country schoolmaster confirmed his unorthodox suspicion that children were in possession of "spiritual truths" hidden from adults. Even before entering the classroom, Alcott had taken strong exception to the lingering doctrine of innate depravity, both in its Evangelical and Calvinistic expressions. "Of all the impious doctrines which the dark imagination of man ever conceived, this is the worst," Alcott wrote in 1831. Alcott believed that the labeling of any of God's creations was not only blasphemy but also a self-fulfilling prophecy. Other American clergymen objected to the doctrine on theological grounds, Alcott on educational assumptions. To Alcott the central problem with American early childhood education was not its Calvinistic preoccupation with sin, but its failure to comprehend the child's ability to transcend evil. Alcott's empirical investigation of his own children, as Charles Strickland has demonstrated, proved that children were often weak and selfish, but were able to overcome their shortcomings through patient and loving early education. "Having made the child perverse by inheritance," Alcott warned gloomy parents and clergymen, "ye contrive, upon principle, to make him so by education."[22]

Alcott was determined to act and soon joined a small band of New England reformers, physicians, and educators interested in the ideas of the Swiss educational theorist Johann Heinrich Pestalozzi. Pestalozzi had divided the learning process into three fundamental steps: observation, description, and naming. The child was first introduced to simple objects and gradually learned to distinguish geometric forms. By analyzing the size and shape of objects, the child learned to distinguish them, eventually giving each a unique name. Mental development of the child, Pestalozzi believed, was simply a matter of change from the simple to the complex. But for Alcott, unlike the European educational reformer, early education was more than simply training the senses. For Alcott, the Pestalozzian object lessons allowed the child to "separate those outward types of itself from their inner connection." The object lesson was only a vehicle to probe the inner spiritual being of the child.[23]

Alcott, moreover, sensed in New England a climate of opinion that by the early 1830s was favorable to educational experiments of all kinds. Accounts of the remarkable success of parents in educating their children at an early age were already appearing in journals and family magazines throughout the region. One account noted that as early as four months, the child could begin to focus on objects and by ten months could, in fact, begin to learn the alphabet with the aid of blocks. So impressed were education-minded physicians like Alcott's brother William with the initial findings that some began to postulate a separate stage of mental development that corresponded with the preschool years. To these advice writers, early childhood was a time of delight in natural objects, animals, pictures, amusements, and recreation; early education should be a time of freedom of action in which the child was a free agent. "A clearer light is falling on the subject of early education, and our methods of attempting to gain access to the mind," one optimistic writer in the *American Journal of Education* noted in 1829, "are becoming more congenial, more intellectual, more gentle, more cheerful."[24]

The immediate object of the group's attention was the establishment of infant schools, an English innovation in education that combined Pestalozzian object teaching and Lockean psychology. In London, the schools had been successfully used as vehicles for the education, and eventual redemption, of the children of the poor. The American reformers, however, had in mind educational experimentation as much as social reform.

Commenting favorably on an early American infant school, the *American Journal of Education* described the endeavor as "something which resembles, not so much a school, as a large nursery . . . the object of which is to provide for its little inmates employment and amusement, not less than instruction." In Boston, the schools soon caught the attention of small groups of socially elite women who undertook the subscriptions necessary to sponsor the new schools. Their dedication made the infant-school movement a small but flourishing enterprise by the early 1830s. Alcott became one of the most enthusiastic supporters of the project, for he thought he saw in the plan a "chance to reduce misery and vice, promote intelligence, virtue and happiness." Open to all classes of society, the infant school was, in Alcott's mind, "among the wisest and happiest agents of Christian beneficence."[25]

In the next two decades, Alcott elaborated his own theory of early education derived from his classroom experience, from observations of his own children, and from European educational thought. His experience in the infant-school movement, however, remained seminal. Alcott fashioned his ideas of early child training on the assumption that the infant already was in "possession of the faculties and apparatus for his instruction." These faculties, Alcott was convinced, appeared much earlier than most American parents and teachers were willing to admit and unfolded in a gradual and harmonious sequence. The process began with the child's animal nature but proceeded steadily to the affections, the conscience, and finally the intellect. Supported by his experience in training his own children, Alcott now believed that the role of the educator was to facilitate the growth of the faculties rather than to "drive or even to lead" the child. First the teacher should appeal to the affections, Alcott advised parents, because he deemed these the "powerful spring which puts the young heart in action, and unfolds all its faculties in the sweetest harmony." In due time, the parent was advised to turn to the conscience, through conversations on topics well chosen to lead the child to reflect about his spiritual nature. In his search for the hidden spiritual faculties of the child, Alcott was more convinced than ever of the need to abandon the catechetical methods of Calvinism and the preoccupation of Evangelical education with training the moral sense.[26]

The Transcendentalist educator put his theories into practice when he opened a school in Boston's Masonic Temple for the education of the children of the city's most respected families. The Temple School was an experiment in Transcendental education, an intent expressed in even the smallest details of its furnishing plan. The headmaster's desk was located in a "commanding position" in the center of the room, while the young children were seated facing the wall so that "no scholar need look at the other." Alcott, who had frequently advised others to teach in imitation of Christ, arranged to have a large bas relief of Jesus "fixed into the book case to appear just over" his head. In the four corners of the room were placed library busts of Plato, Socrates, Shakespeare, Milton, and Sir Walter Scott to serve as constant inspiration to the young scholars. Throughout the classroom were placed "not the ordinary furniture which only an upholsterer can appreciate" but those objects which through daily contact would "address and cultivate the imagination and the heart" of the children.[27]

Alcott chose as his assistant the Salem schoolteacher Elizabeth Palmer Peabody, who had been attracted to Boston by his Transcendental circle. Eager to be at the center of Transcendental thought and educational experimentation, Peabody was ready for the experiment at the Temple School. "I am vain enough to say that you are the only one I ever saw," she wrote to Alcott, "who surpassed myself in the general conception of this divinest of arts." For the opportunity to take part in a unique experiment in Transcendental education Peabody was paradoxically willing to take on the more routine aspects of the school, including procuring students, observing the daily routine, and taking copious notes. As historian Roberta Frankfort has suggested, Peabody saw in the Temple School the chance to test the central premise of her teaching: the moral perfection of the child. Alcott and Peabody could agree that education approached its finest expression when aimed at the "elevation of moral life in society."[28]

Alcott's own efforts were directed toward finding the best methods to locate, stimulate, and train the conscience. The educational experiments took the form of "conversations" with children either in the classroom or in the parlors of neighbors. In both cases, the educational objective was the same; Alcott called the conversations an attempt to "unfold the Idea of Spirit from the Consciousness of Childhood." Using earlier observations of his own children, Alcott had come to view the child's nature as divided into three distinct phases. The animal nature of the child, the first to appear, was expressed as the active child searching for enjoyment by satisfying his appetites. The divine or spiritual side of the child appeared only later after the adult's cultivation of the conscience. "On these occasions, he conversed with them, and by a series of questions, led them to conclusions for themselves upon moral conduct," Peabody noted, "teaching them how to examine their animal and spiritual natures, or the outward and inward life, and showing them how the inward molds the outward."

The educational objective of the conversations, however, always remained the same—the conquest of the lower nature by the higher. Victory could not be simply imposed since the child had to participate in its own education by first distinguishing between its animal and spiritual natures. In this inevitable struggle Alcott was prepared to guide, prompt, and question children through conversations in their attempt to discover the deepest roots of self. The conversations ended when the child was able to distinguish and control his animal nature. For Alcott it was the very beginning of education because the inner evil of the child could now be restrained while the inner good could be released.[29]

Peabody's *Record of a School* (1835, 1836), in fact, placed her at the center of American Transcendental education along with her mentor Alcott. The *Christian Examiner* urged anyone "interested in education . . . and in any degree inclined toward transcendentalism . . . or to a more spiritual philosophy than generally prevails" to read the account of the school. For the most part, Peabody remained the admiring assistant, praising Alcott for creating a school on the assumption "that there is real intellectual activity in these little minds." Throughout the work, Peabody reminded her readers that the older pedagogy was not only intellectually flawed but educationally ineffective, for "nothing is permanently remembered which does not touch the heart, or interest the imagination." But occasionally even Alcott erred and Peabody was uncharacteristically critical in accusing him of "unconsciously leading children into his own views." The liberal Unitarian William Ellery Channing, Peabody's earliest mentor in educational matters, was substantially more skeptical. "I have still doubts. I want proof that the minds of children really act on the subjects of conversations; that their deep consciousness is stirred," he wrote to Peabody. "Then I want light as to the degree to which the mind of the child should be turned inward. The free development of the spiritual nature may be impeded by too much analysis of it." Peabody was learning that the center of educational innovation was often an uncomfortable place and seriously considered Channing's final remark: "The soul is somewhat jealous of being watched."[30]

Some Boston families were more concerned with the social propriety than with the educational effectiveness of the Temple School. In particular, rumors circulated that Alcott had crossed the lines of public decency in his conversation about human reproduction which stemmed from a lesson on the life and birth of Christ. At first, rallying to her mentor's defense, Peabody explained in the second edition of *Record of a School* (1836) that Alcott had only intended a reference to birth as a "spiritual fact," in the Wordsworthian sense. The remarks, however, failed to quiet the school's critics, the most outspoken of whom now saw it not only as indecent but also obscene and heretical. Alcott, whose gaze was apparently fixed on the child and the heavens, failed to sense the growing public outrage and, in fact, intended to publish the full account of the offensive lesson along with others in his *Conversations with Children on the Gospels* (1836, 1837). When Peabody realized that the book would make matters worse, she demanded a disclaimer in the preface which portrayed her as "a passive instrument . . . especially when she felt that she differed from Mr. Alcott on the subject in hand, as was sometimes the case." For Peabody, the decision was a difficult one, for at stake was her reputation for moral purity, an asset which she ultimately judged more important to a female educator in antebellum America than a reputation for educational innovation. She was right. Amidst sharp public outcry and declining enrollments, Alcott was forced to close the school in 1839, bringing to an end the first experiment in Transcendental education in America.[31]

The intellectual legacy of the first American debate over the early education of the child (1830–1860) was complex. Clearly, by the time the debate ended, few approved of the Calvinist tenets of innate depravity, will breaking, and the primacy of literacy. At the same time, the radical departures of the American Transcendentalists had attracted few converts, for most American parents refused to assume the innocence of childhood and declined to make spiritual self-knowledge the objective of early education. Still there was a common body of assumptions, values, and ideas about childhood education to which most Americans subscribed. Though a wide gulf separated Wayland's admonitions for stern family government from Bushnell's plea for a more gentle Christian nurture, most parents of the evangelical persuasion could still agree that spiritual salvation and social stability were the central aims of early education in America. Perhaps in reaction to the Calvinist and Transcendentalist extremes, liberal Protestants at the center began by 1860 to proffer an American vision of early education that assigned central importance to the child, mother, and family. But even Bushnell's qualifications raised as many new questions about the exact method and content of early education as it answered about the underlying conceptions of childhood. When should the child's education begin? Was the family or school the proper setting for early education? What were the relative roles of teacher and mother? What was the proper balance between mental and moral training? Should early education favor freedom or restraint, work or play? What were the relative claims of the individual and society in early education? In seeking answers to these vexing questions—questions that reached beyond early education to social policy—Americans, by the eve of the Civil War, were at least ready to listen to the ideas and consider the institutions of European educational reformers. None would be more triumphantly heralded and vigorously promoted after the war than the educational and social theories of Friedrich Froebel. Even

Alcott, never a supporter of European educational panaceas, wrote in 1860: "The German Kindergarten or child's garden is attracting attention with us. It is the happiest play teaching ever thought of, and the child's Paradise regained for those who have lost theirs." There was as much history as prophecy in his remarks.[32]

2

German Hopes (1848–1852)

Like Alcott's thought, Froebel's educational ideas emerged from a conflict with the strict religious instruction imposed by his father, a Lutheran minister. Froebel later recalled his unhappy childhood, the "gloomy lowering dawn," after the death of his mother. "This loss, a hard blow to me, influenced the whole environment and development of my being: I consider that my mother's death decided more or less the external circumstances of my whole life." But life in the small rural parsonage was also the source of certain childhood joys which Froebel always associated with the "old-fashioned Christian life." His apprenticeship to a forester at age fifteen marked the end of his painful youth. With the inspiration of the popular romantic poets, Goethe and Schelling, Froebel found a new solace in the woods, a period which he called his "religious communion with nature." He later studied briefly at the Universities of Jena, Gottingen, and Berlin; he was excited by the idealistic currents of the day but showed little patience for formal study. Restless and curious, he left the university to find work as a land surveyor, estate manager, forest-department official, and museum assistant before settling down to become a tutor and rural schoolmaster. But Froebel took to heart his father's disapproval of his "shiftlessness" and his inability to "confront the world" by choosing a career, a failure that he attributed to his own "undeveloped state of mental culture."[1]

The transformation of Friedrich Froebel from teacher to educator-prophet came two years later after he attended the Yverdon Institute

(1808–1810) operated by Pestalozzi. He accepted the central principle of Pestalozzian object teaching and soon became an ardent advocate of educational reform. He agreed with Pestalozzi that all education began with sense perception and that objects could be effectively used to excite the child's interest in learning, but he was concerned that the Pestalozzian object lessons alone missed the "spiritual mechanism" that underlies early education. "Several subjects of teaching and education highly important to the all-around harmonious development of man seemed to me thrust far too much into the background, treated in stepmotherly fashion, and superficially worked out," he later wrote in his autobiography. Froebel was searching for a means to unite the child's soul with the faculties of reason, feeling, volition, and perception. The sense-dominated theories of Pestalozzi had stopped short of achieving this spiritual objective. "Pestalozzi takes man existing only in his appearance on earth," Froebel wrote, "but I take man in his eternal being, in his eternal existence."[2]

Froebel preferred idealism to associationalism in constructing his own educational system. At the center of Froebel's educational system lay the idea that mankind was the physical embodiment of God's reason. "In all things there lives and reigns an eternal law," Froebel wrote; "This unity is God." Like the American Transcendentalists, Froebel believed that the material world was only the outward expression of the inner divinity of all things; but he did not regard the universe as static. In a world of constant change in which both living and nonliving matter continually "unfolded their inner essence," childhood held a special meaning, for it was a relatively uncorrupted embodiment of God's reason.

Thus Froebel recognized a correspondence between the evolution of natural forms and the stages of the child's growth, and he considered this perception his most important intellectual contribution. Since all things unfolded their nature according to a divine prepatterned plan, the key to the puzzle of the education of the child lay in discovering the relationship between the child's outer and inner worlds. Froebel elaborated this central postulate in a series of miscellaneous pamphlets and educational tracts, later published as *The Education of Man* (1826). Ponderous in style, obscure in philosophy, and frequently repetitious, Froebel's works were, nevertheless, marked by rare insight into the child's early development. To Froebel, education was simply the process of "leading the child to a clear self-consciousness of the inner law of Divine Unity, and in teaching him the ways and means thereto." His intuitive methods and rhetorical flourishes led one contemporary critic to comment, "The man is actually something of a Seer. He looks into the innermost thoughts of the child as no one else has done." It was an accurate assessment.[3]

Froebel's major contribution was to divide the process of early education between birth and age six into discrete stages of physical and mental development—infancy, early childhood, and childhood. The mental and physical developments, moreover, helped to define the educational tasks at each stage. Moreover, Froebel devised various educational exercises related to each stage. For example, even before the child left his cradle, he was taught simple grasping and holding lessons. Infancy ended when the child became less involved with his own body, and early childhood began with gradual maturation of the intellectual faculties. When the child's will and intellect were sufficiently strong, the child entered school for the cultivation of the intellect, marking the beginning of childhood. Froebel was convinced that his stages were developmental, for each educational task corresponded to an observed mental, physical, or spiritual change in the child. Froebel thus believed he was illuminating "the progressive course of development and education of the child in a logical sequence."[4]

Froebel also rejected the religious strictures of his own childhood and declared that the child, essentially good by nature, was a bundle of possibilities at the beginning of life. "Great was my joy when I believed I had proved completely to my own satisfaction that I was not destined to go to hell," he later recalled. "The stony, oppressive dogmas of orthodox theology I very early explained away." Froebel, however, did allow for certain inner dispositions which could be perverted, through experience or education, toward evil. For example, if not properly attended, the child's disposition to cry could lead to the "most hideous fault" of childhood—willfulness. It was an observation that reflected Froebel's Calvinist upbringing, but he was quick to add that the child's will should never be broken, only properly educated. "All these shortcomings and wrongdoings have their origins in and result from the inability of the parents to distinguish between the child's nature and his essence," Froebel wrote in *The Education of Man*. While the essence of childhood was innocence, the nature of children, or their outward behavior, could sometimes appear evil. "The shortcomings will at last disappear," Froebel advised parents, "although it may involve a hard struggle against habit, but not against depravity in man."[5]

The years between four and six, between the family and the school, most fascinated Froebel. Having outgrown the clumsiness of his infancy and with a new command of language, the child had achieved acute mental activity. Froebel, however, was also disturbed by the emotional and intellectual limits of the cradle and the nursery. In the atmosphere of love that surrounded the family, Froebel feared that parents would be unable to "check and deny" the evil impulses of the child and cultivate his deeper, inner good nature, though he was convinced that the child was not ready for the passive obedience the school discipline required. He reasoned that early education required an institution especially suited to the "wealth, abundance, and vigor of the inner and outer life" of childhood.[6]

Froebel considered several social institutions as remedies. The older day nurseries and orphanages had educated homeless children before German public education, but Froebel rejected the "limited, defensive and negative action of a custodial institution" in favor of a "large, educating, and developing one." Froebel was also distrustful of the various outdoor utopian schemes advocated by the popularizers of Rousseau. He sought to protect the child, then, both from the restraints of a custodial institution and from the dangers of nature in the raw. Froebel later described his search for the elusive "institution for fostering family life" through "self-instruction, self-education, and self-cultivation of mankind." Ultimately, he favored the creation of a new social institution of education—to take its place midway between infancy and childhood, the family and the school, and nature and society.[7]

Froebel called his new creation a *kindergarten* or child garden, a neologism which he thought captured the essential elements of his Romantic theory of education. First, the kindergarten was to be an institution where the child could congregate with his peers outside the restraints of the family and the school. At the same time, the protective gardenlike atmosphere of the kindergarten would guard the child against the corrupting influence of society and the dangers of nature. In the child garden, the mental, physical and social faculties of the child could be cultivated, unfolded and ripened. In the end the term *kindergarten* signified for Froebel more than an institution—it was an approach to early child training. "I desire that in the future all institutions in Germany for the education and care of little children, all that are based on games and occupations, all that worthily correspond to the child's nature and the man's being, may be called by this name *kindergarten,*" he wrote to his cousin in 1840.[8]

Froebel was careful to point out that the educational advantages of the kindergarten did not all come from the spontaneity of the child. For the first time in the kindergarten the child was placed under the instruction of a trained adult—a woman who was neither as emotionally attached as a mother nor as emotionally distant as a primary teacher. Training and expertise in child development and care were to be counterparts of sensitivity to children in the kindergarten. A trained "kindergartner" was placed in charge of the child's physical, social, and spiritual development in a community of his peers. "Now the aim of the institution is to make the needs and requirements of the child-world . . . correspond to the present stage of humanity," Froebel concluded, "and to provide appropriate plays and means of employment, and consequently of instruction and cultivation."[9]

A pleasant physical environment was an important part of the kindergarten, and Froebel recommended the use of an adjoining garden or at least a brightly painted, sunny room filled with plants, animals, and pictures. He warned that a kindergarten should not be furnished with adult tables and chairs or cramped into a space too small for the vigorous activities of childhood. Unlike the traditional classroom, the kindergarten was to be furnished with desks and chairs scaled to the size of the child and provided with room enough for the romping of young children. Froebel envisioned a space filled with the sights, sounds, and objects of early childhood. Not hornbooks and catechisms, but rather the simple shapes, sizes, and colors which delighted the child and formed the basis of early impressions comprised the stock materials of the kindergarten.[10]

Froebel called these simple geometrical playthings the "gifts" and "occupations." According to the German idealist, these forms were the metaphysical core of early education which Pestalozzi had failed to see "beneath" the outward sense impressions created by objects. As historian Dominick Cavallo has pointed out, Froebel's educational insights closely paralleled those of the American Transcendentalists. Both German and American romantic educators believed that the playthings of young children were, in fact, "objectified properties of mind." By presenting the forms to a child in an orderly sequence, the kindergarten teacher could prompt the child to intuit metaphysical patterns previously thought to be beyond the child's comprehension. Early education was really a problem in applied philosophy, and the educational apparatus simply a pedagogical tool to help the teacher reconnect "alienated" thought and sensual information. The kindergarten apparatus, Froebel believed, was itself a material expression of his metaphysic of education—"man lives in a world of objects which influence him and which he wishes to influence."[11]

Since education and development were coextensive, training could begin at the earliest moment. In fact, when the child entered the kindergarten he was already familiar with the first two gifts—solid geometric forms that had been used by the mother in the cradle to cultivate the child's early sensual and physical development. For example, Froebel's first gift was a colored woolen ball used in exercises initiated by the mother not only to develop the child's senses and muscles but also to "confirm, strengthen and clear up in the mind of the child feelings and perceptions . . . and awaken spirit and individuality." Froebel's followers believed that even in the cradle the child was able to intuit the concepts of "freedom" and "unity" symbolized in the motion and the sphericity of the swinging ball.

By the age of five, the child was ready for the more complicated forms and exercises of the kindergarten. Froebel astutely observed that "children of five years . . . can build in common at the same time." Unlike the geometrically simple solids of infancy, kindergarten gifts three, four, and five were more complicated dissected cubes or building blocks with which the child was taught to build. "As the divisions of the cube increase in variety and complexity, he finds he can produce more and more perfect forms," from which association leads to the "idea of organic connection" as the "regulator of instinctive activity," wrote one of Froebel's commentators. After mastering the prescribed manipulations of the blocks, the child was introduced to a second educational sequence, the occupations. In the weaving, bead-stringing, sewing, and stick-laying exercises, the child was now taught to create his own forms. But the educational theory behind the occupations remained the same; the physical, cognitive, and social development of the child were related in an elaborate pedagogical program that presumably reflected underlying metaphysical realities.[12]

The seemingly simple games and play were also linked to the fundamental moral lessons of the kindergarten: individual and social order. For example, when the child was given his third gift, a building cube, he was taught to carefully remove all of its contents. The teacher might interrupt to point out the difference between the original unity of the cube and the elements that composed it, comparing the child to the class, the individual to society. No random spill was permitted, for each small part belonged to the whole, and, even in play, the child was taught to respect the underlying order of the material world. As the child advanced to more complicated exercises, such as building houses and other structures, he was asked to reflect upon larger patterns of order in society. No Froebelian exercise was complete, however, until the blocks or all the games were returned to their containers—a final, concrete reminder to the child of God's plan for moral and social order.[13]

Instruction in the kindergarten gifts and occupations also included other children. The spontaneous activity of the child, or "self-activity," first given expression in the gifts and occupations, was finally harnessed in the songs and games of the kindergarten, which often included moral lessons. For example, a morning lesson in the use of a building block might be concluded by a game of singing and marching with other children. Most Froebelian games began with a large circle. Children were instructed in rhythmic movements while a trained kindergartner accompanied the game on the piano. Gradually the original large circle was broken into smaller circles, but the game would not end until all the children were again merged into a single circle. "I am convinced that in this way we may not only arouse and illuminate the ethical feeling of the child, but also strengthen it and elevate it into practical activity; and, finally, that this practical moral activity will recoil with blessed effect upon the nature and development of religious aspiration," Froebel wrote. The abstract and individual play with the building block had been generalized and underscored by the "social principle" of the game. This educational tenet in particular attracted the Transcendentalists, for they believed that the songs and games of the kindergarten provided the essential counterpoise to the gifts and occupations. Social harmony tempered self-direction. In the process, the child had learned the simple social rule that "every part is necessary to the whole."[14]

Froebel grounded his educational plans in his perceptions of the social position of women in Germany. At the heart of his understanding of the "woman question" was his belief that modern industrial society had separated the roles of "mother" and "woman," previously bonded in "primordial union." The unfortunate division of roles, Froebel had come to believe, affected both the poor and the rich, both women of leisure and working women. He observed that upper-class German women in the mid-nineteenth century had almost entirely abandoned their role as mothers, preferring to delegate responsibilities to wet nurses, governesses, and teachers. For the working woman, on the other hand, the "struggle for existence" separated her from the daily tasks of motherhood, for she was forced to place her children in day-care facilities. Once lost, childrearing skills were difficult to regain; Froebel showed how the two classes were related through a highly developed economy of domestic services. For "rich or poor, high or low, cultured or unlettered," Froebel argued, "the imperfect attainment of ends by the one class brings about disadvantage to the other." Ironically, women from diverse social backgrounds came to share the same misfortune: poor child management. In an open letter to the women of Germany, Froebel railed against the "shameful ill-management of children," which he attributed to "ignorance, perversity, distortion, and even the absence of womanly child-loving sensibility."[15]

The separation of women's roles, however, was not irreversible. Froebel, in fact, made the search for a "means to mediate" the women's selves and restore the "primordial union" a central objective in his educational plans. He early dismissed the use of political action, though at times he appeared sympathetic to the suffrage movement. While deploring the "present position" of women in society, when woman's work was "so rigidly defined by man's will, even to the fettering of some of its noblest impulses," Froebel remained convinced that "emancipation" would come through the reform of childrearing and early education and not through politics. He advised that emancipation was not something that could be wrested from a male-dominated world—women would have to work out their "own salvation through their own labor." In fact, Froebel defined emancipation as "reconciliation and contentment richer than the common use of the term." The search for freedom through social feminism, then, became a question of mediating "the external relations of women's lives, the civic and social demand upon them, and the claim of the child's being." Froebel soon became convinced that a statement of a "simple easily managed method of children's care" was only the first step in restoring dignity to women's most sacred role. The training of women in his principles of childrearing and early education—first in Germany and later throughout the world—became Froebel's self-proclaimed mission.[16]

The centerpiece of his educational scheme was the Universal German Kindergarten (1840), an elaborate plan for the training of women in kindergarten principles and techniques. In his plan, Froebel proposed gathering into one institution the scattered training institutions for nurses, domestic servants, teachers, and charity workers. The facility was to be located in the small German town of Blankenburg, where the educator planned to locate a model kindergarten, a training institute for kindergarten teachers, a publishing house for kindergarten tracts, and a factory for kindergarten equipment. He planned to underwrite the venture by first enlisting women throughout Germany to become "shareholders" in the kindergarten center. Froebel even suggested that middle-class women could pay their own way by organizing themselves into "Ladies Working Societies" that would produce handcrafts. Labor and materials would be contributed and the proceeds could be used to purchase shares in the school, at the same time demonstrating the "true German womanly spirit." These were to be no "mean trade or professional unions," but rather small unions of middle-class parents and teachers who would spread the kindergarten message through "harmonious cooperation" of families and schools.[17]

Froebel was particularly interested in training American women who recognized their role as mothers and teachers more than did women in other nations but who considered school work only as "a convenient pastime between their own years of school and marriage." Though Froebel had not visited the United States, his observations were startlingly close to the experience of Mt. Holyoke women who, as historian David Allmendinger has shown, were searching for a "bridge over the longer interval needed to start their own homes and families." To Froebel America offered an ideal opportunity for the establishment of the kindergarten training institutes. The training course needed in America, the German reformer assumed, was not for either nurses or kindergarten teachers, but rather for mothers; in it they could be instructed in the physical care of children and in self-improvement through play. In 1848 Froebel wrote to his nephew Julius in America to inquire about the possibility of establishing an American kindergarten training center which would be operated by women familiar with American customs and fluent in English. "Everything should be prepared in America and the way, so to speak, be paved, in order that the work might commence properly," the reformer noted.[18]

Froebel had earlier recognized the potential of America for the growth of the kindergarten. "We must emigrate to the country that offers all the conditions for the existence of a genuine human family life which renders the development of pure humanity possible, where such a life is at least sought and can freely develop," he wrote as early as 1826 in *The Education of Man*. "All those conditions we find in America." His vague commitment was reinforced after meeting a German-American physician in Heidelberg in 1844 who was studying the "newest European discoveries in his science, meaning to introduce them in America." "He urged me most earnestly to go to America, where he was sure that I would reap an immediate harvest from my self-sacrificing labours." It was a conversation Froebel never forgot. Like other educational utopian thinkers of nineteenth-century Europe, Froebel continued to speculate about the possibilities of the New World and gave America a central place in his scheme for the universal "regeneration of mankind."[19]

The Revolution of 1848 and the subsequent conservative backlash aimed at social-educational movements of all political hues increased Froebel's interest in the United States as a home for the kindergarten. Carl Froebel, the educator's brother, made matters worse for the kindergarten movement when, writing without Froebel's permission, he made an implicit comparison between revolutionary politics and education in his pamphlet *High Schools for Young Ladies and Kindergartens* (1851). Shortly after its publication, the Prussian government banned kindergartens as an arm of the socialist movement, and despite the influence of Froebel's conservative followers, he was unsuccessful in having the prohibition rescinded. "If they will not recognize and support my cause in my own fatherland," Froebel wrote, "I will go to America where a new life is unfolding itself and [the] new education of man corresponding with it will find footing."[20]

Froebel never emigrated nor realized his utopian dreams for spreading the kindergarten to America. His Universal Education Institution, located in the small southern German town of Keilhau, operated a model kindergarten for several years, published some pamphlets, and trained a few kindergarten teachers. The modest enterprise, however, never attracted the

10,000 kindergarten disciples from Europe and America whom Froebel envisioned. Froebel's vision of a "Kindergarten and Training School for Kindergartners in America" also faded. In utter despair at the closing of the kindergartens in his homeland, Froebel desperately inquired about the possibility of establishing kindergartens in the United States. "I have sent off a very definite statement to the United States, where I have a most estimable energetic brother-in-law," he wrote to a friend in 1852. "I have put my trust in him from youth up, and I am without fear or trembling, without nervousness or apprehension as to my personal concerns, therefore." A more candid glimpse of the plight of the aging prophet is clear in the correspondence with his nephew Julius Froebel, never a supporter of the kindergarten cause, who lived in America between 1850 and 1857 after fleeing Vienna for political reasons. He corresponded with his uncle about his visions of social-educational reform and American realities. America was a country which "rewarded work," Julius advised, and "those whose major loves were beer, cigars, and music should remain at home." Perhaps chiding his visionary uncle, he noted that America had no room for "dreamers and romantic weaklings." Froebel died June 21, 1852, an embittered man whose hopes for social-educational reform in Germany were extinguished by the political banning of the kindergarten and whose plans for the transfer of the kindergarten to America were largely unrealized.[21]

3

American Realities (1848–1872)

Froebel's despair was premature. Always sensitive to the latest trends in German philosophy, literature, and education, the *Christian Examiner* introduced its American readership to the Froebelian kindergarten in 1859. According to the liberal Unitarian paper, Germany already had led the way in the fields of Biblical criticism, natural history and *belles lettres*, and now was pioneering in a new system of early education that promised to "begin education at the very threshold of life." "The leading idea of Froebel," the editors correctly observed, "is that education should develop the individual according to the peculiar tendencies of his nature, not according to any arbitrary standard, and that these tendencies are manifested at a very early age." The *Examiner* also noted the political vulnerability of social-educational reform in Germany, a land where the "hopes of political freedom . . . have again been blighted," an apparent reference to the banning of the kindergarten by the Prussian government eight years earlier. While Froebel's German followers were heartened by the political views reported in America, his disciples were also misled by the overoptimistic tone used to describe American social and educational realities. The kindergarten movement was transplanted to America by the German disciples of Froebel only after the encounter with American culture produced marked changes in Froebel's social and educational thought between 1848 and 1872.[1]

The Revolution of 1848 brought Germans who were familiar with Froebel's ideas to the United States. Men like Adolf Douai, William Nicholas

Hailmann, and John Kraus left Germany to pursue careers in education in America. Few of these German educators had been direct disciples of Froebel. Their careers had been spent in the gymnasia and colleges of Germany and not in popular social-educational reform movements. Still, these teachers shared the bond of liberal education and politics with the Froebelians and preferred to leave Germany rather than change their politics. Emigration tended to reinforce their tenuous commitment to the Froebelian movement. In a new country they were free to experiment with kindergarten reforms in the flourishing German-American academies. Hailmann probably spoke for the others when he paraphrased Froebel after arriving in America: "Here, more than elsewhere, family education is entrusted to women; here, more than elsewhere, the adaptation of the females to the calling of teacher, particularly in elementary education, is recognized."[2]

Carl and Margarethe Schurz, also political refugees of 1848, immigrated with dreams of political and educational reform. "What I am looking for in America is not only personal freedom," wrote the more politically intense Carl Schurz, "but the chance to gain full legal citizenship." Margarethe Schurz channeled her interests in social change toward education rather than politics. Born to a prosperous and cultured Hamburg family, Margarethe's interest in education prompted her to enroll at age sixteen in the lectures of Friedrich Froebel, where her meticulous note-taking, no small accomplishment given Froebel's rambling lecture style, gained her the instructor's praise. Her German kindergarten activities, however, were cut short when she met and married Carl Schurz.[3]

Persuaded to come to America, Margarethe at first dropped these activities. In sharp contrast to her husband's taste for public life, she preferred the privacy of domestic life in the small German-American enclaves. The rapid acculturation of their children, however, reawakened her interest in Froebel. "The old people have preserved the tradition of the German spirit and German training, but they were unable to bequeath this tradition to their children," Carl wrote to his wife in 1867. The Schurzes, like other liberal German families, felt caught between a "stupid Pennsylvania Germanism" that resulted from the total isolation from American society and the "waves of Americanism [that would] soon overwhelm the second and third generations." Margarethe believed that without the kindergarten, their German cultural heritage would be lost forever. "The mission of Germanism in America," Carl wrote, "can consist of nothing [short of] a modification of the American spirit, through the German, while the nationalities melt into one." The Froebelian kindergarten became the educational answer for the Schurz family. Based on her memory of Froebel's lectures,

Margarethe in 1855 established a small family kindergarten in Watertown, Wisconsin.[4]

In sharp contrast to the romantic nationalism that inspired the emigration of the Forty-Eighters, the second wave of German Froebelians, encouraged by Peabody, came to America to achieve social-educational rather than political goals. To be sure, the Froebelians continued to cloak their aspirations in political rhetoric, but the revolutionary ferment of 1848 was gone. Bertha Meyer, the sister of Margarethe Schurz and a leader of the English kindergarten movement, for example, was explicit about the shift from political to social-educational objectives in her popular manual, *Aids to Family Government* (1879). "What the idealism of the previous century thought to gain by violent and revolutionary means," she wrote, "the realism of our day is [sic] gained by patient and practical effort." The kindergartners of the 1860s and 1870s hoped now to export to America not political revolution but social reform through family and kindergarten education.[5]

Froebel's view of the United States as a country hospitable to the kindergarten became part of the official ideology of the Froebelian movement and was repeated over and over in the lectures of German kindergarten trainers. Perhaps the most important spokeswoman for the introduction of kindergartens to America was Bertha Maria von Marenholtz-Bülow, a leader in the influential Hamburg Froebel Union and president of the German Froebel Society. She considered it her prime mission to train German women as kindergarten teachers and governesses in accordance with Froebel's dream of the American kindergarten movement. "Upon America, where, in truth, a new world is forming, which possesses all the creative powers of a young state," she told her trainers, "where the individual enjoys full liberty, and no restraint prevents him from carrying out his own designs in his own way, we look as the field of our richest harvest."[6]

To capitalize upon the new possibilities, Marenholtz-Bülow encouraged some trainees to consider emigration. "Besides founding kindergartens the most important thing is to instruct the young women in general to be able for education of the next generation," she wrote. In her remarks, she implied that international extension was essential for the growth of the movement. "I think you, in America, will succeed in this task much easier than we can here in Germany, where we are so often hindered by social laws and the rules of government."[7]

One of the first of Marenholtz-Bülow's students to emigrate with the intention of earning a living as a kindergartner was Matilda Kriege. Though her exact reasons for leaving Germany are unclear, she did assume that "American kindergartens were much more popular and [better] paying than the German." However, her attempt to found a kindergarten in New York City met with "prejudice against German kindergartens," which made the chances for earning a living almost impossible. Her arrival in Boston in 1868 was greeted without ceremony, but the novelty of the kindergarten did not escape public notice. "This lady was a personal pupil of Froebel," the *Boston Transcript* announced, "and has brought with her from Germany the material and apparatus for the kindergarten proper as taught in German cities."[8]

Kriege's Boston kindergarten fared little better than her New York project. She admitted two age levels by dividing the school into sections for children of ages 3–4 and 5–6. But even the age spread failed to attract enough students to cover expenses, and the kindergarten closed. Kriege again blamed the local newspapers which she said mistakenly publicized the school as a "German Kindergarten." She protested—in vain—that the purpose of the school was not to increase the "rivalry among nationalities," and she disagreed with editors who thought that "Froebel's system is adapted to the habits and manner of life in Germany." The failure of Kriege and others was nonetheless instructive, for though the German trainers attempted to reach an American audience, they had not learned how to do so. It was a lesson the next émigré would master.[9]

By training and birth, Maria Boelte was the most influential German Froebelian in America in the early 1870s. The daughter of a prominent German lawyer and magistrate, Boelte enjoyed a childhood of "much social cultivation," later recalling that her father's position "gave us every advantage." At age eighteen she entered the somewhat frivolous social life of upper-class young German women until she was persuaded by her aunt Amely Boelte, a popular German writer and enthusiast of the Froebelian kindergarten, to lead a more productive life. Against her parents' wishes, Boelte moved to Berlin in 1854 to formally enroll in the kindergarten training program conducted by Froebel's widow. After two years of course work she was ready to launch her career in London, where kindergarten instructors trained in Germany were in demand.[10]

The London years helped to transform Boelte into a leader of the growing international Froebelian movement. "The kindergarten in London consisted of poor children, who often had to be washed in the basement," she later recalled, "and clean linen aprons were put over the dirty clothes." Boelte's experience in England forced her to reflect upon both the pastoral ideology and the upper-class leadership of the German kindergarten movement. "The visitors consisted mostly of ladies belonging to the aristocracy, who often were accompanied by their children," she wrote. "It was curious to see these pretty, carefully kept, but spoiled children, how they watched the poorly dressed, bright, active and well-trained poor children." Boelte began to admire the deep "sense of activity and social functions of English education," which she curiously attributed to the Lockean tradition, but she found the English children cold and indifferent to the melodies and poetry of the German kindergarten. Boelte returned to Germany in the fall of 1867 and devoted herself to private kindergarten training, first in Hamburg and later in Lübeck.[11]

The London experience also sealed Boelte's commitment to the kindergarten movement: "I look upon those years as very successful ones, as I had every facility to carry out Froebel's ideas." Unlike the economic and political protest movements of the same period, the Froebelian movement attracted upper-class German women who were interested in improving the child-training skills of domestic servants and working-class women. This mission appealed to Boelte. Her complete conversion to the cause was not marked by the sudden religious inspiration that characterized later generations of American kindergartners but rather by the disciplined benevolence of European *noblesse oblige.* "I loved the kindergarten too well to give up," she wrote after the London years, contrasting her professional commitment to the indifference of others in the movement who, when "they learned the routine . . . were finished and done." On the contrary: "I had only one objective in view, namely to prepare myself as thoroughly as possible to be able myself to do the right work in regard to the kindergarten by and by." She dedicated her life to the training of "women in every position in life [to] accept the principles of the new education of mankind."[12]

Elizabeth Peabody first met Maria Boelte in London in 1870 after extensive correspondence with Amely Boelte, Maria's aunt. Even the optimistic portrait of American opportunities painted by both Peabody and John Kraus, however, could not persuade Boelte to come to America. "Many characteristics of America give great encouragement," Peabody later wrote. "We are not dragged back, as they are in Europe, by old customs, whose roots are intertwined with the heart strings of inherited sentiment." Peabody was not to be discouraged and began to prepare an American audience for the arrival of the German kindergarten trainer in her "Plea for the Kindergarten," alluding to Boelte as an exemplar of high German teaching standards. Peabody's early appeals were unsuccessful, for Boelte initially favored kindergarten promotion in the rural villages of Germany, as Froebel also preferred.[13]

Boelte's international urban experience also left her with a sense of dissatisfaction with the progress of the movement in the small towns of southern Germany, where the kindergarten was meeting resistance from a "stubborn country folk" who "adhered . . . strongly to their old customs and habits." In the large northern German cities of Dresden, Bremen, and Hamburg, the kindergarten reformers were more active. Here the children of the well-to-do were educated in private kindergartens, and poor children were given a free kindergarten education in municipal or charity kindergartens. Boelte admired the work of the Hamburg Froebel Union, which she described as an association of upper-class women "who devoted time and money to doing good work." The social realities of Germany in the 1870s, then, frustrated the efforts of Froebel's disciples who were seeking to implement his plans for universal domestic reform. Not surprisingly, many German Froebelians like Boelte were eager to explore domestic reform with a new audience of women in England and America. Boelte reached the decision to immigrate to the United States in 1871 with the urging of Elizabeth Peabody. "I received your letter inviting me to come to America," Boelte finally responded, "and although my work and home ties were very dear to me I resolved to go to America for the sake of the cause."[14]

Peabody had her own difficulties in America, for her efforts to raise the salaries of the German kindergartners were meeting only limited success. At times she was able to secure a large donation, such as the gift of $1000 from the American tragic actress Charlotte Cushman in support of Kriege's normal class, but more often the contributions were small. Peabody's friend Anna Lowell, for example, responded thus to her solicitation: "If you are getting up subscriptions for a kindergarten class you may put us down for twenty dollars. That is a small sum, but just now we are engaged in so many various projects that we cannot promise more." Peabody's dream of creating an endowment of at least $2000 to fund the salary of a German teacher through small contributions was as unsuccessful as her attempt to become the trustee of a $10,000 fund that would have allowed her to "open a free normal school to those qualified to enter the study." Without funds to establish an American kindergarten training school, Peabody turned to the flourishing American female academies in order to place the German trainers.[15]

Peabody found Boelte her first position in a well-known private school for girls in the Gramercy Park district of New York. The director, Henrietta B. Haines, had become interested in the kindergarten program several years earlier while visiting London and offered Boelte a one-year contract to demonstrate Froebelian practices by operating a model kindergarten at her school. Apparently Haines had no intention of changing the curriculum of the female seminary, which stressed preparation for marriage and the refinements of domestic life. She saw kindergarten skills as a natural complement to seminary training. Peabody diplomatically concurred, calling kindergarten training "the highest finish that can be given to a woman's education." Still the offer appealed to Boelte, who was familiar with the training of the daughters of the well-to-do and hoped to gain the time and resources needed to plan a German Froebelian kindergarten training school. "During my first year's work in America I did not wish to open a regular Training School for Kindergartners," she later wrote, "because I had first to organize my kindergarten and make it a 'model' as far as that could be done during one year's work . . . a thing entirely overlooked in this country."[16]

The kindergarten program at the Haines School had only limited success during its first year, 1872–1873. American mothers were reluctant to send their children to the novel school, but resistance gradually broke down. The school opened in September with an enrollment of nine children, which increased to thirty-two by the winter term. Peabody suggested to foreign teachers that it would be "harder work to govern American children. Their vivacious temperament, their lively energies, need 'conscious law' as a curb, rather than a spur." Traditionally, Europeans attributed the boisterous character of the American child to the leveling influences of democratic family life and common-school education. German kindergartners, in fact, were concerned about reports of disorder in American schools from children raised without notions of rank or class, but they also welcomed the receptiveness of American children to new ideas. Perhaps to allay exaggerated fears, Mary Mann, Peabody's sister, put the challenge in another light. "In America, where the excitements of opportunity are literally infinite, the importance of training the speculative mind and immense energy of the people to law, order, beauty and love . . . is incalculable."[17]

German trainers seemed at first better prepared to deal with American children than with American parents. Like Kriege, Boelte stressed the practical side of American national character and tried to modify the German curriculum accordingly. "Games most successfully carried out in Germany or England," she wrote in 1873, "are often not accepted by American children, if brought to them unaltered; but, if slightly changed, are at once seized upon enthusiastically." Boelte's early views on the preferences of American children reflected her recognition of the need to adapt the Froebelian songs and games to an American social setting. "It seems almost as if the little Germans would carry out the ideal side, take to the symbolical game at once," she wrote, "whereas the little Americans want to have *the practical side*." Boelte concluded that in many cases "the American children must be taught *how* to play" and would later become "twice as happy and childlike."[18]

Taking the opposite position, Peabody suggested that the Germanic songs and games might be beneficial to the "English turn of mind" in American education. By this she apparently meant the overly reflective, analytical side of American early education. The "rich, slow moving melodies," she argued, would force Americans "to pause at times in our rush of life, and allow ourselves to feel the mystery and the prophesies that hang around the sacred hour of childhood." But even the best efforts of German trainers and American promoters were unable to put an end to the sniping of many American parents who considered the foreign nature of the curriculum and instruction in the kindergarten a serious drawback. They were concerned about the German songs and games, but were even more worried about the Teutonic English of kindergarten instructors. One parent feared that the use of German words in the kindergarten exercises would create an artificial barrier between mother and child. "Instead of importing kindergartners," an angry parent wrote to Peabody, "we must educate for the art of Americans, who speak to children in the language of their mothers."[19]

With the support and encouragement of Peabody, German trainers gradually turned their attention from teaching children to training parents. Though some Boston mothers were still reluctant to send their children to kindergartens, many adapted kindergarten methods for home use. To do so they required training. As early as 1868, Kriege admitted "twenty American ladies" to a course of afternoon and evening lectures in the theory and practice of the Froebelian kindergarten. The demand for the training course soon exceeded the supply of seats, a response which Boelte also experienced in New York. In addition to teaching the kindergarten children and two primary classes, Boelte gave evening lectures to American women on the theory and practice of the Froebelian kindergarten education. "The new feature of a 'mothers class' that I had added was a great additional power, and the ladies in it became my strength," the German trainer readily admitted. In all, 130 students and teachers were trained during the first year of the Haines School kindergarten program. But Peabody was more encouraged by the quality than the quantity of early training. "Everything depends on the quality of the first kindergartners we train—their spiritual, moral intellectual quality," Peabody added. Only training would spur the American kindergarten movement by guiding the parent "to do for the children the right thing," and by educating "the community to require it done as a general thing."[20]

In order to meet the growing interest in kindergarten training, Kriege compressed the two-year German training program into a seven-month American crash course. By offering instruction in the gifts and occupations four afternoons a week and practice and observation in the kindergarten two mornings a week, she hoped to acquaint American parents and teachers with the essentials of Froebelian childrearing and early education. Her lectures covered the "moral and religious culture, hygiene and physical needs of children," while the American women also received practical instruction in the use of music, freehand drawing, and modeling. Kriege justified the changes in kindergarten training, in part, on the basis of educational expediency. "You must first show them practically what it is," Kriege wrote in the preface to her published lectures, *The Child, Its Nature and Relations* (Marenholtz-Bülow, 1872). "This will excite the interest and inquiry and then people will be ready to read something on the subject."

But Kriege was also committed to revealing the underlying scientific principles of child culture. Kriege's classes were similar to the programs the Boston Moral Science Association (1873) offered to young women on life's laws, marriage, and maternity. As historian William Leach has argued, kindergarten training was another attempt to discover rational social laws. Kriege hoped to illuminate these areas "where education is left to chance, or is dependent on the natural capacity and fitness of the parents, the best of whom have no sure guide in their work, and the greater part of whom deal thoughtlessly and arbitrarily with their children."[21]

Kriege's course of study prompted serious disagreement among other German kindergarten trainers in America. John Kraus was particularly disturbed that the shortened course offered by the Krieges—Matilda and her daughter Alma—would result in the preparation of "superficial kindergartners." He apparently shared his discontent with Maria Boelte and raised the possibility of establishing a new American training center that would fulfill the original plans of Froebel. Its purpose would be to purify Froebelian ideology. "When one such normal school shall have been founded," Kraus wrote to Boelte in July 1871, "the holy fire of true enthusiasm for this basis of all education will soon be spread far and wide; and the blessing of the true kindergarten thus be carried straight into the home and family."[22]

By 1873, Boelte was busy revising her plans for American kindergarten instruction in light of her first year's experience. Though she was convinced that there was a real demand for kindergarten training in America, she remained uneasy about the lack of discipline of young women in American seminaries, evidenced in the informality and lack of rigorous training at the Haines School. The German trainer, moreover, had determined that the work load of conducting both a model kindergarten and a training program was too demanding for a single instructor. Neither job was performed well. With Peabody's encouragement, Boelte planned to open a separate training institute the following year. Apparently Boelte simultaneously entertained Kraus's business and marriage proposals, for they agreed to marry and to launch a new kindergarten training school in New York. "It is a great mistake that men are excluded from early education in this country," Kraus added at the time of his decision. "In Europe it has become an acknowledged fact, that kindergartens become only a success when able men and women work together." Alma Kriege, the daughter of Matilda, joined the staff to take over the operation of the model kindergarten in October 1873 when the New York Normal Training School for Kindergarten Teachers, Kindergarten and Adjoining Classes was opened to the public. Kraus-Boelte was now finally in a position to bring pure German kindergarten training to America.[23]

Joseph Payne, an English educator and lecturer at the College of Preceptors in London, provided a candid description of German training methods based on a visit to the Gotha Normal School for Governesses in 1876, a school he called a "kind of practicing ground for the kindergarten governesses." Instruction was rigorous; lectures on the method and use of the kindergarten blocks were delivered orally and no note taking was permitted. At crucial points in the lecture, the Froebelian materials were distributed to the students in order to lay the ground work for "clear representations in the mind." For example, a lecture on the concept of "unity" between education and philosophy was followed by a practical exercise using kindergarten blocks. "Every student was required to do herself with the cube what she was as a teacher to require from the children." The repetition of the lessons Payne called "wearisome," and he decided that "the teachers of the kindergarten governesses in Germany certainly give their pupils extremely little credit for native intelligence." Training of kindergartners in Germany, Payne concluded, did not follow the Froebelian dictate of learning by "self-activity since the kindergartners are told everything."[24]

German kindergartners in America held similar views on trainees though their ideas were often masked. For example, Kraus-Boelte envisioned the kindergarten normal school as an inverted social and administrative pyramid. "So deeply are we impressed with the importance and utility of the kindergarten, and with the high qualities of the teacher of the very young," Kraus-Boelte quoted one German trainer, "that we are more and more disposed to believe that the true order in rank and promotion among the teachers should be, to speak in paradox, downwards." By this she presumably meant that the closeness of the classroom teacher to the kindergarten child made her position ultimately more important than the trainer's or supervisor's. Inspiration or sympathetic understanding of the child, however, came only after mastery of the hundreds of questions, attitudes, thoughts, and fancies of children that the kindergartner might encounter in the classroom. "An industry and patience far beyond any need by the teacher of more advanced pupils, are required by the highly cultivated men and women," Kraus-Boelte announced.[25]

German trainers in America also viewed their strict methods as a reform measure in a double sense. First, Kraus-Boelte believed she was simply answering Peabody's call for "an exact statement of Froebel's art and science of education in its severity," which had been "extensively travestied in this country." Second, German Froebelians identified their efforts with the movement for normal school reform. They saw no contradiction in the strict training sequence that they proposed to implement and the goals that American educational reformers had established for the normal school. "The American Normal School, in order that its diploma shall mean anything," wrote reformer Anna Brackett, "has therefore to distinguish between the chaff and the wheat and then, decidedly and with authority, to separate the one from the other, retaining only the wheat." German kindergarten trainers had proposed to apply this standard in training the first generation of American kindergartners.[26]

Support for German kindergarten training also came from American women outside of the kindergarten movement. Catherine Beecher, whose principal activities and writings had made her a spokesman for domestic reform before the Civil War, endorsed kindergarten training for American women in 1872. The rigor of German kindergarten methods and training, Beecher felt, could help restore dignity to domestic science and thus enhance woman's role. The task, however, would not be easy, for everywhere in postwar America she found the homemaker under assault. Beecher argued that war itself had drawn American women from their proper place in the home to serve as battlefield nurses. Industrialization had further degraded woman's domestic role, and the recent waves of immigrants, unschooled in the domestic arts, threatened to displace the American woman from the home entirely. Finally, the suffrage movement threatened to inundate the American woman with "grave and complicated responsibilities." Amidst an otherwise gloomy picture of domestic reform in postwar America, the kindergarten was a welcome sign. Not content with endorsing German training schools, Beecher projected her own vision of an ideal "woman's university" that would include kindergarten, primary school, preparatory school, college, and professional school, "an institution embracing the whole course of woman's training from infancy to a self-supporting profession, in which both parents and teachers have a united influence and agency."[27]

Most American women were content in the early 1870s with less ambitious objectives for kindergarten training, and a few considered enrolling in Kraus-Boelte's two-year training course in New York. Unlike Kriege's abbreviated twenty-six-week course, the curriculum of the Seminary followed German precedent in demanding one year of course work and one year of practice teaching. The first year was viewed as "test work," a period in which both the trainer and trainee assessed the latter's suitability for the kindergarten vocation. "The object of the course is to give members of the class a clear conception of Froebel's pedagogical aims in his several gifts and occupations," Henry Barnard remarked in the *American Journal of Education* (1873), "and to show the deep significance of the child's natural play, and breathe a true spirit into employments which become otherwise an incomprehensible mechanism." The trainee first observed in the classroom and only gradually assumed all duties of a kindergarten teacher. Not until the second year did trainees actually teach the kindergarten child.[28]

The course of study consisted of lectures, reading, and practical exercises in kindergarten theory and technique, a program that at times made little distinction between the education of the child and the training of the teacher. Since a metaphysic of education embraced both child and adult, the trainee's understanding of the Froebelian gifts and occupations unfolded parallel to the child's own experience. Beginning with the simplest geometric forms, students worked through the entire sequence of gifts and occupations. As in Germany, the study of each educational device was accompanied by a lecture on an appropriate, complementary moral lesson. Using Froebel's *The Education of Man* and other educational tracts, Kraus-Boelte outlined not only the educational tasks at each stage of the child's life but also the accompanying physical and mental changes. By definition, disagreements were impossible. Kraus-Boelte neither entertained questions nor let the students interrupt. Payne had in mind the imperious methods of the Gotha Normal School when he commented, "Even in Germany, the land of pedagogy, teachers very often abuse their proper function," but his remarks were also appropriate for the New York Seminary.[29]

The operation of a model kindergarten at the Seminary was an integral part of the training, for without a functioning kindergarten Kraus-Boelte felt that kindergarten training would be no better than normal-school preparation. "They should be professional or nothing," she wrote of the entering kindergarten students, "and they cannot be professional . . . unless they have such means of giving the best facilities for illustration and practice of the principles taught." The affinity of the training program and demonstration kindergarten, however, was professional only within the limits of a nineteenth-century social-educational movement since the practice kindergarten was used only to illuminate the relationship between child development and the "universal laws of education" already postulated by Froebel. The demonstration school, then, became integrated into the normal department since both were choreographed to illustrate Froebel's laws of education. A strict regimen was maintained at all times, since Froebel believed that the kindergarten should reflect world order. "The serpent of disorder did certainly tempt, now and then," Peabody wrote after a visit to the kindergarten of the Seminary, "but the human embodiment of the saving love was at hand, with timely advice."[30]

Much of Kraus-Boelte's social thought was rooted in the mid-nineteenth-century German childrearing reform, which differed substantially from American efforts at domestic reform. By the early 1870s, European social reformers had come to fear that the abandonment by upper-class women of their responsibilities as guardians of the next generation would lead ultimately to social chaos. With the tasks of nurture and education turned over to domestic servants, the important early training of the child had been placed in the hands of those who were least prepared to perform it. The children of the poor were even worse off, for these youngsters received no training. If the social malady of the rich was the neglect of their children, the remedy was rigorous adult training in kindergarten theory and in the techniques that would allow upper-class women to better train domestic servants and to occasionally work among the poor. Only a fraction of the German women who entered the kindergarten training courses were expected to teach kindergarten, but all were encouraged to gain the information and skills necessary to supervise a governess or to directly educate their children according to Froebel's system. Domestic servants were also eligible for training and, once trained as kindergarten nurses or governesses, would be better selected, better educated, and better paid in their "legitimate status as a deputy mother." Trained mothers, in turn, would be free to undertake the higher duties of cultivating the child's moral, physical, and mental development.[31]

Drawing upon European expectations modified by American experience, Kraus-Boelte and Peabody hoped to admit two types of American women to the New York Seminary. Though the kindergarten advocates never clarified their thinking about the socioeconomic status of kindergarten trainees, they were certain that the Seminary would attract applicants from two pools: female academy students and recent immigrants. Kraus-Boelte's experience at the Haines School had already demonstrated that well-to-do and middle-class women were interested in learning the kindergarten skills for home use. "It is from the most advanced classes of high and normal schools, public and private," Peabody agreed, "that the pupils of our training classes should come, and from the most refined circles of private life—remembering that these are not identical with wealthy and fashionable ones." At the same time, Kraus-Boelte planned to recruit recent immigrants to be trained as nursery governesses who would work for the more affluent. The German trainer reasoned that domestic kindergarten work would be preferable to factory and other manual-labor positions. Again Boelte's views were apparently influenced by Peabody. "The Irish nature is not altogether bad material for the production of good motherly nurses," Peabody had suggested in her well-known *Training Lectures for Kindergartners* (1886), "but it must not be left wild; it needs a great deal of discipline." In this scheme, working-class women without a high-school education would be taught the simple, practical kindergarten skills (the gifts and occupations) and not the finer points of Froebel's theory and German philosophy. "In America more than elsewhere, we must expect to find multitudes attempting to do what is beyond their power, and the profession of education, in common with all other spheres exhibit this fact," Kraus-Boelte later quoted normal educator Anna C. Brackett.[32]

In order to carry out her educational and social visions, Kraus-Boelte implemented a strict, albeit subjective, admissions policy. Graduation from high school was not a formal requirement, but she did expect literacy, culture, and refinement as the *sine qua non* of admission to the Seminary, and she tested all candidates for their knowledge of music, art, and literature, giving some preference to applicants with vocal or instrumental abilities. But the real criteria for admission to the Seminary were determined during a lengthy interview with the director, for she alone would be able to distinguish between the true kindergartner's "quick, responsive, the real, and the genuine" sympathy for children and the common "artificial or simulated" approach to early education. The ideal kindergarten teacher, Kraus-Boelte told one American candidate, was a young woman who combined "a spiritual comprehension of [child nature] with the dexterous handling of the kindergarten materials." Kraus-Boelte took admissions very seriously and reported turning away "some tired out school and music teachers and some shop girls." It was not so much German snobbishness as ideological zeal that made the interviews rigorous.[33]

Finding qualified kindergartner candidates was obviously a more difficult task than she had expected, and Kraus-Boelte admitted only one trainee in the first year although she had no trouble filling the evening classes. Kraus-Boelte was encouraged by the number of American mothers interested in the home use of Froebel's blocks but was disappointed in the number of American women who were willing to give "their whole time and energy to the cause, enabling us to enter as deep a study of the system as we choose." Still the German trainer hoped to limit enrollments to the "better—if not best class of cultured women" in the United States.[34]

The lack of applicants in the nursery governess program forced the foreign trainers to revise their social expectations when the program failed to attract even a single respondent. An incredulous Kraus-Boelte commented, "Abroad nurses are trained after Froebel's principles, whereas in America there are no nurses to be trained." The attempt to recruit recent immigrants, especially Irish women in Boston, as kindergarten governesses also ended in failure. Since there was widespread fear that the waves of recent immigrants in the 1870s were lowering school attendance figures, the admissions difficulties troubled Peabody and Kraus-Boelte. The German trainers somewhat haughtily explained that recent immigrants were frequently more interested in the opportunities of the marketplace than in the discipline of kindergarten training schools. "The American girl 'aspires' to other, though not always better things," Kraus-Boelte observed in her early lectures. "A situation in a shop, or a position as a teacher stands in her eyes higher than employment as a 'first class' or so-called 'nursery governess.'"[35]

By the mid-1870s, several German kindergarten training schools had made some adjustments to American society. The contrast between the European and American leadership was dramatically illustrated for Matilda Kriege when she visited Germany in 1873 to attend an international Froebelian conference. "It was as high toned and intellectual an assembly as I ever saw," Kriege reported to her American friends. In Europe only "ladies of the highest rank and character take the lead." Also missing in the American movement were the domestic servants and kindergarten nurses. In Europe the kindergarten nurse, Kraus-Boelte noted in a final lament, was "esteemed and loved by all members of the family." Presumably, in a republican nation, domestic work was a sign of servitude and consequently the object of disdain. Lacking aristocratic leaders and working-class followers, the kindergarten cause in America would be in its basic structure different from its German counterpart.[36]

In order to give the new social basis of the American movement an ideological legitimacy, German and American advocates returned to Froebel's writings, particularly noting those passages in which he called common kindergarten training and education for all classes the sign of a "progressive culture." American kindergarten advocates, moreover, had come to believe that the kindergarten movement had been held back by the class bias of German leaders and began to object to the class-conscious interpretations of Froebel. "But should we give the masses the commonalty, and to the ungifted, the education of the most highly cultivated classes," wrote Baroness von Marenholtz-Bülow in her *The New Education by Work* (1876), "there might be no more unhappy beings than learned men, on the joiners bench, and the artist as a chimney sweep." In preparing the American translation of this Froebelian tract, Mary Mann added the disclaimer that many of Froebel's comments "do not apply in our own beloved country, whose political institutions present no barrier against the rise of any man to the height of social circumstance which his abilities and education would adorn." Even without Mann's overstatements, the German Froebelian movement by 1872 was well on its way to becoming an international social-educational reform movement with an important American following.[37]

Transplanted to America between 1848 and 1860, the kindergarten remained a captive of the German-American community for the first two decades. The efforts of American reformers like Elizabeth Peabody to free the movement resulted in a second migration of German-trained kindergartners to America between 1860 and 1872. In the process of transfer, the Froebelian movement changed from a class-structured political movement to a middle-class social-educational reform movement. Still, before the mid-1870s, most American parents remained ignorant, suspicious, or fearful of sending their children to a German kindergarten. Kindergartens and training institutions had been established, but the kindergarten idea was still in search of an American following. Ironically Kraus-Boelte herself concluded, "Froebel's principles and theories can only be successful in foreign countries, then, when gifted, intelligent, pedagogical persons take it in their hands, and arrange it according to the minds and spirit of the people."

4

Saint Louis (1872–1880)

The rapid expansion of the kindergarten movement after 1873 began in Saint Louis, a center of midwestern commerce and manufacturing and the second-fastest growing city in the West. The city's immigrant population swelled between 1860 and 1870, absorbing large numbers of Germans. At first the German population supported local neighborhood kindergartens and later provided a base of popular support for the introduction of the kindergarten to the public school. Under the stewardship of William Torrey Harris (1835–1909), the superintendent of schools, and Susan Blow, a local convert to Froebelianism, the kindergarten "experiment" prospered and attracted its first large American following. By 1876, Saint Louis provided a national model for the training of kindergarten teachers and the operation and management of kindergartens.[1]

Harris was well prepared to manage both the practical and philosophical aspects of the kindergarten program. A Yankee schoolmaster, he adopted the West shortly after the Civil War and there quickly established himself as the leader of a small group of schoolteachers and German immigrants devoted to the study of Hegel. The Saint Louis Philosophical Society (1866) and the *Journal of Speculative Philosophy* (1867) earned the city a reputation as the American center of idealist philosophy. In the first issue of the journal, Harris announced his blueprint for the study of philosophy in America: "Reason shall find and establish a philosophical basis for all those great ideas which are taught as religious dogmas." Another Hegelian put the matter more simply: the Saint Louis movement was in the "deepest sense religious, not as a formal but as a universal."[2]

For Harris, Hegelian philosophy also provided the key to the history of education, for he believed that American education was really in the third stage of a dialectic of world history. During the late Middle Ages, the institutions of the church and state had reawakened scholarly interest in the study of national literatures, placing a new emphasis on literacy and education. Rousseau's *Emile*, for Harris the central document of the Romantic revolution in education, challenged literacy as the central vehicle of education, for it supported "object learning" over "book learning." American education, formed in the period 1790 to 1860, grew, then, in the clash of "anti-book" and "book" learning. The growth of American industry and cities (material forces) had affected the outcome only indirectly, for education worked through the relatively fixed social institutions of the school, the church, the state, and the family. Yet urbanization and industrialization, Harris concluded, had placed a new challenge on the administration of school systems.[3]

Harris's own life (1835–1908) provided a personal yardstick with which to measure the dramatic changes in American education. He grew up in rural New England, a Congregational Calvinist by "family and education." He was educated in both rural (North Killingly, Connecticut) and urban schools (Providence, Rhode Island). Harris strongly protested against corporal punishment and the martinet system of instruction based on the timed responses, military in character, of the pupil. "I came to detest the city schools very bitterly," he later recalled, "because I loved the individual freedom and hated mere forms as such."[4]

Harris marked his meeting with Amos Bronson Alcott at Yale in 1856 as the beginning of "freedom and insight" in his own education. As a college student, Harris was looking for a "new and better order of things" and dabbled in phrenology, spelling reform, gymnastics, water cure, dress reform, and mesmerism. Alcott's lecture in New Haven, "Orphic Seer's Conversation," occurred at a critical intellectual juncture for Harris, a period he called his *Aufklärung*. Rebelling against Calvinism, Harris was ready for Alcott's Transcendentalism, and the lecture was the beginning of Harris's "descent below the surfaces of illusions of common sensuous experience and tradition." Transcendentalism was "glad tidings" to the student, for in it he found for the first time a life of the mind that allowed the "emancipation of the soul from prosaic bondage to the present here and now." Harris left Yale without graduating the following year (1857), prepared to search for the "three moderns"—science, literature, and history. In Saint Louis the young man declared his intellectual freedom, finally renouncing Calvinism for Hegelianism as the key to all learning.[5]

His early childhood experiences, like Froebel's and Alcott's, later raised doubts concerning the function of public school education. As a teacher and principal in the Saint Louis public schools, Harris concluded that the classroom was only a subordinate institution in the moral instruction of the child in an evolving "modern urban civilization." Family and church provided the basic rudiments of education—moral discipline—before the child entered the public school. To Harris, the central educational goal of the public school was clearly to amplify the "semi-mechanical moral virtues" of regularity, restraint, and punctuality. The difficulty lay in preserving at the same time the "spontaneity and free insight" of childhood. Like other educators of the period after the Civil War, Harris was ambivalent about the impact of industrialization; he sought to promote its economic advantages but feared the loss of the values associated with rural education.[6]

After the Civil War Harris invited his old teacher Alcott to visit him in Saint Louis and address his Hegelian circle, which included both schoolteachers and philosophers. Alcott was cordially received, but the trip, like so many of Alcott's sallies, was an intellectual fiasco. The Saint Louis Hegelians found little inspiration in Alcott's "conversations," which the acerbic Denton Snider, *philosophe* and group historian, labeled "mystic oracles—often dark, tortuous and riddlesome." Snider reported that Transcendental thought "simply exploded in mist" under the penetration of Hegelian dialectical argument. The careers of the two educators suddenly seemed to stand in sharp contrast. Alcott, the intuitive rustic educator, was the master of the parlor conversation while Harris had become an urbane administrator, successfully managing a huge public school system through applied idealistic philosophy.[7]

Elizabeth Peabody also was impressed by the opportunities in Saint Louis for the kindergarten when she learned of Harris's work, probably through Alcott. Immediately the promoter entreated him to "make Froebel's kindergarten a part of your public school system." Peabody desperately needed to demonstrate the usefulness of the kindergarten after so many kindergarten failures on the East Coast and decided to tour the Midwest to promote the cause. Though she had not included Saint Louis in her itinerary, she invited Harris to attend a kindergarten lecture in Chicago in the summer of 1870, adding that "I still hope to make you a convert to my system." Harris declined, but her visit to Chicago confirmed Peabody's suspicions. "In the West I was agreeably surprised to find a large number of men who did enter to the idea and saw that if the adult did his duty to the child," she wrote Harris on August 25, 1870, "it might be as perfect in its evolution from the first as any of the unconscious forms of nature."[8]

The continuing relationship of Harris to the Transcendentalists was a puzzle. The key lay in Harris's sense of the dramatic changes taking place in American society. The failure of the Transcendentalists to understand the growth of cities and industry made their thought, however brilliant, "antique." To the Saint Louis Hegelians, Alcott remained a "seer, wrapped in a vision," Peabody an antebellum moral crusader. At the same time, the New England Transcendentalists continued to pose the central question of education for Harris—to find an educational program that would harmonize the "discipline" of education with the "spontaneity" of childhood. A too literal interpretation of Wordsworth's *Ode* had pressed Alcott's and Peabody's thinking to the limits of educational usefulness. If Calvinism and conservative Evangelicalism had destroyed the educational values of freedom and insight for Harris, the Transcendentalist theories of education had only confused them. Harris hoped to resolve the "dilemma of American education" by introducing Hegelian reason, thus providing a middle way between the permissiveness of Romantic education and the discipline of religious education.[9]

Benefiting from Alcott's mistakes, Harris built the Saint Louis public school system on a foundation of empirical rather than Transcendental assumptions. He organized the lines of responsibility in the school system and allowed each school principal considerable autonomy. In return, school principals reported detailed information concerning salaries, costs, and attendance to the office of the superintendent. Harris, further, began an extensive program of school visits in order to gain an even more detailed picture of the operation of a large urban school system. Above all, he wanted verified information about real children and not Transcendental theories about childhood before revising the school system to meet children's needs. He published his findings rather than filing them and he circulated the reports to teachers, principals, and superintendents in other cities. Harris again parted ways with Alcott, this time substituting a rationalized bureaucracy for visionary individualism.[10]

Harris's interest in efficient administration soon extended beyond the school system to the families of schoolchildren, and in 1868 the superintendent ordered a survey of Saint Louis neighborhoods in order to assess educational needs. Harris collected data on the class, ethnicity, and age of attendance of Saint Louis schoolchildren. The report disclosed alarming inequalities in public education and highlighted the deficiencies in the factory and levee districts of the city. Harris was particularly concerned about the early departure of slum children, for the surveys indicated that the child of working parents often began school at age seven and left to work at age ten. The children of the poor received only three years of education, a statistic Harris found shocking not because it reflected inequality of educational opportunity but because it posed a threat to the order of civil society.[11]

Harris's interpretation of the statistics was guided by a Hegelian view of institutions and social process. In modern urban society, the superintendent reasoned, the traditional social institutions of education—family, school, church, and state—had moved into a new alignment. The church had ceased to play the dominant role in the early education of the child. The family had become an emotional rather than an economic bond and could no longer fully educate the child for his future role in civil society. The state had unwillingly become the guarantor of vocation. The new functions of institutions laid an even greater stress on the transition from family to school, for at a critical juncture in his development the child was exposed to the debilitating influence of the street. Philosophy now guided administration: in the slum Harris feared that Plato's "divine sense of shame" would be lost.[12]

Hegelian philosophy not only helped Harris to conceptualize public problems but also provided certain clues to their educational remedies. The child was born into a "sacred circle" of family life, the natural social institution of man, and lived in "common joy and grief." The child learned the paradoxical lessons of "love" and "authority" in the family, for here parents introduced him to feelings of "love and confidence" and at the same time to the "mysteries of the world." The contradictory forces were the makings of a new synthesis when ultimately the child, through the principle of "self-activity," launched his own family life.[13]

The Hegelians paid particular attention to the transition from home to school, since education was a process that began at birth when the child was still in the family. In three successive life stages—infancy (1–2), childhood (2–12), and youth (12–21)—the individual confronted the institutions of family, school, and vocation. The "struggle" between "self" and "institution," in fact, defined the "synthetic" nature of education in two ways. Individually, the "inner" self of the child was subordinated to an "ideal" self; socially, the individual combined with others to form society. The end product was a "rational" individual able to live freely and independently in society. There was, however, a relentless social pressure behind the Hegelian view, for Hegel taught that in the end "the family rears the children not for itself but for civil society."[14]

Peabody followed the emerging Hegelian interpretation of early education in Harris's reports. Always the promoter, she found another opening wedge for the kindergarten in his arguments. "The necessity for what is called discipline in your primary schools would be all but superseded if children were first trained to create order from within, which is Froebel's idea," the Boston reformer chided Harris. "I should think if you let them run wild till they are seven years old, they would have by that time created such chaos or disorder around themselves that your primary school would become a battlefield." Peabody knew that in focusing her argument on the themes of civil order and disorder she would attract Harris's attention. What she did not understand was that Harris had already abandoned the Transcendentalist belief that social order was a simple reflection of individual harmony. Harris, like other social thinkers of the 1870s, was searching for a way out of the exaggerated individualism of antebellum reform. As historian William Leach has demonstrated, even Alcott "had completely severed his bond with Transcendentalism" by the 1870s. "The individual sees only himself like Narcissus in the pool," Alcott wrote. "Individualism brings men into opposition to the family, institutions of learning and the state," and "only as it is broken down is there harmony." Harris was interested in the kindergarten but not on Peabody's terms because he believed that the kindergarten required a rational, institutional context. Significantly, Harris declined Peabody's offer to place a German-trained kindergartner in the Saint Louis schools.[15]

At first Harris hoped to solve the problem of school attendance by extending the legal age for public education to include children under six. His suggestion, however, ran into opposition in the school board, which was already struggling with the problem of overcrowding. In 1871 Harris repeated his plea for early education, noting for the first time that the Froebelian system provided "valuable hints" for dealing with the education of working-class children, though he carefully avoided making commitments to the Froebelian movement. At first the superintendent did not favor public adoption of kindergartens but strenuously supported the adoption of kindergarten methods. By 1872 Harris reversed his position and called for the creation of a public kindergarten on an experimental basis for children of ages three to six. The kindergarten, Harris believed, might serve as the transition between home and school that would help reunite society.[16]

His meeting with Susan Blow in 1872 helped the superintendent translate his vague interest in Froebel into real plans for a program of public kindergartens. Blow was the daughter of Henry T. Blow, a southern Unionist and a leader in Saint Louis business and politics. A sensitive young woman of a deeply religious nature, Blow had learned of the kindergarten while on tour in Europe with her father, a United States minister to Brazil. As a substitute teacher in the Saint Louis schools, Blow began to experiment with the new technique and thus attracted Harris's attention. Their friendship, and the beginning of a lifelong intellectual companionship, was ensured when Blow was asked to join Harris's philosophical circle.[17]

Reared in a home life of "blue Presbyterianism," Susan Blow had been a studious, religiously introspective child. Her parents spared little expense in her education. At first she was tutored at home by governesses in French and religion and later studied in a local Presbyterian minister's small school for boys. Instruction was catechetical and Blow later recalled the weariness of reciting passages from *Magnall's Questions*. "It is held up now as a specimen of all that is bad in the textbook line." Concerned by his daughter's religious moodiness and overscholarly nature, Blow's father established a small private school where her preoccupation with religious questions nevertheless continued unabated, primarily through her reading of the Scottish divines. "I read mainly religious and theological books—sermons—Neander's *Life of Christ*—some of his church history and some philosophy among other things." Blow also apparently participated in the periodic religious revivals that swept through the school, for she noted that her teachers at times dismissed class in order to encourage the students to "attend to the more important matters of their soul's salvation." Blow never recorded the emotional experience of conversion because she "felt throughout her youth that she was a Christian." But it was an unstable sense of salvation: "I was always trying to read books which would confirm my faith and was fond of citing things like, 'Doubt of any kind can be removed only by action. The end of man is an action, not a thought, though it was the noblest.'"[18]

Blow's formal education began at age sixteen when she was sent to the private female academy of Henrietta B. Haines in New York City. "There I gained a great deal though the school was not a thorough one," Blow later recalled. "Miss Haines felt nothing of a two or three hundred year mistake in an historical date and the sciences were taught as superficially as possible." Blow read the Romantic poets Schiller, Browning, and Tennyson "by the yard" but "gained no real insight" into Emerson's thought. The theological tracts of her youth, however, continued to hold her imagination. "Mainly I fed my soul on Robertson's sermons which I still think very remarkable." She attempted to read Hegel and readily admitted that she did not "in the least understand." As early as the seminary years, her devout mother commented prophetically that "your religion is the governing principle of your life."[19]

Blow returned to social and intellectual isolation in postbellum Saint Louis, for according to one observer she was "too bookish, displaying too much erudition" to succeed in the social role of daughter of a wealthy congressman and yet intellectually too immature to join the Hegelians. When

President Grant appointed her father minister to Brazil, Blow seized the opportunity to travel first to South America and later to Europe where she first learned of Froebel's kindergarten. But the splendors of Italy and Rome, not Germany, raised new intellectual aspirations in the American girl from Saint Louis. Europe was a "revelation," she later wrote to Harris. "I found myself when I got back to America with a store of sympathies and sentiments quite *alien* from any I had felt before."[20]

Blow's initiation into the "sacred fellowship" of the Saint Louis Hegelians made the return easier and ultimately marked the end of her long intellectual isolation. She began to attend the afternoon and evening lectures on German Idealist philosophy. At first the scholarly, often pedantic, lectures on Kant, Fichte, and Hegel left Blow with "sealed eyes and untouched heart," but hearing Harris speak, she felt the walls tumble. "That afternoon was the most solemn and resplendent of my whole life," she later wrote. "I beheld Eternal Reality." Blow suddenly felt that the years of religious questioning were over, for philosophy and reason had laid bare the mysterious puzzles of theology. "I looked into myself and found necessary and universal ideas," she wrote. In the rationalized conversion experience, "my intellect was reborn."[21]

Intellectual companionship did not end her search for personal fulfillment. "All this time I was conscious of two things—an irresistible impulse toward action and hunger for something which might seem worth doing," she later wrote to Harris. "I suppose I had the feeling the Catholics call Vocation." It was a yearning that Blow shared with other women of mid-Victorian America. Writing of the work of the "Catholic sisterhood," social scientist Ella Giles Ruddy remarked that church work was "worthy of imitation by unmarried Protestants." But Blow's vocational alternatives were sharply limited by the social prominence of her family, her mother's own passivity, and her father's strong feelings about "women's spheres" in society. Her father adamantly opposed Susan's entry into public life or charitable work. "Had my father permitted I should have gone into some definite work long before I did, but I would never have done anything against his wish," Blow later recalled. "I remember definitely saying to myself that I would be ready for work [and] when the right moment came God would show the work; Christ waited until he was thirty and should not I be willing to wait for the chance to do the little I was able to do?"[22]

The exact direction of Blow's vocational calling became clearer as a result of her friendship with Harris. Working as a substitute teacher in the Saint Louis schools provided the opportunity to discuss Froebel's educational innovations with the superintendent, and after several meetings Harris encouraged her to study under Kraus-Boelte in New York, a suggestion Blow quickly accepted. "Very shortly after our conversation upon the kindergarten system, and the practicability of its introduction into our public schools," Blow wrote Harris in November 1872, "I came to New York where for the past month I have given the subject careful thought and some practical study." Blow soon became immersed in the details of the German course of study and asked for an extension of her teaching leave in order to gain "a thorough practical knowledge of the system."[23]

Though Blow did not leave a full record of her year's study, the essentials of her experience can be reconstructed from other accounts. The core of American training was systematic study and painstaking drills in the use of the gifts and occupations. In order to gain the necessary dexterity and aesthetic skills, American trainees repeated the simple tasks over and over; it was not unusual for a student to fold hundreds of paper forms, weave countless mats, draw thousands of stick figures, string numberless beads, and sew myriads of prepunched card patterns before her training was complete. In conjunction with the proper use of the kindergarten material, the trainee was also required to study the complementary laws of harmony, color, music, and geometry. At the end of the term, the work was usually presented to the trainer in bound form for evaluation. Kraus-Boelte told one graduating class of kindergartners in a reference to the gifts and occupations: "To know them all is quite a study; to apply them an art; to understand their significance . . . is a science."[24]

But all was not "science" or drudgery. The rigorous training in the use of the gifts and occupations, songs and games of the kindergarten alone did not ensure the success of the kindergartner, for ultimately no books, no educational apparatus, nor any lessons could instill the sensitivity and love of childhood that Froebel required. The long training course was merely a preparation for a more dramatic change of heart in which American trainees, usually in the quiet of their dormitory rooms, renounced some of the aspects of Calvinist or evangelical childrearing and education. "If it were possible every child should be taught by God himself," Kraus-Boelte told the first class of American kindergartners. All training was aimed at that moment of inspiration.[25]

What motivated the first or later classes to undertake the painstaking work or forbear the arrogance of its director is only partially clear. Certainly the chance to work directly with children in an innovative way was reason enough for some to attend. One American student of Kraus-Boelte later recalled, "I was delighted to have the opportunity to see this joyous life with the children that I willingly did the taxing drudgery, though it often kept me up until midnight." Still others seemed attracted by the "scientific" nature of the course itself. "You do not know how mercilessly I have been made to face facts since I have been here," wrote another trainee at the Seminary. "And yet facts are what I need. I have been too visionary, too enthusiastic all my life." Such comments suggest that kindergartners were part of a broader movement of women in American society to "demystify" the most basic facts about maternity. By uncovering the "hidden truths," American bourgeois women gained a certain degree of control over their lives; it was a process of emancipation. Finally, the emotional price American trainees paid for kindergarten instruction was more than repaid with admission into the "sacred circle" of Froebelianism. Nothing could do more to support the dignity of woman's most basic labor: education of the child.[26]

Blow never lost sight of her final objective. "May I hope that your promise to allow me to try the kindergarten experiment will hold good for next fall instead of the winter," she wrote Harris in Saint Louis. "I am personally very much disappointed in what seems to be a necessary postponement, but I am anxious that the experiment should prove a success, and I feel that it is infinitely better to wait than to fail." Blow reassured the superintendent that she undertook Kraus-Boelte's course of study "never forgetting your suggestions of the modifications necessary to be made when a German theory is to be made an American fact."[27]

Blow's kindergarten career began in earnest in the fall of 1873. Harris had recommended that the school board approve the opening of a "play school" on an experimental basis during the fall term. At first Blow suggested limiting the number of children to serve in this "leavening influence." Peabody's request for information concerning the experimental school reinforced Blow's desire to proceed cautiously. "Recognizing that our kindergarten is an experiment and knowing something of Miss Peabody's character," she wrote Harris, "I feel a great disinclination to write anything more than the simple facts of numbers of pupils, hours employed per day, etc." In September 1873, the Des Peres kindergarten, the first public kindergarten in the United States, opened its doors to twenty children. "In my judgment the more quietly and modestly we conduct the kindergarten for the present," Blow noted, "the more probability will there be of showing permanent and satisfactory results."[28]

Harris was also cautious, for the kindergarten had deeper resonances in the ethnic politics of the city. As a center of midwest German population, Saint Louis had been the home of at least one private German-language kindergarten. In addition, Francis Berg, the head of the German-language instruction program, had advocated the public adoption of the kindergarten. Harris, sympathetic to Berg's idea, was nevertheless reluctant to approve it because of his fear of rekindling the bitter opposition among the non-German elements of the city. For a few, the kindergarten was seen as another attempt to "Germanize" the city's schools.[29]

The kindergarten experiment was not without other sources of opposition growing from a more general resistance to educational innovation, based on deep-seated attitudes concerning the relative place of the family and school in early education. Everyone had an opinion on the subject. Some citizens called the experimental program "an educational frill," while other urban parents were worried about the encroachment of the public school upon the family. Primary teachers felt that the kindergarten would make the child "intractable" and unfit for the more important lessons of the primary school. Kindergarten teachers, opponents argued, were exceptional women who would be difficult to find.[30]

Susan Blow confidently dealt with objections to the kindergarten system in her first school-board report (1874). The general tone of the report was positive; she noted that enrollments had increased so rapidly that a second kindergarten was added the same year. Blow reported a 95-percent attendance rate, dispelling the argument that young children could not be depended upon to attend regularly. She also pointed out that physical exercise had proven more beneficial than harmful, contrary to a long-standing fear of educators. Finally, kindergarten students had performed well in primary work, a fact she hoped would allay the fears of educators. Perhaps projecting her own unhappy childhood into the report, Blow concluded that the "strongest claim" of the kindergarten was as an "antidote to the sadness which broods over the minds of the age."[31]

In his reports, Harris was careful to distinguish the Saint Louis kindergarten curriculum, which operated within the strict limits of Hegelian rationalism, from that of other kindergartens. Only those songs and games that served as vehicles to rational development were included in the Saint Louis kindergartens—which, Harris wrote, were not designed as a "paradise of childhood" but as a check on the "gushing hilarity" of childhood to prepare the way for future intellectual development. It was not the teaching of Froebel but the warning of Hegel that underlay the schools: "Education through play is liable to result in the evil that the child learns to treat everything in life in a contemptuous way."[32]

In response to the needs of a public kindergarten program, Blow and Harris fashioned a new theory of childhood education which they called symbolic education. Harris advanced the simple but speculative tenet that the child's thoughts preexisted as feelings and emotions. These embryonic ideal forms, however, could not be cultivated directly as Froebel had claimed. Only through the strenuous training of the intellectual faculties, a process Harris believed led directly to reflection, were feelings given general form or "universality," thus allowing them to become ideas. The difficulty was that the ideas of children were hard to reach during the years between ages four and six, a period in which Hegelians believed the child lived in a world of outer and inner symbols (not sparks, but embryonic ideas). Before age four, the child had an understanding of the material world around him through sense impressions alone and was able to recall and analyze past sense impressions through memory though he was still unable to form abstract thoughts. This psychological and educational lacuna—between sense learning and abstract thinking—was called the symbolic stage because Hegelians postulated that during this brief period the child perceived the world entirely through symbols.[33]

It was an important distinction for the Hegelians because the symbolic stage occurred at a critical juncture in the overall development of the child. During these years, Harris explained, the will of the child united with the intellect to produce attention, analysis, synthesis, reflection, and insight. Harris could not overemphasize the educational, psychological, and social consequences of proper training during the symbolic stage, for unless one reached him through his intuitive understanding of symbols, the child might remain stranded in the sensate stage of learning. On the other hand, if the child remained too long in the symbolic stage, intellectual development might be stunted. Because of the need simultaneously to appeal to and transcend the child's use of symbols, the Hegelians called early childhood "a period of potential individual tyranny." Harris had translated the child-training anxieties of the 1870s into rational terms.[34]

The theory of symbolic education remained heavily indebted to faculty psychology. Harris and Blow explained that during the training of the will the faculties were in constant tension. Play, by contrast, was defined merely as a "repose from tension." Harris even suggested that play served as a "refuge for childhood much as art, music, literature, and drama serve the grown-up." He called play the constructive activity necessary for the "realization of independence and the development of the feeling of self." A critical element of the theory was the Hegelian belief that play in the kindergarten was neither a surrender to individual whim or caprice nor a sign of the inner divinity of childhood, but simply a pause in the steady intellectual education of the child—a step in the creation of the self-creative individual. Anna Brackett, like Blow a student of Saint Louis Hegelianism, perhaps even better understood the implication of symbolic education when she applied it to the feminist critique of society. "Civilization means nothing more than individual caprice subjected to rational will," she noted at the Syracuse Woman's Congress in 1875, "the individual to the general good." Blow, however, had in mind only the education of the kindergarten child.[35]

The kindergarten system of education filled the void by "wisely selecting a series of objects that led to full possession of certain geometric concepts and certain numerical concepts," Blow added. "In all these the child finds relations to the fundamental geometric shapes that he has learned to know, and sees with clearness and precision how to realize ideals." Symbolic education, however, was not simply a matter of presenting the objects that satisfied the child's growing intellectual curiosity. Timing was of crucial importance because the child's faculties developed in a highly ordered sequence; early education began with the senses, proceeded to the will, and culminated in the formation of the intellect. "Here the child climbs up on his symbolic pathway, through play, to Absolute Mind," Harris wrote. The kindergarten material was introduced just at the time that the child "becomes conscious of his power over matter and [his ability] to convert it to use." While the gifts and occupations cultivated the inner symbolic thinking of the child, Harris believed, the songs and games trained the child's social conscience, the most effective check against the "potential tyranny" of the kindergarten child. Organized play activities drew the child away from his exclusive interest in the self. "In the plays and games he becomes conscious of this general or social self," wrote Susan Blow, "and there draws the higher ideal of a self realized in institutions over against the special self of the particular individual." The games of the kindergarten were the "activities and occupations of the world of society" *writ small.* Having formed his own ideals through symbolic training, the child learned to adapt these ideals to others before leaving the kindergarten. Caprice had again been subjected to rational will.[36]

At the same time Blow and Harris were working out a theory of the child's moral nature, development, and education. To the Saint Louis Hegelians, the real nature of the child existed in time and space and was identified with "impulses, desires and animal selfishness." The ideal nature of the child, on the other hand, Harris and Blow identified with "righteousness and holiness." Unlike the Transcendentalists, Harris and Blow believed that the "angelic" nature of the child was only *implicit* and not *explicit* and had to be actualized in social institutions. It was simply a question of real and ideal. In the kindergarten, the philosophically real nature of the child was "annulled and subordinated" and his ideal nature made real in its place. The child experienced a secularized conversion experience, a change in heart from animal to divine, depraved to holy. The Saint Louis variety of kindergarten instruction, then, helped the child to renounce "selfishness without sacrificing spontaneity." Harris and Blow felt that symbolic education provided a better alternative to the moral education of the child than did evangelical methods.[37]

Both the individual and social activities of the child in the kindergarten were also subject to a higher moral law. Gradually the child's conscience evolved (but was not perfected) through individual play and social interaction in the kindergarten. "He sees the ideal laws that are absolutely binding above all temporal considerations; he sees the moral law." The higher moral law, derived from evangelicalism and Scottish Common Sense thought, provided the matrix of cultural values in which the symbolic theory of education operated. Child psychology was important for the Hegelians, but Blow was quick to add that "no self-active being can retain its freedom or self-activity except by conforming to moral law." By redefining the social nature of childhood, Harris and Blow had simply "Hegelized" prevailing notions of evangelical early childhood education. The kindergarten block had displaced the hornbook, Hegelian rational development had dislodged spiritual conversion, but the outer structure of early education still closely resembled evangelical education.[38]

The theory of symbolic education brought Harris and Blow into direct conflict with Peabody, who was increasingly apprehensive about the new departures in Saint Louis. "It seems to me there is an error in your premises; that you make human individuality not a spiritual thing, but a mere affect of animal life," Peabody concluded. "Your individual is only the animal and your rational man . . . is purely a spirit of reason not a spiritual person of heart and will, which the human child is . . ." The kindergarten pioneer was especially concerned about Harris's offhand remarks about the importance of lessons in "politeness" in the kindergarten, for she thought she detected yet another example of the stress on mechanical skills and intellectual tasks at the expense of spiritual learning. "Emerson says the intellect is a sensibility and this involves that the heart is apprehension," Peabody lectured the Hegelian. "The heart knows our immortality, our infiniteness, the intellect, our finiteness. Therefore, education must begin with the heart to do justice to our moral nature, which is the product of our personality." In her impassioned letters to Harris, then, Peabody was expressing something more than the classic tension between "head" and "heart," between rationality and emotion, in American intellectual life. The Saint Louis Hegelians had not simply confused method and education; they had seemingly made spirituality subordinate to rationality. To the Transcendentalist mind, the rationalized bureaucratic school culture of

Saint Louis had not only grown hostile to the kindergarten but also to the spiritual individualism that had been the very engine of antebellum reform.[39]

Peabody had gone too far, and Harris used the occasion to attack the group he called the romantic Froebelians. Harris argued that the kindergarten served an important though limited purpose in American education, for Froebel was "as much a religious [or moral] enthusiast as a pedagogical reformer." Froebel provided an ingenious way to systematize education from the cradle to the school, but the usefulness of his insight had been exaggerated by the Transcendentalists, who claimed no less than the "complete moral regeneration of mankind." Harris now scoffed at Peabody's claim that Froebel had discovered the "eternal laws which organize human nature on the one side and the material universe on the other." The pedagogical weaknesses of Transcendentalism now seemed apparent: by stressing the "gushing hilarity" of childhood, the kindergarten teacher unwittingly restrained the child's intellectual development. "The apotheosis of childhood and infancy is a very dangerous idea to put into practice," Harris warned educators in a statement that summarized the long distance he had traveled from his early intellectual companionship with Alcott. In the 1880s, he called his enchantment with Transcendentalism a necessary step in rejecting "blind obedience . . . to arbitrary authority." It had become nothing more than an intellectual milestone.[40]

Having cut themselves off both from Peabody's ideas and Boelte's students, Harris and Blow set out to win their own converts. The short supply of trained kindergarten teachers for Saint Louis schools was, for other reasons, a serious problem. Harris had already made known his objection against the use of German teachers in American schools, to the distress of Peabody and Kraus-Boelte. The superintendent's fears, however, were not solely political. Harris understood that the kindergarten program required the broad-based public support that only large numbers of volunteers could supply. By using trained volunteers in the kindergarten, Harris hoped to reduce expenses and defuse opposition to German educational reform in public schools. Peabody also knew that the success of the Saint Louis kindergarten depended upon training. "You will see, as I do, that a new primary education is necessary as the underpinning of our public school system and that this will require a new special normal training." Harris agreed for different reasons. As he reminded Blow, "It is useless to expect social regeneration from persons who are not themselves regenerated."[41]

The kindergarten training program in its widest sense was for Blow and Harris an experiment in the social regeneration of parents as well as of children. At first the program attracted only women interested in the novelty of the kindergarten idea, but others soon joined the program, "filled with the sublime enthusiasm" of social reform. For Harris these kindergarten teachers became new urban missionaries working for the "regeneration of society morally and intellectually." Others apparently volunteered merely to learn and apply the kindergarten system to domestic education. The children of the poor, raised on the street, were unruly and undisciplined; the coddled children of the rich and the middle class were equally "incorrigible." Kindergarten training was, then, an educational common denominator that many hoped would solve domestic, social, and personal problems.[42]

Recognizing the importance of trained volunteers for the success of the kindergarten program, Blow visited Germany in 1876 in order to study Froebelian training methods firsthand. In Berlin she worked directly under Froebel's disciples, who apparently renewed her zeal for the study of Froebel's arcane philosophy. "We must, however, look out for one thing, and this is, as the Germans would say, that the *intensiv* may keep pace with the *extensiv* growth," she wrote Harris from Dresden, using the German technical agricultural terms for "highly fertilized farming" and "natural fertilized field farming." Blow presumably wanted to underscore the need for philosophical purism in the kindergarten. "The moment any 'mechanism' gets into the kindergarten it is gone," she wrote Harris. "The teachers must know the why as well as the what and how." The visit confirmed Blow's belief in her vocational choice, the rightness of the Saint Louis cause, and her deep interest in training the next kindergarten volunteers. After the brief study-tour, Blow concluded, "I believe it is possible for us in Saint Louis to make our kindergartens the best in the world . . . if only we are careful in the selection of assistants and can manage to have our teachers keep on studying after they begin independent work."[43]

Blow's absence underscored her growing importance to the smooth operation of the kindergarten program. As supervisor, she was the critical link between the volunteers and the office of the superintendent. The system worked well as long as she could personally certify all kindergarten teachers, but when she left the city, the training program quickly broke down. In 1877 the informal, personal process was replaced by a cumbersome committee method in which nominees were screened by normal instructors, confirmed by the vote of kindergarten directors, and finally approved by a teachers' committee of the school board. As a certifying agent, the board was empowered to issue diplomas for kindergarten assistants or directors. Though the bureaucratic structure saved the program from collapse, its defects revealed the extent to which public kindergartens depended on individual effort.[44]

The Board also attempted to implement a system of quarterly examinations that would replace the system of personal recommendations. Current volunteers were screened for competence in reading, writing, arithmetic, geography, and grammar, and those scoring below a certain average were dropped from the program. Future applicants were eligible for salaries after passing the certification examination of the school board. A premature attempt to professionalize the kindergarten, the examination served only to contract the numbers of volunteers in the Saint Louis kindergartens and threaten the experiment.[45]

Despite the attempts to bureaucratize training, Blow's Saturday morning kindergarten lectures expanded by 1877 into a popular course on art, literature, philosophy, and education. The first training class graduated 13 teachers in 1874; the second, 38; and the fourth, more than 150. Blow's revised course of 1877 attracted an audience of more than two hundred Saint Louis women, largely composed of kindergarten teachers, primary teachers, and parents. The course of lectures covered the gifts and occupations and included long digressions on history, literature, and philosophy to "broaden and deepen" the students' understanding. The course could be taken for self-improvement or as preparation for kindergarten teaching. Women with a vocational interest were later apprenticed as kindergarten assistants and worked under the close supervision of a kindergarten director. "I believe too that the Saint Louis kindergarten spirit was at its highest during this period," historian Denton Snider later wrote; "the primitive purity of the cause had not yet been tainted by success, by fame, by partisan and personal ambition, with its bitter antagonisms."[46]

The sheer physical presence of Susan Blow commanded the respect of the students. "She was small in stature, with a slight, well-rounded, and graceful figure, and keenly intellectual face, and was altogether attractive and distinguished in appearance," wrote kindergarten trainee Elizabeth Harrison. Blow usually lectured from an elevated platform while more than two hundred women were "seated in the small kindergarten chairs on either side of tables which extended across two sides of the large double room." It was a physical arrangement that underscored the relationship of master and disciple. From this position Blow spoke with all the moral authority of a German kindergarten trainer. "Her manner of delivery might be described as that of the perfect sincerity of one who had reached bottom rock of truth and who knew it." Her colleague Denton Snider put the matter more simply: "I was the teacher, but she was the ruler."[47]

Blow began the lectures with some minor aspect of the kindergarten curriculum but always ended on a broader philosophical point. Guest lecturers from the philosophical society were often invited. Harris and Snider, usually speaking on philosophy and literature respectively, were the most popular, for they were masters at relating childhood education and self-culture. One kindergarten student, for example, was captivated by Snider's lecture on Herodotus in which he "discussed the . . . commingling of sense perception and imagination." Together they ranged over the classics: from Plato to Hegel in philosophy and from Homer to Shakespeare in literature, always able, in the end, to turn the point to the kindergarten.[48]

Literature often provided the means to relate loftier themes to the kindergarten. For Harris the poet was a "diviner of truth," giving voice to man's highest ideals in a powerful but less formal way than the rational philosopher. For Blow the study of poetry gave comfort to the soul, previously the province of the church. Though they differed in their approach to great works of art, Blow and Harris agreed that the study of the classic writings of Dante, Homer, and Goethe would help the kindergarten trainees overcome their parochial attitudes toward childhood education. As an experiment in popular education, the classes completed the goals announced a decade earlier in the *Journal of Speculative Philosophy*. Reason displaced religious dogma as the basis for understanding their relationship to socially prescribed duties of motherhood and childhood education.[49]

In the classroom, Blow's intellectual dominance and eloquence first made converts and then disciples of the women she professed to serve. "There must be subordination, prescription, personal discipleship," Snider noted. "She was a will-character and was going to enforce her decree, especially as she now felt herself to be the literary dictator of our Saint Louis work." Blow passed effortlessly from Froebelian stories to Hegelian reflections. "She had studied philosophy under Harris, from whom she learned Hegelian thought," Denton observed, "and she could employ its subtleties and their peculiar technique with fluency and insight." Elizabeth Harrison, one of Blow's most attentive students, spoke for the class when she described the power of Blow's lecture style. "Thought swept on to still greater thought," she recalled. After one lecture Harrison was left pleasantly perplexed with a sense of religious well-being rather than rational enlightenment. "The clear cut logic of Miss Blow's arguments had led me step by step from the commonplace things of everyday life to the possibility of companionship with God."[50]

Blow hammered away at the need to replace religious absolutes taught in childhood with the principles of rational philosophy. Most of the kindergartner students had rejected the Calvinistic doctrine of innate depravity as a childrearing theory but were often left with a religious habit of mind that caused them to have doubts about the moral nature of their children and the methods of their education. The kindergarten lectures attracted women who perceived the reality of evil and the dangers it posed to their children but felt unprepared to meet the challenge without a formal system of religious education. As historian William Leach has argued, Saint Louis women, like other women of mid-Victorian America, were shifting "from abstract and otherworldly concepts of truth to a truth hidden within the reality of physical things." The first step, Blow counseled, was to abandon older religious notions of childrearing. "All the teachings of my childhood and early girlhood," Elizabeth Harrison wrote after listening to Blow, "seemed a mockery, a foolish superstition." But the final conversion of Blow's students to Froebelianism came in the moment of inspiration when the student was able to free herself from religious dogma and accept the rational principles of Froebel's symbolic education. There was an irony in these rationalized conversion experiences, for the new commitment to the kindergarten cause was often more emotional than intellectual. "For the first time in my life I began to understand the meaning of the great Christ life and the Master's teaching, His suffering and death," Harrison wrote after attending a Saturday morning lecture. "It was no longer a theological dogma that one must accept in order to be saved, but a luminous, glorious invitation to come up higher to lead the life of true humanity." If Blow's long pilgrimage in a religious wilderness had ended in her conversion to the ideas of Froebel and Hegel, it was an experience she wanted to share with other women in her generation.[51]

Harris's departure for the East in 1880 signaled the break-up of the Hegelian circle in Saint Louis and the end of the kindergarten experiment in the public schools of that city. The kindergarten program had been an experiment in applied philosophy. Prompted by a sense of social urgency, Harris and Blow had hoped to replace an older theological view of childhood education with social views of Hegel and Froebel. Briefly the philosophical circle and the school system expanded to meet the need to retrain the public. At its peak, the Saint Louis experiment created a system of free urban public kindergartens, an occupational subculture, and a wide base of public support. Yet the goals of Harris and Blow were unfulfilled, for they had planned to provide more than a structure for understanding social change; Hegel and Froebel were to replace the social and religious uses of orthodoxy. Hegelianism, however, remained cryptic to most Americans, and without the constant supervision and instruction of Harris the experiment collapsed in Saint Louis by 1884. At the same time, kindergartens modeled after the Saint Louis schools had already expanded to other American cities by the 1880s, in part because of the favorable publicity given the kindergarten at the Centennial Exposition.

5

The Centennial Kindergarten of 1876: Popularization

Visitors to the Philadelphia Centennial Exposition of 1876 were thrilled by the evidence of the nation's technological and industrial progress in its first hundred years. At the fair Alexander Graham Bell first displayed his telephone, Thomas A. Edison his automatic telegraph, and George Corliss his massive steam engine (William Dean Howells had called it "an athlete of steel") that provided the power for the entire exposition. Beyond the major exhibition halls were countless minor buildings containing, in the words of Centennial historian James D. McCabe, not only the delights of a "cosmopolitan culture" but also the machines, tools, products, seeds, natural wonders, and educational aids that had made the country strong. In the Woman's Pavilion, which was "devoted exclusively to the exhibition of the results of woman's labor," were displayed a patent stove, a fountain griddle greaser, and a new attachment for a sewing machine. In keeping with the Centennial theme of progress, however, the Woman's Planning Committee hoped to do more than exhibit the "petty prettinesses" of woman's work. With the full cooperation of the Froebelians, a working kindergarten was installed in the Woman's Schoolhouse to illustrate the latest thinking in early education. "As the kindergarten is the ground from which the schools of the future will grow," one writer at the Centennial noted, "it will receive much attention in the *New Century,*" the Centennial publication of the Woman's Committee, printed on the fair grounds.[1]

American Froebelians at the Centennial hoped that broad public exposure at the fair would demonstrate that the American public was at least ready to listen to their message. But the exposition would also provide a showcase of American education for visiting foreigners. While American educators hoped to mount an impressive display of the American system of universal popular education—the common school ideal—Froebelians were eager to show that the latest German thinking in early education had been absorbed into American schools. For kindergartners the fair was an unprecedented opportunity for both national and international education and publicity; for businessmen, it demonstrated the new commercial opportunities for educational toys and equipment. Together, the sights, the tastes, the sounds, and the visitors themselves, as Lawrence Cremin has pointed out, made the international exhibition part of a lost tradition of mass popular entertainment and education. "The culture obtained by the millions of our people who have found in the fair a mine of information and suggestion," wrote McCabe, "must have a beneficial effect upon the national character."[2]

More than ten million Americans attended the Centennial and many visited the five separate kindergarten displays. One of the most popular exhibits at Philadelphia was the separate Saint Louis kindergarten display managed by Susan Blow. In addition to the Saint Louis exhibit, manufacturers of kindergarten equipment and publishers of kindergarten literature displayed their wares and encouraged the public to use them in their own homes. During June and July 1876, Blow herself conducted classes in the Saint Louis version of the kindergarten. At least two "non-authorized" kindergarten exhibits also were available to the Centennial visitor, but the most popular was the "Centennial Kindergarten," a working school in the Woman's Pavilion that employed a trained kindergarten teacher to conduct a daily lesson with local orphans. To Harris, a Centennial commissioner, the great lesson of the Centennial was the beginning of a mass popular system of American education.[3]

Though most kindergartners wanted a national exhibit at the Centennial, they lacked the organizational resources to mount it. Though some belonged to the American Institute of Instruction and some to the National Education Association (NEA), neither organization fully represented the growing ranks of the kindergarten movement. The NEA, an outgrowth of the National Teachers Association, originally formed in 1857 to represent teachers' interests on bread-and-butter issues, was a more logical choice, for by 1870 the Association represented a broader range of philosophical issues in American education. By contrast, the American Institute of Instruction (AII) was dominated by a group of schoolmen whose increasingly well-defined sense of group professional identity, however broad and democratic, relegated early education to the woman's sphere. Froebelians addressed the AII but rarely acted through its offices. Members of the NEA, on the other hand, were particularly interested in the educational innovations of Germany, and by 1876 the kindergarten department had become the "live department" of the organization. Though the philosophy of the kindergarten was debated in both the NEA and AII, both organizations still lacked a plan for its national dissemination.[4]

The educational debate in the NEA began in 1873 with a meeting of a special Committee on the Kindergarten chaired by William N. Hailmann, a Swiss-born educator, kindergarten advocate, and principal of the German Academy in Louisville, Kentucky. Hailmann held a messianic view of the American kindergarten in which the United States, free of German repression, would provide the natural setting for kindergarten expansion. Hailmann selected a roster of influential friends of the kindergarten to serve on the committee: Henry Barnard, Bronson Alcott, Elizabeth Peabody, William T. Harris, and Adolph Douai, a group he called "clearheaded, true-souled men and women . . . from city and country, from manufacturing and agricultural districts."[5]

The final report of the committee (1873) affirmed the value of the kindergarten but qualified its conclusions. "The immediate aim of the kindergarten," the committee agreed, "is to make children happy." Yet the NEA also recognized the enormous obstacles posed by a public that believed the family was the center of early education, a place where the three R's formed the basis of all later learning. The kindergarten committee also noted that the American public still drew a sharp distinction between play and work and was deeply suspicious of the educational value of play. Despite certain reservations, committee members concluded that the kindergarten would spread naturally in America, "bringing a higher humanity, produced by the work of the mothers, through the perfect education for their sacred calling." The NEA had not fully understood the important changes in popular American attitudes toward play and early education that would dramatically accelerate the growth of the kindergarten movement in the years after the Centennial.[6]

One of the most important steps in the popularization of the kindergarten came from the efforts of manufacturers to capitalize on the leisure time of the new urban middle class. Milton Bradley was typical of the manufacturers of the new childhood equipment who exhibited their wares at the Centennial. Like other men and women active in the kindergarten movement, Bradley had grown up in rural New England, although unlike most New Englanders, he was not a product of a strict Calvinist upbringing. Raised in a Methodist home, Bradley was educated in the standard reading of the region: the Bible, *Pilgrim's Progress*, and *Poor Richard's Al-*

manac. Education in the family drew a sharp line between play and work; games of chance (cards) were excluded, but games of skill (chess and checkers) were permitted. Unlike Harris, Bradley did not attend college though he briefly enrolled in the Lawrence Scientific School after graduating from Lowell (Massachusetts) High School, where he learned mechanical drafting. Family financial ills ended Bradley's formal education, and the young man found employment in bookbinding and lithography during the 1860s.[7]

The Civil War drastically changed Bradley's fortunes. As a draftsman he was called by the Springfield Armory, but was asked to produce games rather than guns. He made "game-kits" for soldier knapsacks: nine-games-in-one, including chess, checkers, and backgammon. One new game, "The Checkered Game of Life," was so popular among the soldiers that charitable organizations ordered large quantities and distributed it gratis to the men of the Union Army. Sales reached 40,000 copies in the winter of 1860–1861. The rules were simple. The players advanced through a highly moralistic board of eighty-four squares (red squares were neutral and white squares were good or bad). Squares of "Disgrace" and "Crime" led losers ultimately to "Ruin," while the more fortunate proceeded to "Happy Old Age." As historians David Adams and Victor Edmonds have shown, Bradley was capitalizing on the mid-Victorian fascination with the relationship of "virtue" to "success." By the rules of his own game, Bradley was a "successful man" in 1876. In the decade after the war, the Milton Bradley Company produced thousands of games and "parlor amusements" designed to be played by children and adults in the comfort of their homes. Overwhelmingly the games appealed to the national postwar nostalgia for "lost childhood," and perhaps lost innocence. "Happy Old Days in Old New England," and "The Old Homestead," and "Sliding Down Hill" were among the company's best sellers. A Centennial pamphlet advertised Bradley's key to success: "Old games which cheered our evenings years ago are gladly remembered and invited especially on a holiday." At the same time, Bradley helped to open a new market for children's games and sentimental family amusements.[8]

At the height of his commercial success, Bradley was introduced to the kindergarten. The businessman first learned of the gifts and occupations from Springfield's colorful German music teacher, Edward Wiebe. Wiebe had received kindergarten training in Germany directly from Froebel's widow before emigrating to the United States in the 1860s. He never forgot the appealing German melodies and completed a manuscript on kindergarten songs and games, *The Paradise of Childhood: A Practical Guide to the Kindergarten*. Though he found little interest in the German system of education among New Englanders, Wiebe took his book to Bradley, who agreed on the beauty of the songs but rejected it for publication because of its difficult and obscure language.[9]

Bradley's meeting with Elizabeth Peabody changed his mind about the kindergarten and eventually made a convert of him. The businessman later described his "educational awakening" after listening to Peabody lecture on the kindergarten. "Miss Peabody's talk carried conviction to my mind and heart, because there was something within me which sprang out to give her words welcome." After his educational conversion, Bradley agreed to manufacture the kindergarten blocks and publish Froebelian literature. Against the advice of his business partners, Bradley also undertook the publication of an illustrated and lithographed edition of Wiebe's *The Paradise of Childhood*. Despite its initial poor sales, Bradley committed the company to manufacture a complete line of "kindergarten toys" even though his partners told him that the new venture would lose the company even more money. Bradley's behavior, unusual for a businessman, needs some explanation.[10]

The answer lay in the new market Bradley envisioned for his "occupational material for the kindergarten" and other educational toys and devices. Before the Civil War, American toy manufacturing was still in its infancy. Since the eighteenth century, imported "toys" and "fancy goods" had been bought only by the affluent, while handcrafted toys, made at home or produced by small family businesses, were in common use. Wood turneries, tin shops, and iron foundries found extra revenue during slack periods by reproducing miniature objects and toys for children; carpentry shops produced infant furniture for a new market. Mass production and a new leisure class after 1865 changed toys from a novelty to a new industry. The toy market became part of a general commercial revolution, which for the first time in American life included the child as a consumer. New shops or "toy stores" especially tailored to the children's trade, such as F. A. O. Schwarz in New York, Fabricius in Saint Louis, Hollowbush in Philadelphia, and Schwerdtmann in Baltimore grew in the 1870s and 1880s. Many were founded by German immigrants. Though Germany continued to dominate the toy industry until World War I, the American market was growing, a fact reflected in "toy departments" like the pioneering one in Macy's. American businessmen, interested in the new market for Christmas gifts, also began to merchandise toys throughout the year.[11]

The commercial success of toy and amusement manufacturers did not escape the watchful eye of the American ministry. Occasionally a zealous evangelical clergyman would sermonize against the growth of the new industry, warning parishioners of the perils of play. One Lutheran minister

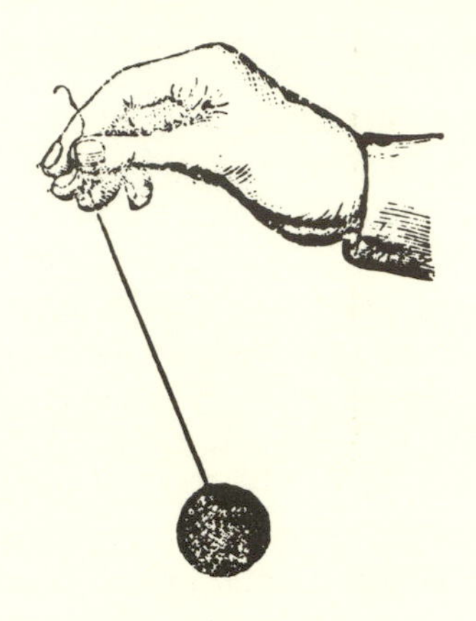
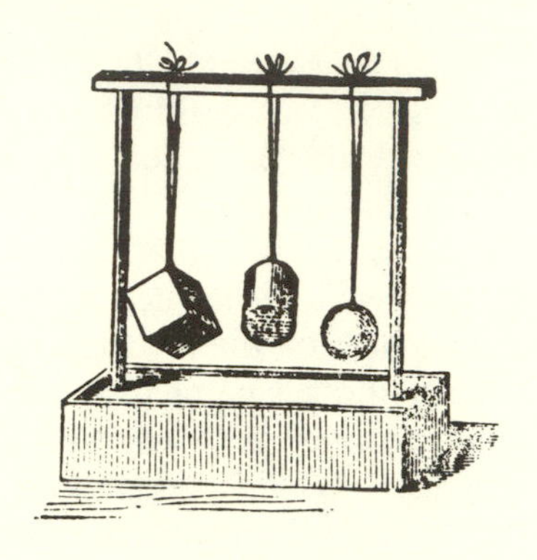

Froebelian Gifts: Gifts one and two. (NEA, *Addresses and Proceedings* 1877:217–218)

thought that the new amusements were at war with the "duties and happiness of domestic life . . . the snowy whiteness of woman's character . . . and the loveliness and grace of childhood." Other clergymen specifically took aim at the snares of toy advertisements. "A Christian household must not sit down and play at Whist," the Presbyterian minister Marvin Vincent facetiously told his flock, "but they are engaged in a Christian and laudable manner if they spend an evening over Dr. Busby, or Master Rodbury Cards." Some Protestant clergymen, perhaps following Bushnell, were willing to give play and amusement a new respectability even before the Civil War. The Reverend James L. Corning wrote in his *The Christian Law of Amusement* (1859) that any game or amusement which promotes "mental and/or moral culture" is sanctified. He conceded that "play is the great business of childhood."[12]

A new advice literature on home or parlor amusements, also reflecting changing public attitudes, advocated a union of moral purpose and domestic entertainment. "Every parent must feel that in the attractiveness, cheerfulness, and pleasure of home lies a great safeguard in the minds of children against the pernicious fascination of vicious and foreign pleasures," wrote the author of *Family Pastime* (1885), "and every parent should seek, therefore, to render the allurements of home superior to

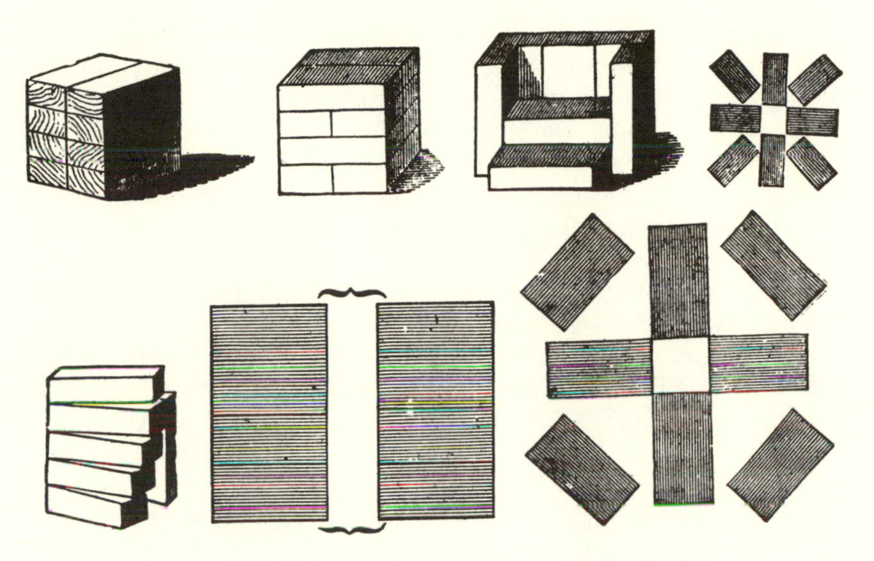

Froebelian Gifts: Gift four. (NEA, *Addresses and Proceedings* 1877:217–218)

those of the world." Other authors went beyond the limits of accepted evangelical purpose and encouraged parents to share the playfulness of their children. "We are terribly troubled about our dignity," Frank Bellew wrote in the preface of his *The Art of Amusing* (1866). "All other nations, the French, the German, the Italian, and even the dull English have their relaxation . . . but we, a political or prayer meeting is about the most hilarious affair in which we ever indulge." By the beginning of the Gilded Age, many Americans were ready to learn how to relax in the company of their children, but they had not shed all of their conservative ideas about the role of play in early education.[13]

At the Centennial, Bradley exhibited his "kindergarten blocks" to this new American audience, as did twenty-two other exhibitors of toys and educational equipment. Milton Bradley made strong claims for the educational utility of his building blocks. The Bradley "occupational material" did not merely entertain, it educated. Another firm, Ernst Steiger Company (founded by a German emigrant), a New York book publisher and manufacturer of educational aids, made similar claims for the educational benefits of its products. Steiger warned parents not to waste the child's valuable home play hours in undirected games. Both Bradley and Steiger recognized that educational supplies were another profitable new aspect of the children's market. The Bradley Company produced "Bradley's Language Tablet," "Bradley's Word Builder," and "Bradley's Sentence Builder." The Steiger Company supplied globes (parlor, scientific, and school), maps, and planetariums. Steiger and Bradley, however, were businessmen with a purpose. Suppliers of kindergarten material, the companies also promoted the educational value of their other goods. Steiger even claimed that home education prepared the child for a vocation and eased the "crisis" of finding a livelihood.[14]

Steiger was not new to the world of international expositions. The New York publisher first gained fame at the Vienna International Exhibition (1873) for his comprehensive exhibit of American newspapers. The display, containing more than 6000 specimens of American journalism, saved the Americans from an otherwise "disgraceful" showing at the fair. One European critic, in fact, praised Steiger as an example of "German individuality and German intelligence" operating "over yonder." Three years later Steiger welcomed the opportunity to display his educational publications at the Centennial, in part to sell his educational products but also as a means for correcting the deficiencies of American education. In his first publication, *Der Kindergarten in Amerika* (1872), a tract written to encourage German-Americans to establish kindergartens and educate their own children, Steiger argued that the kindergarten was even more important in America than in Europe. American public schools, crowded and ethnically diverse, lacked the necessary physical, moral, and intellectual discipline. He noted that one need only look at the fat American children to gain the outward evidence of the problem.[15]

By 1876 Steiger's sectarian approach to the kindergarten in America was changing. With Peabody's encouragement, he began to aim his publications at a larger American readership and undertook the publication of a series of instructive pamphlets, or Kindergarten Tracts, now in English, which could be used to establish home or neighborhood kindergartens. In fact, Steiger agreed to supply Kindergarten Tracts and materials for one year at the fair grounds free of charge. By the Centennial, Steiger's acculturation was complete.[16]

Businessmen like Bradley and Steiger also used advertising to sell their products and in the process often disregarded ideological niceties. Bradley, for example, wrote, "In our miscellaneous list of home amusements we have introduced many features of the Kindergarten occupation," casually renaming the kindergarten blocks "The Original Kindergarten Alphabet and Building Blocks," "The Little Object Teacher," and "Alphabets and Objects Bewitched." Bradley, however, also claimed the endorsement of kindergarten purists for his wares in a leaflet distributed at the Centennial:

"Our material has been prepared under the direction of PROF. WIEBE, Miss Peabody, Madam KRIEGE and others, with the desire to, as far as possible, adapt it to the wants of American Parents and Teachers." The kindergarten was a cause, but it was also a business. Not to be outdone, Steiger issued a *Kindergarten Catalogue* which he called "a list of the Most Complete Assortment of Materials, Gifts and Occupations carefully manufactured in accordance with the directions of Mrs. Maria Kraus-Boelte and other Authorities on the Genuine Froebel system." Together with Bradley's building blocks (priced between 30¢ and 75¢), the kindergarten material provided an inexpensive means for American parents to sample kindergarten education. "These [products] have been used in select schools with much satisfaction and are very valuable in the home." For the first time, kindergarten education seemed to be within reach of most Americans.[17]

Sensitive to the limits of commercial endeavors, Peabody was determined that not only manufacturers publicize the kindergarten at the Centennial. She had given some thought to the role that international exhibitions played in encouraging educational innovation in general and the kindergarten movement in particular. The kindergarten, she pointed out, had been represented in every major foreign exhibition of the nineteenth century, beginning with the original kindergarten exhibit at the London International of 1852. The Philadelphia Exposition of 1876 was simply too great an opportunity to be left to the commercial exhibits, for she realized that Americans and foreigners would form their opinions of kindergartens based on impressions from a few displays. The reformer resolved that the kindergarten be displayed in its "most advanced American form." Peabody called for no improvements to the Froebelian system, an apparent jab at Saint Louis schools, but a kindergarten "only an American can keep." By this she meant an actual working or demonstration kindergarten that would show the "powers of maternal love." If the kindergarten had been successful through displays of Froebelian equipment alone at European exhibitions, how much more so would be demonstration schools using American children taken from a "loveless, motherless" environment.[18]

Preparations for the Centennial Kindergarten were hampered by the lack of a national organization, and Peabody was forced to work through a local group, the Froebel Society of Boston. In purpose and membership the organization was modeled after the London Froebel Society, which was also founded in 1876. The membership contained some of the most socially prominent women of Boston, including Mrs. Louis Agassiz and her daughter Pauline. The purpose of the Society was to disseminate Froebelian ideas by establishing private kindergartens and training schools throughout the United States. The society also helped to support the publi-

Froebelian Occupations: Paper interlacing and pea work. (NEA, *Addresses and Proceedings* 1877:222–227)

cation of the *Kindergarten Messenger,* a small journal Peabody established in 1873, aimed less at defending "Froebel's method" than at providing a forum for American women to learn to identify Froebelian literature. "Our reason for being," Peabody noted, was to encourage American women to form study groups or "Parents' Unions" in order to establish neighborhood kindergartens. By 1876, however, Peabody was apparently able to convince the membership that support of the Centennial should be their first national project.[19]

The immediate challenge before the Froebel Society was to raise funds for the salary of a "Centennial kindergartner." Peabody reminded members of the Society of the "great responsibility to the kindergarten cause" borne by this individual, because only a trained kindergartner could discourage "pretenders at the fair," contrast kindergarten and primary instruction, and demonstrate the importance of kindergarten training. Through the Centennial exhibit, she argued, "the minimum of fair conditions for a genuine kindergarten will thus be advertised." Raising the money was no easy task, for Peabody had difficulty even in sustaining her magazine's subscription lists in the East, a fact made clear in 1876 when it was absorbed as a department of the *New England Journal of Education* under the edi-

Froebelian Occupations: Stick laying and pricking or perforating. (NEA, *Addresses and Proceedings* 1877:222–227)

torship of Thomas Bicknell. Despite the financial difficulties of the journal, Peabody was able to raise the needed funds for a "Centennial kindergartner" through its pages.[20]

The Froebel Society of Boston eventually selected Ruth Burritt, a primary-school teacher from Wisconsin, to manage the Centennial Kindergarten. Like many primary teachers in her generation, Burritt had become dissatisfied with the rigid methods of American common schools. Trained in kindergarten methods under Kraus-Boelte in the 1870s, Burritt was probably one of many American women who wandered into the Froebelian movement as much out of exasperation with old methods of instruction as out of ideological zeal for new techniques. Teaching kindergarten at the Centennial appealed to her because it was the perfect opportunity to show thousands of other American parents and teachers a way out of the routines of early education in home and school. For Burritt, kindergarten teaching was a form of emancipation, though perhaps less strident and more socially acceptable than the other activities taking place in the Woman's Pavilion. The Centennial indeed marked the high point in her career. Here she was placed in charge of eighteen orphans from a local charitable institution, the "Northern Home for Friendless Children." Before large au-

The Centennial Kindergarten. A classroom demonstration at the Philadelphia International Exposition (1876). (*Frank Leslie's Historical Register of the Centennial Exposition, 1876*, p. 118)

diences she conducted a full day of kindergarten exercises, using Boelte's methods and Bradley's products. Daily, the children marched across the fair grounds singing Froebelian songs to the delight of the crowds and press. Throughout the day Burritt paced the children in games and handwork, taking time out only for lunch.[21]

The Centennial Kindergarten gained public notice far beyond the fair grounds. Entrepreneur-journalist Frank Leslie, using a new approach to graphic journalism, captured, and perhaps stimulated, some of the public fascination with the kindergarten. By dividing an art assignment among several artists, each working on one section of the picture, Leslie was able to produce a woodcut within twenty-four hours. The use of multiple woodcuts helped record the immediacy of events better than any technique to date. The illustration of the "Centennial Kindergarten" that appeared in Frank Leslie's illustrated newspaper and was reprinted in his *Historical Register of the Centennial Exposition* was in effect a snapshot without a camera of a kindergarten lesson in progress. Leslie pictured one child holding a Bradley "alphabet block" while the children were seated in Steiger's kindergarten furniture. Leslie was even able to record the public reaction to Burritt's kindergarten lesson. There was a hushed excitement in the faces of more than forty adults packed into an alcove of the Woman's Pavilion schoolhouse.[22]

Local reporters focused some attention on the Centennial Kindergarten amidst the hundreds of competing displays. *The Philadelphia Ledger* called the kindergarten one of the most interesting displays of the fair. "The blessing of Kindergarten training is one of the great discoveries of our day," one reporter wrote. "The rich are seeking it for their children everywhere, and charitable institutions are providing it for their little orphan inmates." *The Ledger* reported that visitors overflowed the gallery space of the demonstration kindergarten and crowded into available space in the doors and windows, noting that "thousands thronged to see the new educational departure and remained hours afterwards to ask questions."[23]

One of the curious visitors was Mrs. Anna Wright, whose personal impressions of the exhibit might have been lost had it not been for its influence upon her famous son, Frank Lloyd Wright. Her story of her trip to the Centennial, however, also reveals much about the impact of the fair on other women. Originally from Wisconsin, Mrs. Wright married an itinerant music master and lay Baptist preacher from New England. Shortly after moving from the Midwest, the Wrights visited the Centennial. An animated woman interested in education, Mrs. Wright engaged Burritt in conversation. Her excitement about the Froebelian method that day was captured years later in her son's autobiography: "At the Centennial at

Philadelphia, after a sightseeing day, mother made a discovery," he recalled. "The Kindergarten! She had seen the 'Gifts' in the Exposition Building." Here was a new departure in education, and like many other parents who visited the exhibit, Mrs. Wright was eager to share the discovery with her children.[24]

The Wright home kindergarten was probably typical of the do-it-yourself approach to kindergarten education following the Centennial. Reluctant to enroll their children in private kindergartens, many American parents were nonetheless willing to try out kindergarten methods at home. "She was eager about it now," Wright wrote in his autobiography. "Could hardly wait to go to Boston as soon as she got home—to Milton Bradley's." After the Centennial, she ordered a complete set of Steiger's kindergarten tracts from a Boston bookseller and acquired a complete set of Froebelian gifts and occupations from the Milton Bradley Company in Springfield. "Here was something for invention to seize and use to create," Wright later wrote. "These 'Gifts' came into the gray house in drab old Weymouth, and soon made something begin to live there that had never lived there before." Though the Steiger material contained ample instructions and illustrations, Mrs. Wright was ready to learn more and enrolled in Kriege's training class. "Mother would go to Boston, take lessons of a teacher of the Froebel method and come home to teach the children," her son later wrote. Her excitement was contagious. "What shapes they made naturally if only you would let them," recalled the famous American architect.[25]

Not all visitors to the Centennial Kindergarten shared the energy or excitement of Mrs. Wright; certainly few had so gifted a child. But the lesson of the exposition was not lost on other parents. After visiting the Centennial, one enthusiastic woman from the Midwest wrote a short manual on kindergartens for use in small towns where training, equipment, and literature were scarce. Nora A. Smith encouraged mothers first to form small study clubs in order to educate themselves using the inexpensive Steiger tracts as texts. Study the "kindergarten bible," she advised parents, "till the truths it holds have taken root in the heart and life." Smith's message was clear: hire a trained kindergartner if possible, but American women could also undertake kindergarten study alone. "There is nothing more valuable to neighborhood life than a kindergarten," she concluded, "no, not even the church itself, of whose work it should always be a part."[26]

Not all public reaction or press coverage of the kindergarten exhibits was favorable. The wide variety of kindergarten products, theories, and practice confused many editors. The American Kindergarten, the Centennial Kindergarten, and the Saint Louis Kindergarten all offered adaptations to American educational needs, but the nuances were confusing. Steiger's and Bradley's products stressed the home use of Froebelian blocks, while others stressed the need to establish separate kindergartens. While many Americans recognized the advantages of the new form of education, most were unwilling to incorporate the kindergarten as a permanent feature of the school system. Americans were cautious because they still feared the foreign character of the kindergarten as much as the possible encroachment upon the family.[27]

Some of the strongest criticism was leveled at the Saint Louis kindergarten exhibit, the intricate handwork of which annoyed many reporters and visitors. Even Elizabeth Peabody admitted that the Saint Louis kindergarten exhibit left a "sad impression" on the public, who thought the handicraft "too perfect" to be the work of children. A writer in the *New England Journal of Education* was less charitable in striking out at the complex ideas embodied in the display. "The elaborate European philosophic system of school culture can not be swallowed whole," he wrote. "Like the theory of evolution it makes too heavy a draft upon the eternities to satisfy our swift American people." Others thought that American parents should study the ideas of Froebel and temper them with "American common sense" before establishing kindergartens. The Centennial Kindergarten, by contrast, probably suffered from its association with the more radical feminist activities of the Woman's Pavilion. One parent called the Centennial Kindergarten "a conspiracy to rob mothers of their little ones for the benefit of the kindergartners." Only in areas of the "extreme wealthy or the extreme poor," she predicted, would mothers be willing to give up their children to the kindergartner at the tender ages of four and five.[28]

Not surprisingly the sharpest criticism came from conservative evangelicals who saw the kindergarten displays as a sign of the growth of Bushnell's brand of liberal Protestantism. The new attack rested primarily on social rather than theological grounds. Conservative evangelicals argued that the kindergarten system would destroy family life by exempting the mother from duties incumbent upon her. At stake was nothing less than the moral purpose of wedlock, which was to provide religious education for the children. To these pious evangelicals, the liberal theories of clergymen like Bushnell and educators like Froebel were still seen as the opening wedges of social chaos. One critic noted that European "romantic notions" of education would bring about social instability by estranging the child from the family. "The family is the elementary unit of the state," he wrote. "Destroy the family, and you subvert the state." By the Centennial, however, these die-hard conservative evangelicals seemed to be in the minority.[29]

While conservatives considered the kindergarten too lenient, many more liberal Protestants believed that the kindergarten was too restrictive. Where evangelicals feared that the child's will would not be broken in the playful surroundings of the kindergarten, moderates believed that the demands of the kindergarten would be too great. Some Protestant parents still believed that early childhood was a "joyous period" when the child should be free from all the responsibilities of adult life. "The first seven years should be the growing age, not the thinking age," wrote one liberal parent. "Who would wish to increase the sorrows, or lessen the joys, [of infancy] by confinement and strict observances of rules." It was, moreover, the Christian nurture of the family that the kindergarten seemed to threaten. "Take a child from its home and away from its mother, and you give it a stone for bread," the parent concluded. It was precisely such fears that other exhibitors hoped to calm in their "unauthorized" kindergarten displays.[30]

Another exhibitor, E. M. Coe, used the Centennial to win converts to her modified American kindergarten system. An outsider to the kindergarten movement, Coe was an honors graduate from Mount Holyoke College. She took her first position as head of the Female Department of Towonda College, a small school in Pennsylvania, but soon grew tired of private school work. "At times I became almost disgusted with the profession, on account of the superficial work done in the schools, made superficial by the desire to please the pupils, and court the patronage of parents," she wrote. Restless in private female schools where teachers spent all of their time correcting "bad habits previously formed," Coe turned to painting with a "passionate fondness." At the same time she felt that "God was fitting her for the great work" of the kindergarten.[31]

Her "American Kindergarten" exhibit at the Centennial marked the end of her vocational search. Unlike the German kindergarten, her American kindergarten was fitted to a people whom Coe described as individualistic, religious, and "eminently practical." Objecting to the emphasis on group games, she claimed to offer individual kindergarten instruction: "In this country the *individual* occupies the highest rank." In order to meet the religious (evangelical) needs of the American people, this unorthodox kindergartner introduced Bible lessons into the kindergarten. One lesson, "The Temple of the Living God," required the child to erect the temple walls with kindergarten blocks. Coe also appealed to "American practicality" by redesigning the Froebelian gifts and occupations, creating new materials that she called the "great world of form," and including pencils, slates, and books along with the geometrical forms of the kindergarten.

Coe's advertisements were even more revealing: "All the Froebel IDEAS adapted to American Wants."[32]

Coe's free spirit angered orthodox Froebelians. "America is a land of dabblers," John Kraus wrote after seeing her kindergarten. "Everywhere there are people who pretend to have kindergartens, without even knowing what a kindergarten is. Quacks seem to make money out of the popularity of the name." The commercialization of the kindergarten at the Centennial angered him, but Kraus was even more upset by the religious overtones of some of the exhibits. He called the "American Kindergarten" an example of the "religious sentimentalism [which] unfortunately still is a power in the land of freedom." By this, Kraus meant evangelicalism and not the rationalized religion of Saint Louis Hegelians. Coe's curriculum, the German educator warned, was nothing more than a "stream of fetid cant, thick with the most shameful hypocrisy." To Kraus the problem with this kind of American moral education was that it changed "love of truth into blind devotion of visionary imaginings." Peabody agreed, noting that moral training was unnecessary in the kindergarten where the "actual exercise of (spiritual) powers" made evangelical education useless. "One could just as well speak of American Christianity, American Beatitudes, American Sermon on the Mount," Maria Kraus-Boelte added, "as to speak about an American kindergarten, adapted to American wants."[33]

As editor of the *Kindergarten Messenger*, Peabody also responded to the commercial kindergarten exhibits at the Centennial. The kindergarten pioneer, in fact, spent several months at the fair, visiting each pavilion and studying the details of the exhibits. In a series of articles, "Letters to the Boston Meeting of Kindergartners," Peabody reported her observations. Not surprisingly, she railed against the "ignorant claims" of Coe's American Kindergarten, while praising the skilled approach to "moral education" of Ruth Burritt. Peabody gently chastised Milton Bradley for including alphabetical letters on his blocks. Kindergarten promoters, in short, were learning the real price of popularization: commercial distortion.[34]

Harris viewed the educational implications of the Centennial from an entirely different vantage point. As a Centennial Commissioner for the state of Missouri, he was able to spend ample time at the fair, considering the hidden educational meanings of the pedagogical displays. Swedish woodworking (sloyd), Russian manual training, and the German and American kindergartens, he concluded, were all educational reforms that reflected the industrialization rather than the moral regeneration of America. Harris observed that in their own lifetimes most Americans had witnessed the "swift passage" of a nation of loosely joined villages content with mounting agricultural fairs to a complex industrial nation capable of sponsoring an international exhibition. The educational exhibits at the Centennial indicated the need to include the kindergarten in a mass system of popular public education. For Harris the kindergarten had already outgrown the limits of antebellum Transcendentalist education.[35]

"Americanization" was a term that also came surprisingly easy to Harris, though he did not have in mind "popularization" of the "American Kindergarten" of the Centennial. For Harris, "Americanization" was a process of accommodation of theory and practice in childhood education. Since theories of education and national cultures were related in a dialectical fashion, Harris told an audience at the NEA, the meaning of the Centennial lay in the appearance of a new set of industrial and social conditions that would necessitate a redefinition (or synthesis) in American education. The Centennial posed two options. The child could learn the necessary manual and rational skills in the public school or in the private kindergarten. Either the American primary school could become "kindergartenized" or the kindergarten could become "Americanized."[36]

Harris clearly favored the public school option, a position most other public schoolmen would not take for twenty years. The primary school still held the keys to the development of the child's rationality, the nub of Harris's theory of education. The "old regime" of the school had squandered spontaneity in "an utterly unnecessary manner," Harris argued before the NEA. Overstressing mechanical discipline, Harris contended, had changed the American child into a human "machine governed by prescription and conventionality." The "Americanized" kindergarten promised to locate a center of education midway between the new education and the old. By engrafting the kindergarten onto the public school, the school system encouraged the growth of intellectual "self-activity" in the proper years: before the rational culture of the primary school.[37]

For Froebelians "Americanization" was an unfortunate word. Peabody and Kraus-Boelte feared that Harris's position would be confused with the popularizations of the kindergarten at the Centennial. Peabody warned Harris that there could not be any improvement of "laws which are internal and inborn." Kraus-Boelte explained that there can be only one kindergarten system; the method was a discovery, not an invention, and since it therefore was not intrinsically German it could not be Americanized. Implicit in their remarks to Harris was the sense among Froebelians that the exposure and publicity of the Centennial had somehow gone awry. While thousands of Americans had been exposed to the ideas of Froebel, still others had been introduced to distortions.[38]

To most kindergartners the growing pains of the kindergarten movement at the Centennial—commercialization, popularization, and regionalization—were valid costs of public exposure. The awards made by outside Centennial judges were taken seriously, for they provided the first yardstick of the growing popular appeal of the kindergarten. Milton Bradley received a bronze medal for his efforts in stimulating kindergarten publications. Ruth Burritt was cited for her "moral energy, great heart, and cultivated skill" in her work with orphan children at the Centennial kindergarten. Susan Blow accepted an award on behalf of the Saint Louis public schools "for excellence of work and for the establishment of kindergartens as part of the public school system." In the popular spirit of change and innovation prompted by the scientific and technological exhibits of the Centennial, public resistance to the German educational theories of the kindergarten momentarily abated. While many mothers were persuaded by the Centennial kindergarten exhibits to enroll their children in private kindergartens, others were beginning to apply Froebel's educational thought to the educational problems of an industrial civilization. No concern would receive more attention from kindergartners than did the plight of the urban child.[39]

6

The Free Kindergarten Crusade (1873–1893)

The brief optimism of the Centennial Exposition failed to dispel the problems of four years of economic depression (1873–1877). Displays of Swedish woodworking (sloyd), Russian manual-training tools, and Froebelian kindergarten blocks provided no immediate solutions to the economic hardships of the 1870s, which were particularly acute in American cities. Even public education seemed unable to meet the needs of the children of the poor urban immigrants in the cities. Relief societies were swamped as children joined the growing number of jobless adults on the streets. The problem of urban childhood, Jacob Riis reported, had become the single gravest "arraignment of a Christian civilization" in an age of prosperity.[1]

Some socially concerned Froebelians responded directly to the economic hardships of urban children by establishing charity kindergartens in working-class neighborhoods. These tuition-free kindergartens provided direct relief to the children of the poor through food, clothing, and education. At first this relief was a form of kindergarten alms, but gradually these reform-minded kindergartners expanded their vision of educational philanthropy. Free kindergartners believed that the urban child could be taught habits of cleanliness and discipline during the day while working mothers could learn the principles of Froebelian child nurture in evening classes. The free kindergarten would also serve as a community center for adult education classes and home-visit programs. By reaching the child at an early age, free-kindergarten adherents hoped to eliminate the problems of urban poverty, help the immigrant mother, save the child, and improve the nation.[2]

The establishment of more than one thousand free kindergartens also dramatically transformed the structure and ideology of the kindergarten movement during the 1880s. Perhaps most obvious was the change in motivation among the first generation of American-educated Froebelians. "In examining the motives which actuated the members of these associations," the Commissioner of Education reported in 1888, "it is evident that the philanthropic, the charitable, has been more dominant than the strictly educational." Beneath the terse report of the Commissioner was a major shift in the social thought of Froebelians from the Transcendentalist faith in individualism to a more guarded optimism in an urbanized American society. The new ideology of the free-kindergarten crusade drew as heavily from the social teachings of Evangelical Protestantism and scientific philanthropy as from the outdated reform ideas of Froebel. Not only did the revised ideology attract new adherents—philanthropists, reform editors, and charity workers—but it also served to vastly expand the rank and file of the kindergarten movement. Enlivened by new ideas and new members, free kindergartners began to explore new institutional settings for social and educational reform; before the conclusion of the debate, they had placed free kindergartens in orphanages, reform schools, church missions, public schools, and social settlements. "The movement needed to be illustrated on a large scale," wrote free-kindergartner-turned-historian Nina Vandewalker, "and the value of the kindergarten as a child-saving agency demonstrated."[3]

One of the earliest attempts to use the kindergarten as a child-saving agency was made by Felix Adler, son of the leader of American Reform Judaism. One year after the crippling railroad strikes of 1877, Adler opened his "Free Kindergarten" to the children of the unemployed. Motivated by the need for immediate relief for the children of the jobless, the reformer provided clothing, hot lunches, and personal-hygiene facilities. The urban child received formal instruction in the Froebelian gifts and occupations under the constant "watchfulness" of a Ladies Committee. But Adler had in mind something more than the "negative advantage" of rescuing the child from the street. Two years after the first free kindergarten, Adler opened his "Workingman's School," an institution that would extend the advantages of kindergarten education to children of ages thirteen and fourteen. Together the schools provided working-class children with Adler's keys to the virtuous life: ethicalism and vocationalism. The "Free Kindergarten and Workingman's School" had become a social experiment aimed at giving a "new dignity of intellectuality to labor and to the workingmen as a class."[4]

The roots of Adler's school lay in the Ethical Culture Society formed in

1876. Affirming the "universal message" of the Hebrew prophets over the "particularism" of Judaism that stressed regaining a homeland, Adler sought a religious creed in which the ethical obligations of man would replace the sectarian message of organized religion. As a student at the University of Heidelberg in the 1850s, Adler had come under the influence of neo-Kantian idealism. The young student was persuaded by the argument that neither the existence nor the nonexistence of God could be demonstrated. But the similarity to Saint Louis Hegelianism ended here, for Adler insisted on the "ethical" as well as the "rational" nature of man. By transforming Kant's "categorical imperative" into an "ethical imperative," Adler believed he had the essentials of a socially relevant religious thought. The Ethical Culture Society of 1876 was to be the great instrument of his thought.[5]

Adler's Ethical Culture movement soon drifted toward education as the center of its programs. Adler believed that poverty had disrupted the natural ethical education of the family and vocation, and therefore that industrialism posed human and educational rather than class or economic problems. Distrustful of the "apocalypticism" of both Marx and Jesus, Adler retreated to a program of transcendental education. "There is a divine power in the world, not individual, manifest in the moral law as revealed in human experience," he wrote in his *Ethical Philosophy of Life*. Like the educator-prophets Alcott and Peabody, Adler understood the transcendental role of the teacher in drawing out the divine in human nature. The parlor conversation had been a limited forum, and Adler sought now to work out his theories in urban educational institutions. The "Free Kindergarten and Workingman's School" was to be the showcase of Adler's philosophy, and soon early education proved to be the most successful element of Adler's initiative after community fears had subsided and the advantages of hot lunches, supervised play, and formal instruction had become apparent. Within two years, free kindergarten education had become a permanent feature of the school. Adler believed that ultimately all social institutions would be brought into a new equilibrium, allowing the complete ethical and vocational education of the individual from childhood to adulthood.[6]

The success of the free kindergarten, however, was soon obscured by popular fears of the "Workingman's School." Most educators and charity workers were unwilling to lend support to the school because the name was identified in the public mind with the radicalism of the early labor movement. For example, in Chicago, where labor tensions ran high in the early 1880s, Ethical Culture sponsorship of free kindergartens was delayed a full decade. Even those who understood the conservative aims of the movement were critical of Adler's program. As Commissioner of Education, Harris agreed that education should be responsive to economic hardship but believed that manual training at the "Workingman's School" sacrificed reading, writing, and arithmetic skills needed by the children of the working class. As did others, Harris feared their illiteracy more than their idleness. Blow recognized and welcomed the limits of educational reform movements. "I am glad I am sure about education," she later wrote, perhaps disingenuously, to Harris. "That gives me something to work for. Social questions I do not understand and I can't agree or disagree without knowing more about them."[7]

Harris's own efforts to expand the kindergarten enrollments in poor urban neighborhoods began in Saint Louis (1873–1877), then the only American city in which the urban poor could obtain a free kindergarten education. The scope and definition of the Saint Louis experiment, however, fell short of the goals of the new reformers. Harris hoped to use the kindergarten only as an auxiliary to the school system. Firmly convinced that the main avenues of socialization remained the family, the church, and the state, he was unwilling to extend the kindergarten influence to the home. The kindergarten was a one-way bridge between the home and the school; on it the child moved into the world of Hegelian institutions. As an administrator, Harris clearly recognized that his power lay in the school system and not in the urban neighborhood.

Social questions were very much on the minds of other free-kindergarten advocates. In fact, as labor tensions attendant on immigration mounted throughout the 1880s, a pervasive fear of the children of the newcomers gripped many American cities where socially elite women were particularly vocal in outlining the dimensions of the coming educational crisis. In Cincinnati, for example, Mrs. Alphonso Taft, mother of the future president, was convinced that because of his home life the "mind of the child of the workingman needs training more than the mind of the child of the higher life." To others the specter of a generation of poorly educated children of immigrant workers was all the more loathsome since they believed that ignorance could not be contained by class boundaries. Taft spoke for others when she voiced the fear that the "stupid and stolid" children of working parents challenged the well-being of all classes in the public school, where they formed a "clog and hindrance, absorbing the time and energies of the teachers to remedy previous neglect." The note of urgency was more significant than the perception of events in such pronouncements. Lay reformers recognized that a wide distance still separated Adler's and Harris's conception of the proper education of the working class but advised others that time might be running out. "Do we want a more conscientious class of working people, those who are good and true and honest, and who believe that work is better than beggary?" Taft questioned. "If you want this, train the children."[8]

Beyond fear lay a new interest in environmental determinism as a counterpoint to moral self-sufficiency in the social thought of free kindergartners. As convinced as many were of the existence of a "blot upon our boasted civilization," free kindergartners were equally sure of its root causes. "In close proximity to the wealthiest, most luxurious homes stands the miserable tenement house and the shanty, where a number of our little pupils live," one free kindergartner reported. For the first time, the potential kindergarten child was seen as a victim of his environment, not as a Wordsworthian babe fresh from the hands of God and trailing clouds of glory. Both romantic views—childhood seen as virtuous or as debased—provided ample material for inflamed rhetoric of urban social reform. "Their bodies are becoming diseased by neglect, their minds brutalized by contact with indecent sights and sounds, and their souls, oh! their poor souls, hardened by contact with lying and thieving, and swearing, they are almost squeezed out of existence," wrote a free-kindergarten director in self-righteous indignation.[9]

At the same time, the educational implications of the "social question" were fully occupying Harris's attention. Specifically, Harris had refined his views on the role of the kindergarten in social reform and presented them in an 1880 report to the American Social Science Association (ASSA). Founded in 1865, the ASSA was devoted to broad "social inquiry" but made little distinction between questions of "social reform" and "social policy" in its early years. Members of the association considered themselves men of enlightenment interested in a wide spectrum of social problems—sanitary conditions, poor relief, prevention of crime, law, prisons, and the education of the poor. The ASSA, according to historian Thomas Haskell, was founded on the naive assumption that the "ills of society might vanish if only enough right information could be assembled in one place and brought to the attention of rational minds." Spurred by such sentiments, ASSA members went about their business in an orderly manner, organizing the association into four departments: Jurisprudence, Finance, Health, and Education. As a leader in both Hegelianism and education, Harris was a likely choice to chair the Education Department, a post he held between 1878 and 1886. It was just the kind of organization in which Harris worked best, for he could range freely between pure social thought and its institutional applications. Under his leadership, the Education Department examined public schools, reformatories, colleges, and lyceums after first investigating the social function of the kindergarten.[10]

Harris appointed a subcommittee on kindergartens that included an old colleague, Henry Barnard, and a newcomer to the kindergarten movement, Emily Talbot, a founder of Boston University and an advocate of public kindergartens. The report reiterated the articles of faith established during Harris's years as school superintendent in Saint Louis. The committee noted that the kindergarten would be most useful in instilling "habits of personal neatness and cleanliness, courtesy and deference to others, punctuality and regularity, and proper use of language" among the children of the working poor. Ever mindful of Hegelian principles, Harris added that the kindergarten must be managed "so as to aid and not hinder rational purposes." But there was also a new urgency in the message of the kindergarten subcommittee to the ASSA. "From the fact that social science seeks to discover the sources of evil in civilization," the committee concluded, "it is interested in any devices that will reach the proletariat and neutralize the seeds of perverseness and crime in their earliest growths." Harris and his colleagues were more convinced than ever that "no device promises fairer results in this direction than the Kindergarten."[11]

The ASSA report came after a decade (1870–1880) of debate among reformers, educators, and philanthropists over the impact of the city on the child. By 1880, however, both the setting and the content of the child-saving debate were beginning to change. Impatient with the highly generalized discussion of child saving before the ASSA, more practical social reformers had formed a companion organization earlier in the 1870s, the National Conference of Charities and Corrections (NCCC). While the parent organization continued to treat the theoretical issues of "social economy," the NCCC membership concerned itself with the immediate problems of "what to do with the poor . . . the insane . . . and the criminal classes." For almost a decade the two organizations met jointly until the widening gulf between social theory and practice prompted the NCCC to meet separately after 1879.[12]

The new debate over child saving took place in the context of the emergence of "scientific philanthropy." Faced with the virtual breakdown of the poor-relief system in the years after the depression of 1873, charity workers sought new principles upon which to base good works. Most professionals agreed on the need to replace the old system of direct relief to the poor through outdoor programs of almsgiving. Poverty workers found new broad areas of agreement: efficiency, regulation, and direct contact in work with the poor of the cities. As historian Robert Bremner has shown, philanthropists sought to demonstrate that "true charity was a matter of the head as well as the heart."[13]

The very basis of child-saving work was transformed under the new principles of scientific philanthropy. When charity reformers rejected the older "moral-fault" explanation of crime and pauperism among children, Mary Mann's brand of kindergarten charity and temperance suddenly seemed old-fashioned. Only a decade earlier the Transcendentalist naively hoped that the kindergarten would prompt a change of heart and thus influence men to "stay home from the grog shop to hear their four year old babies sing." Free kindergartners, influenced by scientific philanthropy, now doubted whether individual regeneration could precede social reform in the city. Empirical evidence suggested that the child was molded at a very early age by his environment, probably before the age of six, and in the slum was more likely to become a criminal or a pauper. Free kindergartners had to act quickly because the urban child was literally doubly disadvantaged by his environment. Thrust out of the family, he was exposed to the debilitating influences of the street just at the time he was most vulnerable. Science supported the arraignment presented by the social reformers; most new charity workers agreed with Riis's view that the "tenement stamps the child's life with the vicious touch."[14]

Scientific philanthropy underscored the urgency of the problem of urban childhood but provided few new solutions. By the 1880s, two approaches—institutional and family—dominated the discussions of charity workers. Both systems had roots deep in antebellum reform. Institutional child savers favored the separation of the children in foundling hospitals, reform schools, orphanages, and asylums. Products of the Jacksonian search for an ordered society, the institutions were designed to counter the disorderly conduct of dependent children with the routine of institutional life, shielding the child from hunger, abuse, and neglect. The second school of thought favored the "placing-out" of children in foster homes in the country. Charles L. Brace, a pioneer of the New York Children's Aid Society, argued that the child in a rural home was removed from the evil influences of both city and institution while the home life was reestablished in a healthful environment. Professional quarrels over solutions, however, did not obscure a broad consensus among child savers on the problem of the urban child. Removal of the child from the baleful influence of the urban environment either to an institution or to a foster home was the solution to the problem of crime and pauperism.[15]

The search for "scientific principles" had only heightened the old debate over child saving. Institutional approaches that undermined the home, "the fortress of the American people," seemed flawed to many charity workers. "We may accept institutions as stern and sad necessities and use them as a physician uses a drug, to help nature throw off the disease, not substitute it for the steady, curative treatment which comes with long, faithful nursing," wrote one reformer. At the same time, the placing-out system was especially vulnerable to the attacks of the social workers. Unregulated and inefficient, the system seemed wedded to the excesses of individualism which characterized benevolence before the Civil War. Tales of mismanagement, careless placement of children, illegal and exploitive apprenticeships, and general lack of supervision fueled the debate. Critics charged that the system had only swollen the ranks of the paupers and criminals in the West. At the same time, Riis himself noted that thousands of children remained trapped in the city. Bolstered by new facilities and methods, advocates of the institutional approach joined the attack. One proposal, "the cottage plan," which favored smaller units of children under the care of a "Christian lady," aimed at restoring the broken or inadequate family life of the urban child. One prominent charity worker, taking pride in a model institution, remarked at an NCCC annual meeting that "Our object is to save, not scatter."[16]

The new view of urban poverty challenged both approaches to child saving as remedies that received the child after the "stamp of the tenement" was already upon him. Data on the high rates of crime and pauperism in poor neighborhoods seemed to confirm the environmental explanation. Even when the family survived, charity visitors observed, the figures of crime and pauperism remained high in the city. Absent from the home for long periods, the working mother often became the unknowing and unwilling agent in the delinquency, truancy, and ultimate indigence of her children. Ignorance added to the neglect by the urban immigrant mother. Unschooled in the new facts of diet and health being uncovered by the child-study movement, the poor mother was unable to raise her children properly. The logic of scientific philanthropy led social reformers to search for preventive and, inevitably, educational measures. "New methods of education are opening a new era in the intellectual and moral development of children," Anna Hallowell told a committee of the ASSA in an address on the care and saving of neglected children.[17]

Within the NCCC charity workers began to stress the environmental causes of poverty, preferring "social misfortune" to "moral misconduct" as the explanation for the problems of urban children. They firmly believed that the intemperance, immorality, laziness, and dishonesty of the parent would, lacking intervention, imprint the child. Women working in organized charity now emphasized the imprisonment, ill health, neglect, unemployment, and ignorance of the working parent as the chief causes of urban poverty. Based on "scientific principles" of charity, charity workers were searching for a means to reach into the urban neighborhood and to save the child from social misfortune. "The old benevolence was simply relief. Then came the idea of reformation, then prevention, and now at the end we have an idea that is above them all," noted W. Alexander Johnson. "We want to apply benevolence to the betterment and enrichment of life."[18]

One solution to the problem of urban childhood came from outside the professional channels of child saving. The first generation of American-trained kindergartners, the students of Blow and others, seized upon the problem of the children of the poor as their own special province. Speaking before the NCCC and other charity organizations, a few courageous kindergartners declared that the kindergarten was a scientific child-saving agency. Froebel's advice to visit the kindergarten child at home was now seen in the new light of scientific charity; suddenly the kindergarten seemed up-to-date. Trained kindergartners could instruct the child in the gifts and occupations and the working mother in Froebelian principles of hygiene. By reaching the child before the stamp of the ghetto had molded him, the free kindergartners hoped to prevent the growth of future generations of the paupers, criminals, feebleminded, and insane that were filling American institutions. One reformer noted that the child was the "whole problem of charities and corrections" and that the free kindergarten provided the answer. "There is as much science in charity work, as in any other work," California kindergartner Sarah Cooper wrote after attending the 1889 meeting of the NCCC. "We need to understand how to administer it. I expect to devote the rest of my life to benevolence as far as I can."[19]

Cooper's life is important because, perhaps more than any other kindergartner's, it illustrates the combination of Christian benevolence, what historian Page Smith called the "Protestant Passion," and scientific philanthropy that underpinned the free-kindergarten crusade. Sarah Cooper, a little-known Bible teacher in San Francisco, had become increasingly dissatisfied with the rigid Bible lessons based on the life, death, and resurrection of Christ. After a visit to a local kindergarten in 1878, Cooper adapted kindergarten pedagogy to her Bible-class work. Cooper's Sunday-school reform work might have remained a matter of local interest except for her friendship with her second cousin, Robert G. Ingersoll. Her association with America's leading infidel raised the suspicions of orthodox members of her church, and Cooper's work in the modest kindergarten Sunday school became the basis of a heresy trial.[20]

A deeply religious woman, Cooper had suffered greatly in the early years of her marriage, losing three children by disease and her husband by suicide in 1885. Her own hardships brought her closer to Ingersoll, in whose deep humanitarianism she found comfort. Rejecting his agnosticism, Cooper nevertheless shared some of Ingersoll's dissatisfaction with orthodox Christian theology and frequently wrote to her cousin about the need to replace the concept of a vengeful God with a theology of domestic love. For Cooper, Christian nurture in the family became the foundation of evangelical Christianity, for it supported parental and maternal authority, which she called the pillars of "love" and "law." In Froebelianism, Cooper found the extension of these Christian principles.[21]

Cooper quickly adapted the kindergarten technique to her Bible-class work, for she hoped it would prompt evangelical Christian women to update their teaching methods, extend education to the children of the poor and rich alike, and revise their narrow views of Christianity. In particular, Cooper at first hoped to reform the Sunday school. She told her adult Bible class that the traditional Sunday school methods and lessons were inadequate in two important respects. First, Evangelical Protestant texts had failed to stress the importance of the material, bodily, and spiritual development of the child. "Froebel, the founder of the kindergarten, was one of the most devout men," Cooper wrote. "He insisted that the spiritual and physical development of childhood should not go separately." Second, the Sunday school excluded children outside the church.[22]

Cooper's Sunday-school work aroused uncertainties in James B. Roberts, an orthodox deacon and elder of the church. Believing in a literal reading of the Scriptures, Roberts began an informal investigation of the new teaching methods. After he had visited the kindergartens of the city, the deacon's suspicions grew. Instead of children in earnest prayer, he found children at play. He was also upset by the kindergarten songs and games, which lacked any mention of Christ. The metaphysics of Froebel's games so bewildered Roberts that he began a formal inquiry into Cooper's right to teach in the Presbyterian church.[23]

A panel of churchmen requested evidence in 1881 that the Bible teacher was "thoroughly orthodox and Calvinistic in her beliefs" and possessed the "intellectual endowments" of a Christian woman. When Cooper asked for a formal hearing, the request resulted in a heresy trial. The formal charges of the Presbytery of San Francisco revealed the deeper meaning of the trial. In addition to several general indictments, Cooper was charged with teaching "allegorical and mythical interpretations of the scriptures" and holding "sentimental and humanitarian" views not in accord with the orthodox creed of the Presbyterian church. As her friend Commissioner of Education John Eaton recognized, Cooper was on trial for her Froebelian ideas, thereby drawing national attention to the kindergarten movement. The most prominent kindergartners of San Francisco were called to testify concerning the Christian orthodoxy of kindergarten teaching—a difficult task. Kate Smith (later Wiggin), the young, attractive head of the Silver Street Kindergarten, became a key witness. When Smith cited the Lord's

Prayer as an example of Sunday-school teaching that did not mention Christ's name, the charges soon collapsed. Cooper was eventually cleared and invited to remain a member of the church. Voluntarily withdrawing in 1881, she joined a Congregational church where she continued her kindergarten Bible classes. The trial helped to popularize the free kindergarten and at the same time to sever its work from the churches.[24]

The trial reinforced Cooper's conviction that the theology of the church was "husk and dry bones." Writing to Ingersoll, she called the work of the church "organized hypocrisy." Gradually Cooper became convinced that the work of the Bible school teacher lay outside the church. "Thank God it is becoming to be more and more understood that religion is not alone a preparation for some future world," she wrote, "but a grand instrument for the improvement of this." The kindergarten became for Cooper the work of the Christian Church reinvigorated, for it literally followed the Christian teaching: "Whosoever receiveth a little child in my name receiveth me." The immediate result of the trial was to drive kindergarten social reform out of the church and into the slums.[25]

Work in a free kindergarten appealed to other members of the first generation of American-trained kindergartners. Too young to participate in the great moral campaigns of antebellum America, the free kindergartners grew up in an atmosphere of moral fervor that surrounded the antislavery cause. The home lives of Eliza Cooper (later Blaker) and Anna Hallowell, both born of Philadelphia Quaker stock, were typical. Morris Hallowell, Anna's father, risked financial ruin resulting from his outspoken position on the antislavery cause. Jacob Cooper, Eliza's father, volunteered for the Union army at the age of forty when he felt that the cause of human freedom was in jeopardy if the North lost the war. "As the abolitionist surrendered her whole being to the great movement," free kindergartner Amalie Hofer wrote, "so the kindergartner must learn to look upon her work, not merely as a scientific profession but as a Christian movement."[26]

Experience had prepared a generation of American women for the kindergarten movement, but in the 1880s sudden inspiration prompted hundreds of kindergartners to actually enter the slums. Lucy Wheelock was preparing for a college education at Wellesley College when she learned of the free-kindergarten cause. Visiting a kindergarten in Boston, she felt as though "the gates of heaven were opened and I had a glimpse of the kingdom where peace and love reign." Elizabeth Harrison's "conversion" to kindergarten social reform was no less dramatic. As a young woman from Iowa, visiting Chicago, Harrison stumbled on a free kindergarten and training school that opened the door to "a world of glorious thought and inspiring activity." Kate Douglas Wiggin was introduced to Froebel by

Elizabeth Peabody but resolved to harness the "moral energy" of the kindergarten to social problems. "I walked joyously into the heart of a San Francisco slum," she recalled, "and began experimenting with my newly learned panaceas."[27]

As motivation and rationale, Evangelical Protestantism helped to explain the individual choices of free kindergartners. Adherents to the free kindergarten cause had adopted some, but not all, of the ideology of scientific philanthropy. The free-kindergarten program also reaffirmed the Bushnellian belief in salvation as a gradual process of Christian nurture in the family, which they believed had been denied the children of the urban poor who were often literally raised in the streets. On balance, however, the free-kindergarten crusade had not shed all of its deeper religious roots in mid-nineteenth-century social reform. Free kindergartners simply subordinated their concern with individual salvation to the more immediate need for benevolent social reform. Like antebellum Sunday-school teachers, free kindergartners continued to be motivated by what Clifford Griffin called the "infinite concern for other peoples' souls." The benevolent men and women of the free-kindergarten crusade were simply extending sanctifying grace to the children of the urban poor through scientific philanthropy.[28]

Free-kindergarten associations, private voluntary groups that supplied the initial funding, were the vehicles by which the new reformers put the Christian benevolence into action. At first the associations were designed only to meet the immediate needs of the urban child by providing food, clothing, and education. Gradually most associations expanded services into the community: home visits, evening classes for fathers, and afternoon classes for mothers. Most association directors planned for the eventual public school adoption of kindergarten facilities and saw no conflict between bureaucratization and charity. The pragmatic approach to urban reform was now explicit. "The kindergarten association seemed, therefore, to meet the need of the hour," wrote Nina Vandewalker. "It afforded opportunity in part for the acquaintance with conditions that must precede intelligent effort for relief, and furnished an agency by which an amelioration of some of the conditions could be effected."[29]

The free-kindergarten associations sometimes revived older agencies of child relief in the city. When the Young Women's Christian Association of San Francisco was about to abandon its infant school, for example, the Golden Gate Kindergarten Association offered to replace it with a kindergarten. In Louisville and Philadelphia, workers in free-kindergarten associations augmented the facilities of the children's-aid societies with kindergartens. Often the free kindergartens found temporary quarters in the church; indeed, Dwight L. Moody's church served as the home of Chicago's first free kindergarten. The New York Children's Aid Society itself recognized the need for reform of child-saving institutions in the city. Without abandoning the placing-out system, the New York society gradually created a series of urban institutions: a night school, a day industrial school, a lodging house, and a free kindergarten.[30]

Between 1880 and 1890, more than one hundred free-kindergarten associations were formed to carry out similar goals in large and small American cities. In Chicago, New York, and San Francisco, the wives of community business leaders underwrote the initial costs of salaries, equipment, and classrooms for the instruction of the poor. In smaller cities the work of kindergarten associations was carried out through the subscription method, a direct appeal to a large number of small donors. In one small midwestern city with a population of 37,000, for example, contributions of as little as fifty cents per month were welcomed to support a free kindergarten. Church groups and other philanthropic organizations were contacted first in compiling subscription lists. This method was used successfully in Louisville, Cincinnati, and Grand Rapids.

Not all free kindergartens were funded through subscription. For almost two decades in Boston, charitable kindergarten work was the philanthropic concern of one individual—Pauline Agassiz Shaw, daughter of famed Harvard scientist Louis Agassiz. As a young woman, she was enthusiastic about educational experimentation, an attitude spawned perhaps by her unorthodox intellectual upbringing in Cambridge. She supported experiments in sloyd, industrial education, and vocational training. When she married Quincy Adams Shaw, heir to a great copper fortune, she acquired the means to undertake major educational programs. At the urging of Peabody, Shaw soon focused her attention on several failing Boston kindergartens as her principal philanthropic venture. She also opened two kindergartens outside of Boston and within five years was supporting 31 free kindergartens at an annual cost of $200,000. The *New York Times* reported that "few wealthy persons have made better use of their fortunes."[31]

West Coast philanthropists worked through associations rather than via individual subsidy. In California Jane Stanford and Phoebe Apperson Hearst, women whose wealth stemmed from railroad and mining fortunes respectively, were the major patrons behind the Golden Gate Kindergarten Association. First approached by Sarah Cooper, Hearst financed the construction of the Association headquarters and the operation of seven free kindergartens. The "kindergarten angel" of the Golden Gate Kindergarten Association sharply increased her contributions because of the role of the Association in providing relief to homeless children after the San Francisco earthquake and fire of 1906. Christian benevolence and not scientific philanthropy was the basis of Cooper's appeals. In response to Hearst's generosity, Cooper wrote: "It is Christ's plan for the redemption of this world, and He is moving Christ-like souls of this world, like your own blessed self, to turn with infinite tenderness toward the neglected children."[32]

Cooper's organizational genius went beyond fund raising. In her effort to expand the free kindergartens to the worst slum area of the city (the infamous Barbary Coast), Cooper was able to enlist the support of San Francisco's daily newspapers. With a keen eye for public relations, Cooper called the new project an "investment for the commonwealth," and in her reports and interviews always stressed the civic values of the free kindergarten—crime prevention, industrial preparation, and character training. "Hard headed capitalists, who want to realize good per cents on their investments, need only to figure up the relative costs of supporting alms houses, and places of reform and refuge, and what it costs to run a kindergarten, to see where the balance would come," Cooper wrote in another report. With the aid of her Bible-class volunteers, she soon opened other kindergartens throughout the city. Even Susan Blow called the Golden Gate Kindergarten Association "the largest, wealthiest, best organized and most flourishing association for the extension of the Froebel system."[33]

In Chicago the free-kindergarten program grew up against the backdrop of civic pride and social reform. The Chicago Women's Club briefly sponsored a free kindergarten in the city during the 1870s. By the next decade two privately sponsored free kindergartens were opened to the children of the poor, and in 1881 the Chicago Free Kindergarten Association was formed to promote the establishment of kindergartens in the city. The initial meeting included the most important wealthy women of the city, including Mrs. Potter Palmer, Mrs. George Armour, and Mrs. W. A. Montgomery. Within four years (1884) ten free kindergartens served the poor in the Chicago area.[34]

By 1890 there were 115 free-kindergarten associations in the United States, maintaining 223 schools with a combined enrollment of 14,987 children. The success of the kindergarten crusade far exceeded the initial expectations of the free-kindergarten reformers. "These working centers form a network from city to city across our continent. The self-appointed stewards of the new education are a thoroughly organized force," free kindergartner Amalie Hofer wrote. The kindergarten associations indeed, for the first time, formed the basis for a highly unified movement. "The seventy-five officered kindergarten associations form a ganglia of vitalizing centers throughout our country and constitute what we name the kindergarten movement," wrote Hofer at the peak of the crusade. She was correct if overexuberant.[35]

At first the free-kindergarten curriculum followed the traditional Froebelian program. Free kindergartners, in fact, hoped to demonstrate the universal qualities of childhood by applying identical kindergarten pedagogy to both slum and middle-class children. A Louisville free kindergartner wrote: "The minds of the prince and the pauper unfold in obedience to the same divine laws." The physical and social environment of the slum, free kindergartners argued, had marred but not destroyed the child. "However wretched their condition, the element of Hope is never wanting," reported the president of the Cincinnati Kindergarten Association. "The important question is how to reach these neglected waifs of humanity, and save them from the debasing influences of corrupt associations." In the proper educational environment, the free kindergartners believed, all slum children could respond to the Froebelian program.[36]

In the free kindergarten, the slum child was to be introduced to a new world of sight and sound. The contrast between the brightly painted kindergarten room, decorated with plants and animals, and the squalor and deprivations of the slum, was in fact an important part of the free-kindergarten ideology. Some free kindergartners overreacted. "There is danger from over-ornamentation of the school-room by pictures, flowers, birds and other interesting objects, by which the room becomes to the child's fancy a museum," Harris warned social reformers at a meeting of the American Social Science Association. Still free kindergartners took great pains in preparing the classroom for the urban child. "They have come from the tenement houses, where they belong to large families living in one, two, or three rooms," *Harper's Monthly* reported. "There is no privacy in these homes because there is no space for it; privacy is denied the very poor." The abundance of toys and games in the kindergarten, moreover, stood in sharp contrast to the relative paucity of playthings in the slum. In some schools pride of ownership was stimulated by lending or giving the Froebelian "gifts" to the slum families. Reaching the urban family had become a priority of free kindergartners, a curious blend of romantic enrichment and environmental compensation.[37]

The physical realities of life in the slum prompted other modifications of the kindergarten regime. Free kindergartners firmly believed that through ignorance, neglect, or circumstance, the immigrant mother often sent her child to school physically unprepared. In response to the needs of working mothers, the free kindergarten opened its doors early in the morning to receive the children. The teacher first attended to the child's physical needs. "It is not uncommon for the good matron to give a warm breakfast to some child who has come, unwashed, uncombed, and breakfastless, to the one haven of comfort—the kindergarten," Sarah Cooper observed. Personal hygiene and nutrition for the socially minded Froebelians preceded the abstract and at times physically demanding lessons of the kindergarten. Hands and face washed, clothing cleaned, and breakfast provided, the urban child was ready for his morning kindergarten lesson.[38]

Gradually even the smallest details of the kindergarten program were tailored to meet the presumed special needs of the urban child. A director of the Louisville free kindergarten specifically outlined the child's daily regimen in a detailed set of instructions to kindergarten assistants. After an individual greeting, the slum child was seated at an assigned table and set to work. The director advised her assistants to begin with "bright music and rhythm [which] starts good circulation and thus throws off all effects of any ill-usage at home." The morning exercises were concluded with songs and games designed to "promote courtesy and care of others in selection of partners." At mid-morning, the teacher was to "introduce the thought of the day," usually in the form of a story. After lunch the child was again assigned to a table to work with the gifts and occupations. "This gives each child the [chance] to express through materials the individual conception of the thought given in morning exercises," reminded the director. The final exercise of the day was a constructive occupation—"a chance for the child to work independently in drawing, painting, wood, tin, wire, or leather." But even at the end of the day, freedom was not complete, for the child was asked to put the "thought of the day in some permanent form to take home."[39]

Kindergarten education did not end in the classroom, for teachers hoped that the child's morning lessons and exercises would reach the urban family. "Every kindergarten child takes into its home—even the lowest—a purer, fresher, moral atmosphere," wrote a Louisville free kindergartner. "Where there are two and in some cases three children from one family, the influence carried into the home is doubled and trebled. Does this not change the atmosphere of the home?" In addition to the habits of cleanliness and thrift carried by the child to the home, parents often returned to the kindergarten in the evening for lessons in child care. "The kindergarten in the tenement-house quarter is a fountain whence flow streams of influence that penetrate hundreds of homes and carry cleanliness, kindlier manners, and higher standards of living with them," wrote one observer. The slum child, then, was seen as a wedge into the urban neighborhood. The education of the child was only the first step in a program of urban neighborhood reform. "The social uplift is felt," Richard Watson Gilder, president of the New York Free Kindergarten Association, reported to the National Education Association, "first, by the child; second, by the family; and, third, by the neighborhood."[40]

In order to extend and amplify the impact of the free kindergarten in the neighborhood, teachers visited parents at home in the afternoon. "We must visit those homes, and learn more of the parents, and children, learn more of their habits, dispositions and needs," wrote E. D. Worden for the visiting committee of the Cincinnati Kindergarten Association. In theory, the visitation programs would improve both the classroom work and the home environment by bringing a simple explanation of Froebel's principles to working mothers. In fact, visiting kindergartners often had first to overcome substantial community resistance. One free kindergartner candidly admitted: "We still find there unfriendly influences to gentleness, kindness, goodness and purity." Unable to perceive the impact of their platitudes, the same visiting kindergartner naively reported that "parents in the locality have not so readily appreciated the elevating power of our work." Another free kindergartner told of the sense of wronged "independence and pride" and the "hurtful" effects of kindergarten charity when "habitually exercised."[41]

Free kindergartners also sought to calm community doubts by stressing the importance of scientific approaches to child training. Unlike the antebellum charity visitor, the free kindergartner carried information, not the charity basket. At first the home visits were aimed solely at explaining the morning exercises and programs of the child—the meaning and usefulness of the complicated gifts, occupations, songs, and games. Gradually the kindergarten teacher broadened the discussions to include topics in child care, health, and nutrition. Free-kindergarten visitors also took great pains in explaining the advantages of patience and understanding in child management, since most reformers subscribed to the assumption of widespread use, and sometimes abuse, of physical punishment in slum families.

Group meetings of neighborhood mothers were a natural outgrowth of the successful home-visit programs. "By becoming acquainted with the mothers, the teachers can better comprehend the child-life committed to their care," wrote a free-kindergarten director in Cincinnati, "and the mothers in their turn become more intelligently acquainted with the methods of the kindergarten." At first the kindergarten child was the means to attract the mother to the kindergarten. Wrote Gilder: "There is a very close bond between the kindergarten and the home and the closest of all is, of course, the child itself." At the kindergarten center's group discussions, the common neighborhood problems—housing, marketing, child care and health, and community facilities—were the most important topics of conversation. Gradually the mothers' meetings evolved into community forums and several free kindergartens even elected neighborhood residents to political office. Community work was considered the most important activity of the New York Free Kindergarten Association. "Home visitation, mothers' meetings, and social work are an integral part of the system," Gilder noted, "and with us are being constantly pressed farther and farther."[42]

The mothers' meetings also provided an extraordinary opportunity for upper and middle-class reformers to meet working women in social situations. Working mothers were asked to accept the social conventions of the reformers just as their children were obliged to conform to the kindergarten regimen. "No dainty afternoon tea was ever more thoroughly enjoyed," wrote one reformer after a successful social event. The bittersweet irony of adult behavior was not lost on another teacher, who noted that "race prejudice" had prompted mothers to form "two distinct and rival organizations" in a kindergarten where "white and colored children mingle freely in the games and occupations." But it was class tensions rather than racial divisions that reformers hoped to ease by extending the advantages of club life to the working mothers. "Those to whom the stimulus of the social and literary club has brought the realization of human companionship and helpfulness on a higher plane can appreciate . . . what the revelation of enjoyment" must mean to the working woman. Other free kindergartners recognized the mutual benefits of socializing with "those whom circumstances have separated from us by the wide difference in social position." Free kindergartners also believed that the mothers' meetings helped to free working women from economic as well as intellectual bondage. A Cincinnati reformer recounted the new assertiveness of one immigrant woman who normally worked long hours in a shop with her husband. "I do get so tired of staying at home and never knowing anything. I told him that I wanted to go over there where I could learn something."[43]

Stimulated by the success of the mothers' classes, some free-kindergarten associations redefined their role in the urban community. By extending the social services of the free kindergarten, several associations hoped to meet the demands of both children and adults in the community. At times the objective was realized by merging with other charitable agencies to form social settlements. For example, the Elizabeth Peabody House in Boston, a "kindergarten settlement," was the product of such a union. Staffed by five trained kindergartners, the new settlement was dedicated to "the union of such principles as those of the kindergarten and the settlement." One former free kindergartner wrote that the kindergarten settlement "differs from other settlements in the city in that the kindergarten is not merely an adjunct to other activities, but is their foundation; the source from which the ideals and practical work of the settlement must spring." The distinction, however, was strained; and gradually social settlements in large American cities absorbed most of the functions of the free kindergarten.[44]

Prompted by a similar vision of urban reform, social settlements by the mid-1890s often grew up in the same urban neighborhoods as free kindergartens. The desire of social-settlement workers to create a permanent outpost in the slum was the next logical step. Free kindergartners had already shown the utility of home visiting. Viewing the kindergarten as an "opening wedge" into the neighborhood, one social-settler candidly wrote that the child provided an "entree into the homes of the mothers." Robert Woods of South End House in Boston summarized the benefits of the kindergarten to the social settlement: it was "human" enough to reach the child,"flexible" enough to provide training, and "alive" enough to provide a new tie between the home and the neighborhood. So great was the initial similarity between the programs and services of the free kindergarten and those of the social settlement that one settlement worker called the free-kindergarten associations "social settlements in embryo."[45]

A kindergarten program was often the first social service a new settlement house offered urban residents. As early as 1887, Dr. Stanley Coit hired two trained kindergartners to staff the kindergarten at Neighborhood Guild in New York. The opening of the Hull House kindergarten (1891) provided another example of the cooperative spirit of the two movements. Under the direction of Ellen Starr, the kindergarten at Hull House was one of the first organized activities of the social settlement. For Jane Addams there could be no better means to meet the "objective needs" of the neighborhood, for the kindergarten provided an essential service for working mothers. "They come for all day and the day doesn't mean a school day by any means," one local newspaper recorded, "for those blessed babies are taken there by half past six in the morning and they stay well till their tired mothers come after them, which sometimes means seven o'clock." In addition to a day kindergarten, Hull House provided a visiting kindergartner for sick children and evening instruction in Froebelian principles of child care for working mothers.[46]

But there was a sharp contrast in the social motivations of free kindergartners and social-settlement workers by 1890. Jane Addams herself expressed the difference when she recalled the first kindergartner at Hull House as a "charming young girl [who] conducted a kindergarten in the drawing room, coming regularly from her home in a distant part of the North Side of the city." By contrast the social-settlement worker, usually college educated and unmarried, willingly made the American poor neighborhood her home. "From the special circumstances of their lives, the people who choose to live in the settlement do so, because for them, that is the best way to satisfy the great common desire . . . to participate in the common life and to further order and progress," settlement worker Elizabeth Manson lectured. Such a challenge the free kindergartners did not accept. Even reform-minded Froebelians continued to see kindergarten work as a preparation for domestic responsibility rather than as an alternative to married life. Settlement workers were also critical of the older charity-visiting ideals of the free-kindergarten movement. "When we go to see them we visit, when we return to the settlement we go home," Manson wrote of the Elizabeth Peabody House in Boston. "It is therefore, in our chosen neighborhood that we must live our lives and strive to attain our ideals, social, political, religious, and domestic."[47]

Many social-settlement workers were also familiar with the writings of Froebel. In defining the mandate of the social settlement, Addams herself referred to Froebel. "If education is, as Froebel defined it, 'deliverance,' deliverance of the forces of the body and the mind," Addams wrote, "then the untrained must first be delivered from all restraint and rigidity before their faculties can be used." For Addams and other social-settlement workers, however, freedom from restraint implied more than overcoming the rigid methods of the classroom. In the American slum the social, economic, and political conditions all conspire to restrain the child. Urban education, then, meant industrial amelioration, household adjustment, and a development of a sense of self-worth through work. "The democratic ideal demands of the school that it shall give the child's own experience a social value," Addams later wrote, "that it shall teach him to direct his own activities and adjust them to those of other people." Addams had gone substantially beyond Froebels' romantic notion of individual deliverance, for an industrial society required a collective deliverance.[48]

Addams and other settlement workers, therefore, were convinced that the new social settlements should offer something more than the older free-kindergarten program. In spite of these flourishing clubs for children early established at Hull-House, and the fact that our first organized undertaking was a kindergarten," Addams wrote in her famous *Twenty Years at Hull-House*, "we were very insistent that the Settlement should not be primarily for the children, and that it was absurd to suppose that grown people would not respond to opportunities for education and social life." Gradually social-settlers were able to adapt the free-kindergarten programs to a larger audience in the working-class neighborhood. Mary MacDowell (a Froebelian-trained kindergartner and director of the University of Chicago Settlement) called the mothers' club, an outgrowth of the Froebelian mothers' class, the most important activity of the settlement. Vacation schools, summer kindergartens and playgrounds—all modifications of the free-kindergarten program—soon became permanent features of the social settlement. As the programs and services of the free kindergarten were adopted by the social settlement, one kindergartner called the settlement "a kindergarten for adults." Allied with social-settlers and other urban reformers, free kindergartners would next turn their attention to the reform and education of the slum child in public-school kindergartens.[49]

7

Garden or Laboratory: Child Study and the Kindergarten

In 1883 G. Stanley Hall, the nation's first trained psychologist, startled parents and teachers with the results of a two-year survey of Boston kindergarten and primary children. "The Contents of Children's Minds" was more appropriately a study of the "ignorance" of Boston school children; for urban schoolchildren, predictably, scored poorly on an examination that tested their comprehension of the simple aspects of rural life. Over 80 percent were "ignorant" of the common notions of "beehive," "sheep," and "frog." Hall concluded that Boston schoolchildren could be assumed to know "next to nothing of pedagogic value" at the outset of their education. The study initially appeared in the conservative *Princeton Review* but soon gained wider publicity, for the psychologist spoke with the new authority of German science in America at the end of the nineteenth century. Borrowing his methods from the previous work of the German educator Bartholomai, who tested the "culture capacity" of city and country children in Berlin in 1869, Hall's questionnaire also included a long list of items that were used to test the child's recognition of simple concepts. The content of the examination was devised and refined in the free kindergartens of Boston, but Hall personally supervised the examination of more than 400 children.[1]

In designing the Boston experiment, both Hall and his assistants accepted the prevailing American belief in the benefits of natural education, a romantic theory which grew from the disenchantment with urban education in the 1890s. The central tenet of naturalistic education was that the slow pace of country life and the intimate contact with natural objects provided the child with an education superior to the artificial environment of cities where, as Dominick Cavallo's recent study of the urban playground movement suggests, the sights, sounds, and smells of the city merged into an indirect and overpowering assault on the senses. But the sharpest criticism was moral: country education, proponents argued, instilled habits of discipline, hard work, and virtue, while urban education neglected or retarded the development of the same virtues. To a generation who recalled the advantages of growing up in a more rural America, the questions raised by Hall's study pointed to a crisis potentially moral rather than scientific.[2]

Though Hall's study had broad implications for American society, the results had particular significance to kindergartners. If Hall's findings were correct, the free-kindergarten movement had solved only part of the problem of urban education in the 1880s. Not just the children of the urban poor but all American children had been spiritually robbed by the experience of growing up in the city or, alternatively, of not growing up in the country. Hall compared the results of children in Boston and children in Kansas City, Missouri. In almost all cases, the children living in nonurban areas outscored urban children, and the ignorance of city children began at an early age before the school could intervene. Environment, Hall concluded, was the crucial variable in urban education, a conclusion that supported the efforts of free kindergartners in the slum and widened the scope of the problem to include children living in other parts of the city.[3]

American Froebelians met Hall's findings with mixed reactions. The more adventurous free kindergartners, for the most part, were sympathetic with the psychologist's work. Hall had maintained friendly relations with Pauline Agassiz Shaw, the patron of Boston free kindergartens, who had placed teachers and facilities at his disposal for the study. He expressed his indebtedness in his report. While the psychologist had some unkind things to say about "fashionable private kindergartens," he was favorably impressed by the performance of children trained in free kindergartens. Most kindergartners, however, were cautious and viewed the results of the study as interesting but inconclusive. The survey was an attempt by a man of science to enter the woman's world of early childhood education. Few kindergartners were disturbed when G. Stanley Hall in 1885 left educational reform to pursue an academic career in psychology at Johns Hopkins University.

By the end of the 1890s, the challenge of Hall's scientific child study to the kindergarten was viewed as more serious. Child study continued to attract adherents from the free-kindergarten crusade, a trend that not only raised serious ideological questions but also threatened to splinter the movement. Hall's simple questionnaire had grown into the most serious challenge to the organization, structure, and ideology of the kindergarten movement. The debate over child study versus kindergarten would pit G. Stanley Hall against Susan Elizabeth Blow. It was a clash of personality and ideas that revealed much about the context of nineteenth-century educational reform.

Blow and Hall met briefly at the end of distinguished careers in American education and science, respectively. As spokesmen for competing visions of childhood, they were separated by the deep intellectual gulf between idealism and Darwinism. The apparent distance between Hall and Blow, however, obscured some interesting common social and personal experiences. Born a year apart, both Susan Elizabeth Blow and G. Stanley Hall recalled growing up in homes strictly ruled by stern fathers but enriched by deeply religious mothers. The adolescent period commonly associated with religious conversion was for both Hall and Blow a particularly painful stage of life, an experience not uncommon to the generation coming of age in the years before the Civil War. Recollections of growing up in antebellum America were later important in Blow's idealistic and Hall's naturalistic theories of early childhood education. The two educators held similar visions concerning the goodness of childhood but remained completely antagonistic in their theories of education.[4]

After the Civil War Blow and Hall discovered German Romantic thought. At first, self-education provided for both the answers to earlier religious questions. Under the tutelage of Harris, Blow attempted to build a scaffolding of Hegelian philosophy to replace the weakened structure of her Presbyterian faith. By contrast, Hall threw off the Calvinistic gloom of his New England boyhood in the intellectually open atmosphere of German university life. Apprenticed to the great men of German science, Hall substituted German Romantic thought for the Christian orthodoxy of his childhood. For a brief time, in fact, both Hall and Blow belonged to the Saint Louis philosophical society and were part of Harris's Hegelian circle. However, absolute Idealism was a painful subject, probably because, as Hall's biographer Dorothy Ross has suggested, it remained associated with his earliest sexual traumas. When Hall left the circle of Saint Louis Hegelians for a career in science, his break with Idealism was complete and final. At the same time, the stage was set for his eventual clash with the American Froebelians. Only rapid changes in the growing field of child psychology in the 1880s would bring the two together again.[5]

Before the publication of Hall's Boston survey, little work in the field of the empirical study of the child had been done in America. When the

American Social Science Association (ASSA) met in Saratoga (1882), scientific study of the child was in its early stages in this country, and the literature on infant development was sparse. The ASSA, in fact, was one of the few American organizations to give any credence to the "social science" of childhood before 1880. Turning temporarily away from institutional concerns in 1882, the education department of the ASSA undertook a survey of the literature of the empirical study of children in America. Harris delegated the responsibility of preparing the background report to Dr. Emily Talbot, who later published her findings as *Papers on Infant Development* (1882). The results were disappointing. Bronson Alcott's *Notes on Infancy*, written almost a half-century earlier, was still the only important American contribution to the empirical study of childhood. Hall found the work totally unreliable, for though Alcott's work contained insights on the physical and mental development of his children, it lacked a clear theory of child development. In short, child-study advocates felt that the early work failed to explain the crucial question of child development—how faculties or instincts "evolved" from earlier ones. Interested in a clearer understanding of the moral development of the child, members of the ASSA Education Committee were ready to move beyond the moralistic overtones of Transcendental thought. Laced with poetic interludes from the Romantic poets, Alcott's *Notes* had all the failings of American Transcendentalism as a social science.[6]

Only one other American, the social Darwinist John Fiske, had assigned childhood so crucial a role in philosophy. But Fiske based his theory on totally different principles; where Alcott turned to Wordsworth for an understanding of childhood, Fiske turned to Darwin. In his *Outlines of Cosmic Philosophy* (1874) and his popular pamphlet *The Meaning of Infancy*, Fiske tied childhood to a scheme of cosmic or theistic evolution. Fiske argued that the prolonged infancy of man had been an important advantage over the lower animals in evolution. The childhood of man extended the period of modification and allowed the development of intelligence, social life, moral sense, and language. Fiske's "evolutionism" was a major advance beyond Alcott's discredited "lapse theory" as the basis of American child study. Both Fiske's theory of a single, cosmic, evolutionary process and Alcott's vision of multiple, divine creations, however, were speculative. The American Social Science Association looked for new and empirical bases for the study of childhood.[7]

The stale American debate over the development of the child's moral sense, based on Scottish Common Sense philosophy, was enlivened in the 1880s by the publication of more recent European research. American scientists specifically welcomed the research of Wilhelm Preyer, a professor of physiology at the University of Jena, who was engaged in a study of the development of the child's will. Preyer observed the actions of children, classifying all into voluntary (willed) or involuntary (impulsive). In sharp contrast to the Romantic notion of inborn natural capacities, Preyer's studies led him to reassert the importance of the senses in the formation of the will. Preyer found no evidence of an inborn will, either good or evil, and concluded that willed movements "cannot take place until the development of the senses is sufficiently advanced." The new work provided little new insight into the problem of the moral sense, but the American scientific community found the results significant because they reversed a half-century of Romantic speculation about the origin of the child's actions.[8]

The publication of Preyer's findings, *The Mental Development of the Child* (1882), in the same year as the meeting of the ASSA, was applauded in Europe as the beginning of the new field of child psychology. American reaction six years later was more restrained. G. Stanley Hall called the work a fine example of the "inductive method applied to the study of child psychology." He recommended the book to American teachers "whose job is, unlike in the past, to systematically learn about the child." Not surprisingly, Harris, who attended the ASSA meeting, was less enthusiastic about the new empirical approach to child study, which he called an excellent study of the "quantitative relations of the phenomenal manifestations of the soul." American child experts of both a rationalistic and Idealist turn of mind, in short, seemed to be asking for further evidence on the child's physical and moral development that would throw some light on the old problem of the child's will.[9]

At Clark University in Worcester, Massachusetts, Hall hoped to surpass his European colleague by applying Darwinian evolutionary theory to the study of mental development, fitting the German professor Ernst Haeckel's classic formulation "phylogeny recapitulates ontogeny" to the apparent similarity between the development of the child and the development of the race. The idea of "culture epochs," the notion that the child retraces the stages of civilization in his individual development, was at least implicit in the educational thought of Rousseau, Froebel, and Pestalozzi. But European educational theorists had always lacked convincing scientific proof for their assertions. Hall now sought to amass the new data for human psychology much as Darwin had done for the plant world. The approach yielded immediate practical results, but ultimately Hall hoped to establish a theory of human psychological development patterned after evolutionary theory. Buoyed by the early returns, Hall wrote that child study "has introduced evolution into the human soul for the first time and thus begun a movement bigger than Darwinism."

Hall became the leader of a new popular scientific movement called "child study," which promised a "genetic" rather than "symbolic" understanding of childhood. The study of the child for Hall was "genetic" since it provided a direct link to man's evolutionary past. Compared to Froebelianism, which Hall called symbolic or unscientific, child study seemed to open new possibilities for improving the early education of the child. Even "modern" research based on the false assumption that the child repeated or recapitulated in his own development the evolutionary stages of the race, a restatement of the older idea of culture epochs, seemed preferable to ignorance. The scientific standing of the movement was, perhaps, always less important than its appeal to thousands of American parents and teachers. As Cavallo has argued, scientific child study made the American child again comprehensible by substituting empirically verifiable data for childrearing advice weakened by the decline of orthodox religion and the coming of Darwinism.[10]

Initially child study attracted support from parents, educational reformers, and public-school educators; and Hall hoped to make Clark University the center of the widening circle of support. Accordingly, he founded a new journal, *The Pedagogical Seminary* (1891), as a forum for new literature and a stimulus for educational reform. Hall also began to plan for an "American Pedagogical Society," an organization that would consider the "hygiene, anthropological and psychological principles that underlie education." Laliah Pingree, superintendent of Boston kindergartens and advisor to Pauline Shaw, endorsed the new society. Apparently, Hall accepted kindergarten support reluctantly, for he envisioned child study as a university-based professional and scientific movement rather than as a popular social-educational movement. Froebelians were attracted to the new state and local child-study societies formed as an alliance of public-school teachers, university professors, and parents. Colonel Francis W. Parker, principal of the innovative Cook County Normal School, for example, saw the Illinois Society for Child Study as a new link between "scientific experiment" and the classroom. At Clark University and in the state societies, kindergartners met with university educators for the first time. John Dewey, professor of philosophy and pedagogy at the University of Chicago, was especially optimistic about the potential contribution of child study to pedagogy, noting that the movement had already taught the important lesson that "the school is to the child and teacher the social institution in which they, for the time, live. . . ."[11]

In 1893 G. Stanley Hall, disappointed with the tone of the educational meetings held in conjunction with the World's Columbian Exposition and angered by the omission of child study, convened a "Department Congress of Experimental Psychology" (1893) at Clark University. The meeting devoted itself exclusively to the questions of what Hall considered *scientific* child study. Hall outlined an ambitious schedule of "data" collection: "inventories" of children, measurements, and studies of exceptional children. Since child study had already shown a voracious appetite for facts, Hall tried not to alienate the Froebelians, who had access to a national network of schools, teachers, and children. Accordingly, the irascible but politic president of Clark University sounded what seemed to be a note of accommodation with the leaders of the kindergarten movement. In his opening address to the Congress, Hall noted that the scientific study of children in the United States began "when four kindergartners in Boston, acting under Mrs. Quincy Shaw's lead, took three or four children aside and endeavored to find the contents of their minds." Though cordial, Hall early recognized that an alliance even with the ideologically more liberal free kindergartners would place child study on a weak foundation.[12]

At first Hall relied totally on available sources and the amateur efforts of parents to collect data on child development. Information was gleaned from such popular crazes as "baby biographies," memoirs, and recollections of childhood. Later Hall attempted to standardize his research by issuing questionnaires that presumably measured specific aspects, or topics, of children's behavior or intelligence. These "topical syllabi" covered such diverse areas as children's "fears," "anger," "love," and "religious nature." The questionnaires were mailed throughout the country from Clark to parents and teachers who administered the tests informally, often with the help of local and state child-study associations. The results of the studies were immediately challenged by the scientific community, who charged that Hall's methods were unorganized and unsystematic. Hall countered that the findings were the keys to the mysteries of childhood, both scientific and pedagogic. "These topics are of the most fundamental nature and underlie, and are sure to determine in the end all work of education."[13]

Encouraged by the interest in scientific child study, Hall invited free kindergartners Alice Putnam and Anna Bryan to compose a questionnaire on the kindergarten in 1896. The test included questions from Froebel's philosophy and about the physiological aspects of the kindergarten. Hall and his colleagues stressed school hygiene and asked specific questions on the precautions taken in the kindergarten against "contagious diseases, fatigue, nervousness, and excitement." For the first time, kindergartners were asked to answer hard questions on such "bad habits, as mispronunciation, biting nails, picking the nose, sucking lips or fingers, making faces, stammering, swaying and other automatic movements." The overall tone of the questionnaire was critical, moreover, suggesting to some kindergartners an assumption of the superiority of the clinic or physiological laboratory over the garden as a proper educational environment. The questionnaire forced kindergarten teachers to see their students in the cold light of science and set aside many of the Romantic assumptions of Froebelianism.[14]

Hall was particularly concerned about the growing evidence of possible physical and psychological damage caused by current kindergarten practice. Both Hall and William H. Burnham, a professor in the education department, had early expressed the belief that "the fundamental muscles," the large muscles that control the limbs and the trunk, developed before the "accessory muscles," the smaller muscles that control movement in the face and hands. Burnham declared before the National Education Association in 1893 that the Clark University findings demonstrated nothing less than "a new law of pedagogy . . . the fundamental is developed before the accessory." Burnham and Hall soon became convinced that the Froebelian kindergarten curriculum was, in fact, detrimental to the natural law of development "written in the very nerve centers of the child." If unreformed, the Froebelian techniques might inflict great physiological damage upon the next generation of American children.[15]

Hall and Burnham were also concerned about the child's possible psychological impairment. At a summer conference in New York in 1894, Hall was particularly critical of the size and complexity of the gifts and occupations, which strained the developing muscles of the children and often ended in frustration. "They directly cultivate 'Americanitis' and tend to stamp a neurotic temper on children, because fatigue is the beginning of every disease of the nervous system," warned Hall. Hall's insight into child psychology, however, was limited, since he viewed all mental development through an evolutionary theory of physiological growth. Hall was raising more questions than he answered, but he hoped that some solutions would come from a dialogue with Froebelians at the first summer school of "Psychology and Pedagogy" (1892). Hall began the summer school as an attempt to shore up the weak American Pedagogical Society by attracting "the few best men" in education and psychology to Clark to attend a series of lectures on pedagogy and to conduct "experimental work" in the university laboratories. He changed the objective of the summer school, however, when it attracted normal-school teachers and principals, public-school teachers, and kindergartners rather than university professors of pedagogy.[16]

By harnessing the popular appeal of laboratory science in the 1890s, Hall hoped to make the summer school an even greater success. The psychological laboratory, an academic innovation for which Hall liked to claim credit, was a new addition to the American vocabulary in the 1890s. The laboratory work of J. McKeen Cattell at Columbia University, James Mark Baldwin at the University of Chicago, and Hugo Münsterberg at Harvard University all became familiar to Americans in the nineties. By 1900 the experimental psychologist had entered the growing ranks of "experts" who were advising American parents on child training. The Clark summer school, then, provided a chance for teachers and parents to watch firsthand the work of these new childhood experts. Encouraged by the eagerness of teachers for "scientific" study, Hall recruited William H. Burnham and Edmund C. Stanford from the psychology department to join the summer school staff the following year. Earl Barnes, a West Coast child-study leader, called it "the greatest summer school for teachers that has ever been held." Clark University had become the fountainhead of the popular movement to improve teaching through summer study.[17]

Summer study proved especially attractive to some kindergartners, for it was an inexpensive, quick, and exciting way to supplement their outdated training. The summer course cost twelve dollars per week or twenty dollars for the whole series—a modest tuition for a crash course in child study, experimental psychology, physiology, neurology, pedagogy, history of education, and anthropology. But summer work at Clark University also provided a unique opportunity to take part in "original research." Parents, primary teachers, and kindergartners provided the raw data for the psychologist's scientific work, and Hall interpreted its meaning for use in childrearing and education. The appeal of summer study brought kindergartners from as far as Topeka, Kansas and Salt Lake City, Utah in order to learn about the new child-study methods and findings at Clark University.[18]

Free kindergartners were well represented at the Clark summer program, for they had already shown a willingness to depart from Froebelian orthodoxy. Nora Archibald Smith and her more famous sister Kate Douglas Wiggin represented San Francisco. Alice Putnam, head of the kindergarten training program at Hull House and a leader of the Chicago free-kindergarten campaign, attended the summer conferences. In 1894 Anna Bryan and Patty Smith Hill, two influential kindergarten leaders from the Midwest, attended Hall's course. Bryan, an older woman, trained under Putnam in Chicago but departed considerably from the strict Froebelian ideology in her work with Patty Smith Hill in Louisville free kindergartens. Bryan later left Louisville to become principal of the Kindergarten Normal Department of the Armour Institute. Together women like Smith,

Wiggin, Putnam, Hill, and Bryan formed the nucleus of an emerging group of kindergarten trainers interested in child study. Their positions made them more influential than their small number would suggest.[19]

Susan Blow reacted strongly to the growing influence of Hall's summer study program. "They are allowing themselves to be misled by confident assertions—the truth or error of which they are not capable of deciding," she wrote to Harris in 1896. Harris agreed that the kindergartners knew "nothing about the topic of physiological psychology" and that the science was "in its infancy and its leaders at odds." Still neither Harris nor Blow were in any position to counter the inroads of Hall, for their influence in the kindergarten movement had waned by the mid-1880s. Harris had retired to Concord, Massachusetts, to lead the contemplative life, and Blow moved to Cazenovia, New York, in order to recover from a deepening melancholia associated with her final inability to reconcile her Calvinist faith and Hegelian education. In Concord and Cazenovia, Blow and Harris followed the developments in scientific child study but held deep reservations about the application of the recent findings to education.[20]

As chairman of its education department, Harris attended the 1882 meeting of the American Social Science Association but found little new in the discussion of child study. To Blow and Harris, the latest empirical findings only confirmed the Hegelian notion of "self-activity" in the child. Like his original mentor Alcott, Harris misunderstood the significance of empirical observations of infant behavior, finding only new evidence of the formation of an "ideal" rather than "material" self. As historian Thomas Haskell has shown, Harris's demurrer on scientific child study was really only part of a larger disenchantment with new directions in American social science. While Harris agreed with ASSA leaders on the need to adopt a "scientific habit of mind" that would allow them to "discover interrelationships and dependencies which ordinarily were hidden from view," he sharply disagreed with the view that scientific method could easily explain human institutions. Harris's views on science left the Spencerian Edward L. Youmans exasperated: "His mode of dealing with the subject would seem to leave us no social science at all." Harris and Blow were, however, now in the minority, a trend made clear by the introduction of psychology into the ASSA in 1882 and the granting of full professional rank to G. Stanley Hall as a "social scientist." The kindergarten pioneers, once leaders in the effort to include child study as a branch of social science, found themselves again besieged.[21]

Of the two, Blow seemed at first to be more intellectually adventurous. She wrote to Harris in 1893, "I was full of evolution. I had first begun to see a little into its implications and tried to look at everything from this point of view." Blow's efforts, however, were limited. In attempting to use an evolutionary format for a new edition of Froebel's *Mother Play*, she soon became discouraged and abandoned the whole endeavor. Blow could not understand the widespread interest of American parents and teachers in the Darwinian conception of the child; for her, evolution was a constraining idea and not the comprehensive vision that could replace Calvinism or Hegelianism. She decided to return to the basic ideas of Froebel, and thereafter ignored evolutionary science. It was another example of Blow's pattern of modest intellectual advance, frustration, and an inevitable retreat to the comfort of older ideas. A period of intense personal despair and self-doubt followed her inability to refute evolutionary naturalism and reaffirm Idealism. Exhausted and depressed, she placed herself under the care of James Jackson Putnam, a Boston specialist in women's nervous diseases, who treated her until 1894.[22]

Though the two never met, Harris and Putnam became her intellectual and emotional pillars during this crisis. It was an odd intellectual triangle in which Blow tried to resolve her own religious doubts by engaging Harris and Putnam simultaneously on questions of philosophy and psychology. Through Blow, Putnam was introduced to Froebel and Hegel and Harris to Freud. Both men recognized the importance of Blow's kindergarten work to her recovery. Originally Harris encouraged his former student to write on kindergarten theory as an exercise but later promised to publish the manuscript in his *International Education Series*. Blow began the project with "no disciples in mind," hoping only to regain her health. Writing was therapeutic for Blow, and the completion of the book also marked the beginning of her recovery. Throughout the work she recognized her deep indebtedness to Harris and suggested calling the new book "crumbs from the table of Dr. Harris."[23]

By the summer of 1894 Blow was feeling well enough to call an intimate meeting of kindergartners at her home in Cazenovia, New York. The formal purpose of the meeting was to "define the ideals of the kindergartners" and to "stimulate an interest in literary schools, mothers' classes, classes for young girls who were not kindergartners, and out-door excursions." But the real purpose of the meeting was to provide an alternative to Hall's summer school. Blow contended that these topics rather than laboratory experiments in child behavior were the proper concerns of Froebelian kindergartners. Her plan was to gather only those kindergartners sympathetic to her views. Radical leaders like Chicago's Alice Putnam were clearly not welcome. The scheme depended, moreover, on the intellectual leadership of Harris, the most important spokesman of "rationalist" psychology.[24]

As the titular head of the "old" or rationalist school of psychology in

American education, Harris was expected to respond to the "new departures" of child study. He pigeonholed child study as a branch of empirical or physiological psychology aimed at providing an "inventory of the facts of the mind." By contrast, rationalist psychology was the study of the "presuppositions of mental life," which began with a simple inventory of mental actions but quickly moved beyond it to "reflections on the general form of mental processes." As Harris understood it, child study would be most fruitful in the unexplored areas of "arrested development" (insanity, idiocy, and fatigue). Though child study could help to explain elementary forms of thought, Harris predicted that it would be useless for understanding the higher forms of rationality. After the first decade of child study, Harris concluded that the "basal idea of the free will" remained intact, and therefore that philosophy and not science remained the foundation of education.[25]

Countering the popular appeal of child study among teachers presented a greater intellectual challenge to Harris. In a speech before the Massachusetts Schoolmaster's Club (1895), he first sounded his oft-repeated warning that child study ignored the role of introspection in education. "Introspection is internal observation—our consciousness of the activity of the mind itself," Harris later remarked. The questionnaire method was flawed, he reasoned, because it could not measure introspective thought—the essential ingredient of the child's development. Hall's approach to education missed the fundamental objective of education: "Education attempts to change what is into what ought to be," Harris wrote; "it seeks to realize an ideal." Since to Harris education was an art and not a science, child-study methods would ultimately harm not only the kindergarten but also all of American education.[26]

To the women of the kindergarten movement, the scholarly Commissioner of Education was still a source of intellectual inspiration. At Cazenovia, Harris delivered lectures on "introspective versus physiological psychology," "the three stages of thought," "the will," and "pedagogy." Once again, he repeated the importance of moral or will training in the early education of children. He outlined the three formative stages of Hegelian thought: symbolic thought, the formation of general ideas, and rational thought. The lectures were old wine in new bottles, but Blow hoped the older members of the kindergarten movement would be swayed over to Hegelian "psychology" by Harris's intellectual stature.[27]

To bring his lecture style up-to-date, Harris illustrated his talk with a model of the brain. He began with a history of phrenology, carefully pointing out the mental peculiarities mapped as bumps on the skull. Harris told the kindergartners that phrenology, like faculty psychology, had fallen into disrepute because the definitions of the faculties were imprecise, the higher intellectual powers omitted, and the so-called "protuberances" unscientific. Turning to the model, Harris pointed to the location of the fissures, convolutions, cerebrum, hemispheres, cords, and major ganglionic centers of the brain. But Harris's real intent, unlike that of his child-study colleagues, was to demystify and thus dethrone the empirical study of the brain. His crafty use of the teaching model was a way of quickly dismissing material considerations before turning his attention to the all-important higher intellectual faculties. He concluded: "In the laboratories of the students of psychology, no metaphysical results, nor results in pure psychology of positive character, will be arrived at, it is safe enough to say."[28]

The 1894 Cazenovia meeting was a victory for Susan Blow. The *Kindergarten News* called the meeting "unique—there has been nothing of the kind before it; but we predict that others will follow." The journal also correctly noted that the meeting was really a "consultation" between the kindergarten pioneer and "a few of her intimate friends." Of the thirty kindergartners invited to the conference, almost all were sympathetic to the Froebelian point of view. If the meeting changed few minds, it dramatically altered Blow's rôle in the movement. At Cazenovia she reasserted her authority on kindergarten theory as a final step in her own therapy. The discussions and political maneuvers invigorated the kindergarten pioneer. "But it is my own opinion that when she has once recovered from the fatigue she will be better for having had the meeting," Blow's friend and nurse Cynthia Dozier wrote. "I am quite sure that a new era has dawned for the kindergarten." For different reasons she was right, for the conference had only planted new seeds of discord.[29]

Blow's revitalized leadership was clear at an 1895 meeting of kindergartners in Chicago where disciples of Hall and Blow for the first time met head-on. Hall raised specific criticism of Froebelian kindergarten theory and practice, claiming that kindergartners too often ignored the new scientific contributions of biology and psychology. Blasting the Romantic ideology of the Froebelian kindergarten for blinding its practitioners to the real educational needs of children, Hall listed specific recommendations for improvements. Most of the audience, however, did not wait for Hall to complete the list. Thirty-three of the thirty-five kindergartners walked out, like religious zealots offended by attacks on orthodoxy, when Hall attempted to distribute his latest questionnaire. Only Hall's former summer-school students Hill and Bryan remained. Susan Blow was ecstatic. "I have hold of the kindergartners," she wrote Harris. "That is enough." After a decade of illness, Blow was convinced that she had regained her health and the leadership of the kindergarten movement.[30]

Personal insult soon added fuel to the debate on child study versus kindergarten. At her first meeting with Hall, Blow found the psychologist in an antagonistic mood. "Having seen him, I think less of his kind of child study." Blow immediately stiffened her opposition to the Clark school and naively suggested an alliance with John Dewey or Earl Barnes as an alternative to Hall and the Clark group. Blow wrote to Harris in 1896: "Professor Dewey has got out questions again of Froebelian inspiration." Though Dewey's views on the kindergarten curriculum were unorthodox, his ideas were clearly preferable to those of Hall. The educational implications of child study, moreover, had never been broached within the International Kindergarten Union (IKU), and at the request of Anna Bryan, a special child-study committee was established in 1896 to look into the whole question of psychology and the kindergarten. Blow was willing to make a tactical retreat toward Dewey if she could avoid further confrontations with Hall. In the world of shifting educational alliances at the turn of the century, Blow now saw the benefits of an educational agreement with the Chicago school. Whatever the exact political course, Blow clearly warned Harris that "the child study movement is something the kindergarten will probably have to fall in with."[31]

Developments within the IKU increased Blow's concern about the political challenge of child study. Dewey's influence was growing, a fact evidenced by his appointment to the child-study committee along with James Mark Baldwin and Harris as "guides and philosophers" for the kindergarten movement. Blow had also noted the gradual shift toward Dewey's brand of psychology among some of the younger members of the kindergarten movement. "Of course, this doesn't mean much for the simple reason that the title has already been applied to other trainers in the movement," she rationalized. "But, after all, there is something in a name, and the rank and file may be influenced by the high sounding title." She again encouraged Harris to publish his long-delayed study on psychology as a counter to child study. "I am delighted that you are making it *now* instead of *never* with your psychology," she wrote. "I am sure it will do great good."[32]

By the summer of 1896, Blow had decided that a political showdown with child study was necessary. "I think the time is ripe and the leaders of the kindergarten must decide which way they will go," Blow wrote to Harris. Blow devised strategy to bring the membership of the International Kindergarten Union back into line. Since Chicago was the only child-study stronghold, Blow hoped to isolate it at the next convention of the IKU and thus restore conservative leadership. With some radicals leaving for free-kindergarten work and with some moderate Froebelians disillusioned with

Hall's high-handed actions, she saw the chance for a "fair and good natured fight" for control.[33]

The strategy proved only partly successful. The child-study committee of the IKU gained a sympathetic response to presentations at the annual meeting of 1896. Hall, Putnam, and Bryan, rather than Harris and Blow, commanded the attention of the younger membership of the organization. Hall, in fact, used the occasion to distribute the results of his latest study. Anna Bryan delivered the favorable report of the child-study committee, calling the new methods of child study "invaluable" in developing teaching methods and a "genuine sympathy" for children. But the child-study faction lost ground at the next meeting (1897), which perhaps emblematically was held in Saint Louis. Patty Smith Hill made her professional debut with a hard-hitting paper on the usefulness of child study to the kindergarten. She began diplomatically by noting that child study had only "awakened us to a realization of the true value of many of the great truths of Froebel." But her endorsement of Barnes's concept of "use-interests" and her advice to kindergartners to simply discard the "meaningless drills in forms, surfaces, edges, and angles" gained her few friends in a city where the fond memory of Susan Blow lingered. "That was the first and only time that members of the IKU 'froze us out,'" Hill recalled many years later.[34]

By 1899, Caroline Haven, a child-study advocate, demanded immediate reforms based on the moral implications of Hall's law of "from fundamental to accessory." In an emotional appeal, Haven drew the attention of the teacher to "the trembling of the hand, the tense body, the drawn muscles of the face" of the kindergarten child. Unless there were immediate changes in Froebel's gifts and occupations, some kindergartners feared the possibility of real physiological harm to the child. Moderate Froebelians, on the other hand, thought that the differences were often semantic. "The biologist discusses recapitulation, rehearsals, ontogenetic and phylogenetic development, nascent development, etc.," Lucy Wheelock wrote, "while Froebel's school would use other names, as the mirror of nature, unfolding, race-history, and stages of growth." Wheelock spoke for a growing number of moderates who set long-range theoretical problems aside for short-term practical solutions. Though moderates supported reform, they were reluctant to join new scientific or pedagogic experiments. They believed that further experiments would not continue to reveal new truths and were more interested in putting their own house in order than in conducting educational research. Though the debate would drag on for almost two decades, the election of Caroline Haven, a "radical," to the presidency in 1900 made it clear that child study was firmly established in the IKU. Child-study supporters, early called radicals and later progressives, could now, in Patty Smith Hill's words, "get questions up for discussion, with equal members for and against it."[35]

Criticism also continued to grow at Clark University, where kindergarten reformers joined hands in attacking Susan Blow, now the recognized spokeswoman for the reactionary viewpoint. The 1896 Clark summer conference resolved that "scientific child study is not and never has been antagonistic to our vital principles enunciated by Froebel." By 1896 Hall was convinced that the study of early childhood education had outgrown the summer-school format. Child-study data now had to be interpreted in the light of physiology, anthropology, neurology, and psychiatry before real progress in education could be made. Hall unveiled in the same year his blueprint for a doctoral program in "Psychological Education," a new field that would relate all the disciplines to education. Not surprisingly, Darwinian evolution was the key to both the program and the discipline. Child study, Hall argued, was now passing through "the same stages of academic growth" as experimental psychology. "The great fact is that evolution is at the door," Hall wrote in the *American Journal of Insanity*. "Psychology is now just about where the biological sciences were shortly before Darwin." The Clark University doctoral program in psychology and education was the first step in his ambitious program.[36]

Among the program's first students were two men interested in the kindergarten, Frederic Burk (1898) and Frederick Eby (1900). At Clark Burk and Eby came under the strong influence of Hall, absorbing his views on child study as well as his opinions of the Froebelians. Burk's dissertation, "From Fundamental to Accessory in the Development of the Nervous System and of Movements" was an application of Hall's theory of biological and physiological recapitulation to a case study of the nervous system. In the final section of the study, Burk treated the educational implications of his findings. Eby's study, "The Reconstruction of the Kindergarten," though more ambitious, was mainly a compilation of Hall's observations on the need for kindergarten reform. Together, their work represented the first formal academic critique of Froebel's educational thought, a challenge both to its underlying assumptions and to its logical structure.[37]

The Clark studies carried new meaning to parents and teachers who had come to accept the implications of Darwinian evolution by the 1890s. The "kindergarten age" for some was synonymous with a period of physical growth, a time of education, and a "vestige" of past racial development. Only the most zealous child-study advocates thought they found in their classrooms the record of thousands of years of man's evolution. Burk, speaking before the NEA, for example, noted that the "kindergarten child is still in the deep-worn gorges which his ancestors have trod." But the prospect of taming, educating, or civilizing the primitive child attracted kindergartners to Burk's theories. The educational stakes in the classroom were high, for the evolutionary evidence was two-edged. It unlocked the mysteries of the child and the race but left the specter of "arrested development" over the kindergarten classroom. To Burk and Eby, evolution supplied an inadequate answer to the educational question raised by the child-study movement: What pedagogical methods would best promote future racial development? Hall's students at first suggested turning to the evolutionary evidence for educational answers. According to Burk, the child played "in obedience to physical impulses of his nervous system planted there by the habits of ancient ancestry" and followed a natural pattern from "individualistic" to "socialistic" play. The role of the kindergarten lay in "guarding the child's right to play, and in providing the time and racial incentives. . . ."[38]

A year-long study of four kindergartens in Santa Barbara, California, revealed the pressing need to go beyond evolutionary theory. The study was the first intensive investigation of the kindergarten classroom by a person trained in child study and sympathetic to early childhood education. Working with eight trained kindergartners and 150 children, Burk found little or no support for the idea of "symbolic" education. He found that imitation and analogies in the "kindergarten age" were of "the simplest kind." "There is certainly nothing in the analogizing found in children's natural play," Burk concluded, "to sanction the kindergartner in any strained attempts to arouse spiritual 'adumbrations' in the child through the symbolic games of the orthodox kindergarten." Burk's subsequent studies of the "kindergarten problem" made him even more dissatisfied with Hall's narrow evolutionary approach. To Burk the doctrine of recapitulation now seemed reductionist. What was needed was not outdated scientific doctrines but pedagogical "incentives" to awaken the dormant instincts of the child. Burk's study renewed his faith in environmentalism as a factor in education; he now called it a "selective agent" helping to shape the child's natural development. Accordingly, Burk stressed free play, spontaneous choice of kindergarten material, and imitation in the child's development. For Burk, environment became as important as instinct in early education.[39]

Susan Blow strongly objected to the Santa Barbara study's conclusions. Politically astute, she attacked the child-study proponents on their own ground: "On the whole, the experiment in Santa Barbara would seem to have tested the ability of the kindergartners rather than the interests of the children," she wrote. "It failed in the essential conditions of a scientific experiment, because it did not eliminate disturbing influences." Turning the issue of environment to her advantage, Blow noted that the physical setting of the experiment was inappropriate. The "jumble of materials" in the classroom made any exact statement of educational impact impossible. Finally, Blow correctly observed that the kindergarten director's value judgments, many hostile to the Froebelian viewpoint, influenced the educational choices of the children. Scientific method, Blow learned, could be a resource for both adversaries.[40]

Blow's underlying outrage, later expressed in her *Educational Issues in the Kindergarten* (1909), ultimately distorted her arguments and reduced their effectiveness. She called the Santa Barbara free-play program a "fatal heresy" in early education. Nothing could be more destructive to the moral, social, and educational order of the kindergarten than to give the child free reign in the selection of his own play materials. "By this abdication they reduce the kindergarten games to a hotchpotch not only devoid of educational value," Blow later wrote, "but absolutely perverting in its reaction upon intellect, emotion and will." Underlying Blow's distress was her deep fear that the delicate balance between freedom and restraint, discipline and spontaneity—a central tenet of the symbolic theory of education—was being upset. Free play was only one step from complete disorder in the classroom and moral chaos for the child. To the Hegelian mind, the danger of kindergarten anarchy spilling over to other social institutions was real; the dire consequences of free play, Blow warned American parents and educators, would not be entirely clear until later generations. In the simple departures at Santa Barbara, Blow foresaw the specter of social fragmentation, arrested emotional development, and a generation of children of irresolute character. "The method of the free play kindergarten, which increases the tendency of capricious wills to hesitant and vacillating choices," Blow concluded, "is a parody of all education." If Hegelian symbolic education had subjected caprice to rational order, free play threatened to undo it.[41]

Not easily defeated, Blow turned to writing in order to stem the tide of child study. She projected a long work which would refute the claims of the evolutionary scientists and explain Froebel's "repeated allusions to the parallel between the development of the individual and that of the race." The crux of Blow's argument was that the stages of the child's development were *symbolic* only and not a rapid recapitulation of human evolution. The gifts, occupations, games, and songs of the kindergarten symbolized "the long childhood of mankind." In Spencer and Darwin, Blow thought she had found a new confirmation of the "ideal" evolution of man, for nature remained for Blow the "prophecy and symbol of the human mind." *Symbolic Education* (1898), the final title of the book, suggested Blow's intellectual isolation. She preferred the obscure German word *gliedganzes*, an adjective she roughly translated as "member-whole," to express the symbolism in Froebel's educational thought. She defined this German concept as an attempt to express the apparent contradiction between man's individuality and his organic relationship to nature. Neither the book nor its terms did much to clarify the issues; again Blow had misread the appeal of antiquated German Idealism in an age of evolution.[42]

During this period, both Harris and Blow showed renewed interest in Transcendentalism, especially the writings of Bronson Alcott. Like Alcott, whose memoir Harris was completing, Blow aspired to become the next great explainer of childhood and hoped her book would revive Alcott's "mythological" understanding of children in an age surfeited with empirical studies. *Symbolic Education*, Harris agreed, belonged to the Transcendental tradition of child study that Alcott initiated, and he called her book a reaffirmation of the Emersonian faith in the child's "kinship to the human race—his identity, as little self, with the social whole as his greater self." Harris, apparently in his dotage, welcomed Blow's exposition of *gliedganzes* as "the deepest and most fruitful in the philosophy of education." Prefatory remarks could not conceal the fact that the volume was simply a restatement and refinement of the symbolic theory of early education. Still, Harris applauded the "happy manner" in which Blow explained the complicated growth of rationality as "symbolic education." Harris was apparently engaging in wishful thinking when he wrote that the book would bring the insights of Hegel and Froebel to new "coteries of zealous students of Froebel" in America.[43]

By the turn of the century, the leaders of the kindergarten and child-study movements had reached an intellectual dead end. Hall blamed the Froebelians for the lack of progress in American early childhood education, calling them "an educational sect by themselves" under the leadership of "the extremely able lady who dominates, with her thought and powerful personality, the entire intellectual field of the American kindergarten." "Like a pope intimidates every dissenter," Hall charged, the Froebelians had driven out new insights. Similarly, Blow and Harris used every opportunity to attack Hall's child-study movement. For example, when Nicholas Murray Butler asked Blow to prepare an article on the kindergarten for a collection of monographs for the United States education exhibit at the Paris Exposition, she seized the occasion to respond to Hall. Harris cautioned Blow to write with restraint for a European audience, but later complimented her on her lucid explanation of the "opposing parties."

Harris thought that the work pierced "to the very center of the fallacies which have been put out upon the public in particular by the President of Clark University."[44]

In many ways, Hall's later polemics were ironic, for they forced the man of science into the romantic camp. Somewhat ungraciously, Hall wrote in the *Forum*, "I am a true disciple of Froebel; my orthodoxy is the real doxy which if Froebel could now come to Chicago or Boston, he would approve." By this Hall meant that he stood for a tradition of educational experimentation and innovation begun by Froebel but obstructed by the reactionary American kindergarten leaders. Hall noted that the American kindergartners long ignored Froebel's insight that the "child repeats the history of the race" and focused upon the trivial aspects of the kindergarten curriculum. The worst example of this tendency was the recent American adaptation of Froebel's *Mother Play*, which he called "a decadent new departure of the American Froebelists." The book contained, in Hall's opinion, only minor educational insights that had become "positively unwholesome and harmful for the child and productive of anti-scientific and unphilosophical intellectual habits in the teacher."[45]

Paradoxically, Hall noted the similarities of Froebel's life and work to his own childhood: "He believed in the original soundness and wholeness of human nature, rather than in any Calvinistic ideas of depravity," wrote Hall. Hall found his memories of his mother and his sentimental recollections of growing up in rural New England echoed in Froebel's idealization of the mother as an educator and his pastoral educational ideology. Hall recalled his own mother as a woman at home in nature and health, the model for the "noblest type of American maidenhood." The idealism of the kindergarten also evoked memories of his student years, a time when the joys of Romantic poetry presented a sharp contrast to the strife of professional life. In "natural education" Hall, like Froebel, found the restorative power for a nation robbed of the values of rural childhood by industrialization and urbanization. If Hall could call Froebel a "seer, a mystic, a deep-souled, large-eyed soul gazer wrestling with great conceptions," it was only because by the 1890s Hall himself had watched the same sky and struggled with the same problems.[46]

Hall's unwavering support of evolutionary science as the basis of child psychology made him the easy target of a growing number of disillusioned psychologists. The Harvard experimental psychologist Hugo Münsterberg was a particularly outspoken critic of child study. He warned parents and teachers that "a high tide of confusion and dilettantism" threatened to engulf education and psychology. Münsterberg feared that the "good appetite of psychology" had already grown into a voracity for facts and figures, an appetite that had destroyed academic discipline and common sense. He dismissed Hall's findings as of little or no help to the legitimate branches of psychology—experimental, physiological, and child. Münsterberg explained that the disciplines of education and psychology were separate and that much of the findings of experimental psychology, and perhaps all of the results of child study, were themselves of "absolutely no consequence to the teacher." The Harvard professor told one group of concerned parents "from his deepest heart . . . *simply I do not believe in it.*"[47]

While scientists like Münsterberg attacked child study as "uneducational," educators attacked it as "unscientific." Nicholas Murray Butler and William James joined Münsterberg in his sharp criticism of the child-study movement. Butler, now president of Columbia University, wrote that "child study needs to be saved from its unscientific and hysterical friends." He decried the silly questionnaires, the untrained workers, the undigested results, and the ponderous platitudes that characterized child study. William James simply called the movement a burden to teachers who do not "take spontaneous delight in filling syllabuses, inscribing observations, compiling statistics, and computing the percent."[48]

Dewey also became more outspoken in his criticism of Hall's approach to child study while carefully avoiding alliances with the Froebelians. Dewey, in fact, became as disenchanted with the empiricism of child study as he had with the Idealism of Hegelian education. The problem was that child study's emphasis on the child's stages of development, a reaction to the Hegelian institutional view, had gone too far. In the midst of endless data on the senses, movements, ideas, and emotions of the child, Dewey believed, the "concrete individuality" of the child had been lost. Child study had become "infertile" because "the forest has been lost in the trees." Neither primitive "impulses" (vestiges of past behavior) nor Hegelian "self-activity" seemed to provide the educational key that would unlock the mystery of the child's development. For Dewey, the real educational significance lay in the present and not the racial past, wherefore he found the growing criticism of Idealistic and evolutionary theories of childhood both "wise" and "otherwise." As a spokesman for pragmatism, he had little patience for the formalist positions that sought new, logically fixed principles to replace the discredited ones. Dewey welcomed Hall's scientific "laboratory spirit," while he deplored the estrangement of the movement from experimental and child psychology. Likewise the weighty superstructure of Hegelianism did not obscure the potentially useful concepts of "play" and "self-activity" inherited from the Froebelians. In short,

Dewey believed that the contest about child study and kindergarten was only the beginning, for it provided excellent educational hypotheses that now needed to be tested.[49]

In the absence of a neutral forum, the Department of Kindergarten Education of the NEA turned over its entire 1897 meeting to the psychology of early childhood education. Since both Froebelians and child-study advocates attended, the emotional issues of "science" and "philosophy" dominated the dialogue. By defining ideological terms more closely, however, Dewey gave new intellectual life to the debate. At first he charted a middle course between the antagonistic parties, stressing the potential contribution of both science and philosophy. Diplomatically, Dewey stated that child study was no more a scientific "fad" than the kindergarten was a philosophic "fossil." Child study was merely the "culmination of educational and social forces," he added, "which could be traced to the original insights of Froebel." Wedded to the "modern psychological movement," Dewey concluded, child study still offered possibilities for the reform of elements of the Froebelian ideology, specifically the gifts and occupations, and the theory of play and artistic expression. He agreed with Hall that the kindergarten "toys" were probably the "remains of primitive occupations" but regarded the "culture epochs" theory as invalid. The decision to restrict the kindergarten curriculum to the study of "cultural products" of past epochs, Dewey thought, was pedagogical nonsense. In "Play and Imagination in Relation to Early Education" (1899), Dewey broke with both Hall and Blow and argued that play must be spontaneous and serious, not a mere imitation of the child's environment. The key, for Dewey, was the imagination of the child and not the artifact—symbolic or evolutionary.[50]

Some Froebelians joined the attack at the School of Psychology (1899), a special conference sponsored by the Chicago Kindergarten College under Elizabeth Harrison. Harrison invited Hall's traditional critics William T. Harris and Denton J. Snider as well as Münsterberg. The panelists, from opposing traditions of empiricism and Idealism, formed an uneasy alliance against Hall. The conference brought into serious question Hall's methods of data collection and the evolutionary interpretation. While the meeting produced no consensus on the question of the psychology of early childhood education, it further eroded Hall's support in the kindergarten movement.[51]

In "The Education of the Heart," the concluding speech at the conference, Hall began to wrestle with the "deeper, dark realm" of education. The address was a painful attempt to locate educational values between pain and pleasure, self-contempt and self-complacency, virtue and sin. The psychologist, however, retained his commitment to science as the basis of education. "Genetic psychology is the psychology of the future," Hall could still proclaim. "We must carry the work of Darwin into the field of the human soul." Hall's entry into the "realm of the heart" seemed to some only the latest blasphemy of the evolutionist. "We begin with the heart and go from the heart to the intellect and will," chided Harris. "Evolution begins with a consideration of rudimentary elements, while the higher life begins with renunciation." America's first trained psychologist had forged his own romantic educational ideology based on American views of the natural environment and science. While Hall's studies began to transform the ideology of the kindergarten movement, new forces in American education—professionalization and bureaucratization—were already beginning to change its outward form.[52]

8

Kindergartens Enter the Public Schools

(1890–1910)

The public-school adoption of the free kindergarten became a new priority between 1890 and 1910. Free kindergartners congratulated themselves for drawing national attention to the social evils of urban childhood, but feared their inability to support, manage, and coordinate the thousands of new teachers, children, and schools. It was a qualitative rather than a quantitative change, for the support of free kindergarten systems, most Froebelians agreed, had become a public problem. Other urban and school reformers concurred and began to campaign for the introduction of kindergartens into public schools as a remedy for educational and social ills. Isolated from the graft and corruption of public education in the 1890s, the kindergarten seemed like an appropriate response to the ailing public school system. Jacob Riis amended his gloomy account of urban childhood and called the movement for public absorption of free kindergartens the "longest step forward that has yet been taken in the race with poverty."[1]

By 1890 free-kindergarten associations, which had led the revolt against older notions of child relief, now found themselves in the forefront of the campaign for public-school adoption. This new position resulted from overload rather than from any lack of either interest or initiative. Private kindergarten associations simply lacked the financial and organizational resources to sustain their educational and charitable aims. Lay boards had already proven unequal to the task of managing the sprawling, complex free-kindergarten systems. Paid kindergarten teachers who gradually replaced free-kindergarten volunteers needed direct supervision. But the free-kindergarten associations also feared their ability to meet the challenges of the swelling populations of urban children. Kindergarten enrollments had nearly quadrupled in the 1880s, jumping from 31,227 to 143,720, and no decline was in sight. If the social-settlement kindergarten was effective in the neighborhood, free kindergartners reasoned, why not simply extend its services throughout the city?[2]

There was a new urgency in the demand for public-school adoption because most free-kindergarten associations were in acute financial distress by the early 1890s. The operating budget of the free kindergartens of Boston, for example, nearly doubled between 1882 and 1889, and reached the limits of Pauline Agassiz Shaw's private philanthropy, a fact she called the "inevitable outcome of munificent charity." Under the skillful management of Sarah Cooper, the Golden Gate Kindergarten Association had also grown into what one free kindergartner called "a public school system on a small scale." Cooper estimated that the Association would require an additional half-million dollars by the end of the century just to sustain the current rate of growth. Public schoolmen were also aware of the financial plight of the free kindergarten. "The most eminent educators of the day recognize and endorse its principles and methods," one administrator complained, "but the expense involved prevents its becoming the lower grade of the public school system."[3]

To meet the growing expense of supporting free kindergartens, kindergarten reformers intensified their efforts to raise funds privately. Kindergarten associations continued to seek support through public subscriptions but counted heavily on the contributions of "kindergarten angels." For example, when the New York Free Kindergarten Association hosted a luncheon for kindergarten benefactors in 1895, the guest list included J. Pierpont Morgan, Mrs. Andrew Carnegie, and Mrs. Cornelius Vanderbilt. But as middle-class subscribers by the 1890s were unable to support free kindergartens, private philanthropists soon became unwilling. Free-kindergarten promoters appealed in vain for the unlimited support necessary to sustain their educational and charitable projects. For example, Phoebe Hearst concluded that only public support could solve the long-term financial problems of the Golden Gate Kindergarten Association, despite Cooper's response that the frequent periods of "retrenchment and economy in government" would destroy the "broad planned character" of personal philanthropy."[4]

In response to the financial crisis, free-kindergarten associations reorganized. By separating the management and operations, lay kindergarten leaders relieved themselves of the problems of teacher supervision and devoted their full time to the campaign for public-school adoption. "We are better organized; we have learned how to arrange and plan our work better," reported the president of the Cincinnati Kindergarten Association. Pauline Shaw hired Laura Fisher, a Saint Louis kindergarten teacher trained by Blow, to manage the free Boston kindergartens. Anna Hallowell reorganized the free-kindergarten association of Philadelphia into the Sub-Primary School Society when she recognized the need for a "broader base of support and a more formal organization." Fanniebelle Curtis assumed the daily management responsibilities of the New York Free Kindergarten Association. The divisions between kindergarten promotion, administration, and teaching foreshadowed developments within the public school, for free kindergartners recognized that fund raising, management, and social service were distinct activities. "The American woman has the reputation of attaining a reasonable measure of success in whatever she resolutely determines to do," wrote kindergartner Stella Wood. "The business aspects of kindergartening—reports, supplies, preparation of data, appearance before boards of education—should also be mastered."[5]

The change in organization and purpose was, perhaps, best illustrated by the transformation of the New York Free Kindergarten Association. Founded in 1889 to encourage the establishment of free kindergartens in poor neighborhoods, the Association maintained thirty-three kindergartens that enrolled more than 1700 children by 1899. Only three years after its founding, the Association began to change its strategy. Richard Watson Gilder, the poet-editor of *The Century*, accepted the presidency of the Association, partly on the advice of his friend and founder of the organization, Nicholas Murray Butler; Hamilton W. Mabie, the reform-minded editor of *The Christian Union*, became the vice president. Gilder and Mabie recognized that to be a "more effective instrument" of social and educational reform the Association would have to reach a larger audience. They abandoned the policy of raising funds from the committed for operations and began a campaign to convince the public of the need for public-school adoption of free kindergartens. The New York Free Kindergarten Association, like other groups in American society, had taken the first step toward changing from a strategy of voluntary benevolence to concerted public pressure through the mass media. "The Kindergarten in America is passing out of the merely sensational period of its development," reported another kindergarten association official; "not only the individual philanthropist but the State as a whole must needs have a vital interest."[6]

In most larger cities the campaigns for public-school kindergartens followed a predictable pattern. First, there was an exposure of the corruption and inefficiency of the public-school program in the press. Second, free kindergartners, in alliance with municipal reformers and the press, pointed out the sharp contrast between the ideals of the free kindergarten and the reality of public schools. In free kindergartens dedicated teachers provided needed educational and social services, while primary educators seemed unwilling or unable to meet the social and educational needs of immigrant children. Third, publicity often forced municipal governments to convene special commissions to investigate the condition of public schools, free kindergartens, and other urban child-saving agencies. In Chicago, Cleveland, Philadelphia, and New York, free kindergartners were asked to provide expert testimony concerning the value of kindergarten education. Based on such hearings, school reformers, editors, and school superintendents for the first time began to take the kindergarten movement seriously. As the lines of power and influence within philanthropic associations broadened, some kindergartners hoped to join the wide movement for municipal school reform.[7]

No group was more influential in helping to promote the new strategy than the editors of the liberal New York journals: *Scribner's, The Century,* and *The Forum.* During the 1880s the editors had already described the popular reforms of the decade—kitchen gardens, lodging houses, fresh-air schools, and free kindergartens—and were now recruited to the campaign for public-school adoption. Edward Eggleston, novelist and historian, contributed articles to *Scribner's* on the need for municipal adoption of kindergartens. Mabie, long-time friend of Lyman Abbott, supported public kindergartens in the liberal Protestant press; and Richard Watson Gilder, friend of Jacob Riis, worked for the public adoption of kindergartens in New York City.

As men of letters, the editors first responded to the poetic quality of the free-kindergarten movement. Gilder, in fact, made the kindergarten the subject of his own sentimental poem, "Child Garden." Apparently the often lurid descriptions of the squalor, poverty, and vice of the slum appealed to the middle-class readership of the magazines. *Arena*, for example, described the poverty areas in these words: "putrid alleys, houses filled with vermin human and inhuman, air blue with blasphemy and obscenity." Though prompted in part by a vicarious interest in the "vicious life" of "the other half," the editors always closed with a sentimental appeal to the redemption offered by free kindergartens. *Arena* called the schools "gardens for the child soul" and *Harper's* "fountains in the tenement district." After 1890 the reform editors, however, were able to turn the sentiment of the free-kindergarten movement into social action by spearheading campaigns for the municipal adoption of the free kindergarten.[8]

Joseph Mayer Rice's series on the mechanical methods and corrupt officials of public education was perhaps the most hard-hitting. Rice, a pediatrician, educator, and journalist, visited more than thirty-six cities in 1892 in preparing a series for *The Forum.* His point was that poor teaching and political corruption went hand in hand. Rice argued that when contracts for school buildings, textbooks, and equipment were awarded to political favorites, education invariably suffered. In a system of urban political patronage, hacks often hired untrained teachers. The result, Rice reported, was that public education by the 1890s had degenerated into rote, meaningless drills delivered in an atmosphere of stern discipline. Even in the progressive Midwestern schools, public education had deteriorated under political corruption. "In spite of the fact that the kindergarten has been part of the public school system of Saint Louis for some fifteen years," Rice noted, "its spirit has not extended beyond the kindergarten itself, the children in the lower primary grades being treated with as little consideration as those in the higher grades."[9]

Public and normal schools that had incorporated kindergarten methods and curricular reforms were the only bright spots in an otherwise gloomy portrait of American urban education. In particular, Rice praised the efforts of William Hailmann in La Porte, Indiana, and Colonel Francis W. Parker at the Cook County Normal School. "The feature peculiar to the schools of La Porte is the development of the social interest." Rice also had praise for the teacher-training program initiated by Colonel Parker. Though Rice found "the results as measured on the scale of one hundred are no better and no poorer than those obtained in other progressive American schools," he did applaud Parker's use of Froebel to inspire dedication to teaching among the students. Rice's message was clear: Educational innovation flourished in professionally managed school systems while poor teaching flourished in politically controlled schools. The kindergarten influence again seemed like a panacea for urban public education.[10]

To the editors of the liberal press, educational and political reform seemed to go hand in hand. The campaign for the public adoption of free kindergartens seemed an appropriate response in at least two ways. First, the community-service ideal of the free kindergarten would be a healthy antidote to the self-interest of political bosses. Second, the stress on innovative teaching techniques might provide a model for the reform of the stale teaching techniques of the primary teacher. The most enthusiastic editors also argued that the public-service ideal of free kindergartens might provide a good example for the reform of other municipal services, especially police and health care. Some free kindergartners, however, were wary of joining the municipal reform movement, noting that there was as great an opportunity for failure as for success. "So long as politicians control our public schools," Sarah Cooper wrote in 1893, kindergartens could be abruptly cut from the budget, forcing children "to run the alleys and by-ways, and get a full crime education."[11]

The report of the Harper Commission provided one of the first blueprints for the cooperation of free kindergartens and public schools. The University of Chicago's president, William Rainey Harper, was appointed by Chicago's Mayor Carter Harrison to a special committee to look into the charges of political favoritism in the ward-controlled system of Chicago public education. Harper was to investigate the means by which construction contracts, equipment and textbook orders, and jobs were awarded. Outraged by the extent of the corruption and graft, Harrison charged public-school officials with the "betrayal of the best interests" of the city and in 1898 appointed Harper chairman of a blue-ribbon commission to review the city's entire school system and propose changes in municipal organization and management.[12]

Harper reported that the "school machinery of Chicago [was] largely defective" and proposed sweeping changes in the school system from the kindergarten to the board of education. The university president also favored the immediate reduction of the number of members of the board of education in addition to upgrading their quality. "Only men of the highest quality and enlightenment," Harper argued, should be stewards of the city's schools. At the same time Harper recommended increasing the powers of the city superintendent of education and appointing a business manager to oversee school contracts. Finally, Harper called for the incorporation of the city's free kindergartens into the public school system to improve the overall quality of instruction and provide a first rung to the ladder of Chicago's educational institutions. On it even the poorest child might climb from the family to the university.[13]

To Harper the relation of political and educational reform was clearest in the testimony of Chicago free kindergartners, which he included verbatim in the final report of the Commission. Elizabeth Harrison reported that the free-kindergarten system had been an effective means of "molding both children and adults." Correct speech, good manners, and discipline, she noted, had been the tangible results of the early program of reform. "We have found that parents as a rule are much more willing to take the innocent corrections and suggestions of their [younger] children, than those of older ones," Harrison told the Commission. Harper concluded that the gains of the reform movement could be extended throughout the city by public-school adoption of the free kindergarten.[14]

Cleveland's superintendent of public schools also included the kindergarten in an overall program of municipal educational reform. Under the widely circulated "Cleveland plan" of school management (1894), school administration was divided into two great departments—the management of business affairs and the supervision of instruction. The superintendent was given the exclusive authority to name teachers and maintain the quality of teaching. A business manager, "the natural enemy of contractors and position seekers," was responsible for all nonteaching matters. Though business management and instructional supervision were separated, the Cleveland plan noted that the innovations of the kindergarten could survive only when well-trained teachers replaced political hacks. "The superintendents did not fool with politics; they were not parties to secret intrigues and machinations," the Cleveland reformers concluded. "They made it their business to get good teachers and maintain good schools."[15]

The language of the Commission reports often echoed the naive social optimism of the free-kindergarten movement. The Harper Commission, for example, welcomed the "sweet discipline" that the kindergarten would bring to public education. Optimistically, the Cleveland Commission hoped that the kindergarten itself might serve as a safeguard against future public-school corruption by humanizing and Christianizing urban public education. Minimally, the introduction of the kindergarten would require "increased watchfulness and fidelity . . . greater energy, zeal, and honesty, if it is to be faithfully and intelligently administered." To free kindergartners the language of the Commission reports at first indicated that the public school would provide a sympathetic environment for the kindergarten. Jeremiah Rhodes, a California school superintendent, felt that public kindergartens might demonstrate "the necessity for liberalizing our ideas of public school administration and teaching."[16]

In Boston and Philadelphia, the persistence of lay educational reformers paid off. Elizabeth Peabody's early appeal had ended in failure in the 1870s and until 1888 kindergarten education in Boston remained part of private philanthropy. Yet the path of public-school adoption remained open, for the Massachusetts state constitution contained no provision that restricted the age of public education. Since city rather than state funds supported public education, absorption of free kindergartens was possible without a state legislative change. Through repeated appeals to the City Council, lay reformers were able in 1888 to convince councilmen to provide funds for the operation of nineteen public kindergartens. Similar appeals to the Philadelphia Board of Education ended in a vote to accept the twenty-two private free kindergartens previously operated by the Sub-Primary School Society. The vote marked a complete victory for Anna Hallowell, who had founded the Society specifically to facilitate public-school adoption. In 1881 the City Council granted $5000 toward operating costs and gradually increased the amount until the School Board approved $12,000 for all thirty kindergartens. The following year the Board voted to centralize the kindergartens and absorb the entire operating budget.[17]

In Chicago the kindergarten entered public education after a long period of cooperation between public schools and private philanthropy. The Chicago Free Kindergarten Association provided teachers and specialized equipment in return for space in public-school buildings. The informal arrangement began as a special interest of two members of the Board of Education who were convinced of the "humanizing influence" of kindergartens in the poorer districts of the city. Six kindergartens were already located in public school buildings when the state legislature expanded the arrangement in 1895 by "authorizing school districts managed by boards of education and directors to establish and maintain kindergartens" when empowered by a majority vote. Public kindergarten education for Chicago public schools was easily confirmed by an election in 1899. The incorporation of the kindergarten, however, grew at a much slower rate in the small outlying towns where school budgets were limited. By 1914 only seven towns outside Chicago and Peoria had initiated kindergarten programs.[18]

Chicago, Philadelphia, and Boston provided success stories, but progress toward public-school adoption was slowed when the campaigns became enmeshed in the tedious urban politics of small and middle-sized cities. In these, kindergarten proponents could not so easily argue the advantages of centralization, while the expense of the kindergarten was an effective response for detractors. Though kindergartners were often able to remove local resistance to public kindergartens, they were frequently frustrated by state legal barriers. Even when municipal reform ended in success, most state governments required school systems to finance the programs from local revenues. Inspired by local victories, then, Froebelians hoped to expand the municipal battle into a state and a national campaign.[19]

The formation of the National Kindergarten Association (NKA) in 1909 from the older New York Free Kindergarten Association was an important step in this transformation. New York was a likely place to launch a national campaign because the successful local effort provided an example of cooperation among kindergartners, school reformers, and editors. New York kindergarten and school authorities now wanted to help other communities in the drive for public kindergartens. Unlike the antecedent organization, the NKA was not mandated to become directly involved in local kindergarten campaigns. The NKA was neither ideological in purpose, like the International Kindergarten Union, nor professional in nature, like the National Education Association. Its *raison d'être* was public relations.

Through organized public relations efforts, the NKA hoped to supply legal and financial information to other communities campaigning for the public adoption of kindergartens. In particular, the NKA worked at leading a national campaign to remove legal barriers and promote mandatory establishment of public kindergartens through changes in state laws or constitutions.[20]

The new role of the Association was reflected in its streamlined organization. For the first time, classroom kindergarten teachers and supervisors were notably absent from the leadership. The staff viewed themselves as national public-relations experts rather than local moral crusaders. A field secretary for the NKA prepared and edited press releases, supervised and conducted surveys of local needs, and worked with local authorities. Field demonstrators were sent to public school systems, hospitals, orphanages, asylums, and factories to demonstrate the "practical value of the kindergarten . . . where there is no money for experimenting." In order to reach a national audience, the NKA concentrated on communication and delegated fund raising to others. "Your present staff deserves relief from the necessity of soliciting support," wrote NKA President John Dewey, "so as to leave all its energies for the performance of strictly educational and social propaganda."[21]

From the outset, the NKA recognized the need for alliance with government agencies and other national organizations interested in early childhood education. The NKA coordinated its promotional efforts with the National Education Association, the General Federation of Women's Clubs, and the National Council of Women. But the sympathetic cooperation of U.S. Commissioner of Education P. P. Claxton was even more important to the achievement of NKA goals. "We are now cooperating in conducting a Kindergarten Division of the Federal Bureau of Education, for which the government made no provision, in all the forty-seven years of the Bureau's existence," Claxton wrote. Through the Bureau the NKA was able to distribute circulars, letters, newspaper and journal articles, and films that "broadened greatly the scope of our propaganda work among educators, local authorities, and the general public alike," one NKA official noted.[22]

Allied with the Bureau of Education, the NKA was particularly active in the campaign to remove state legal barriers. Public kindergarten promoters were most successful in California, where innovative legislation, supported by the California Congress of Mothers, provided for city, county, and school-district adoption through a petition process. Between 1892 and 1913, thirty-three other states provided statutory or constitutional amendments that allowed for public adoption of kindergartens, though only three employed the petition process. Amendment of state constitutions was a slower process. By 1916 only three states provided for mandatory establishment of public kindergartens through constitutional change.[23]

Though free kindergartens were usually annexed by the simple action or vote of the city council, the absorption of teachers, children, and classrooms posed more complex administrative problems. The solutions, as historian David Tyack has noted, were often left during the 1890s to the school superintendent. As the chief urban educational officer, the superintendent was empowered to pick supervisors, oversee the operation of the school system, and employ teachers in accordance with state requirements. He was charged with the implementation of the reforms recommended by public commissions and mandated by municipal government. Often the very commission reports that called for incorporation of kindergartens also granted the superintendent the far-reaching powers needed to implement the plans. "The Board of Education had better have nothing to do with them," wrote one superintendent, "if it does not intend to incorporate them into the general educational system." By reform mandate, then, public schools were opened to the kindergarten; by administrative fiat, kindergartens were actually fitted into the framework of urban bureaucratic education.[24]

The attitudes of public-school administrators toward the kindergarten movement had also dramatically changed between 1870 and 1890. Strong superintendents like Harris and Hailmann in the Midwest and John Swett in the West had used their personal reputations as leaders in both German-inspired educational reform and public school administration to mobilize public support for kindergartens. Hailmann, Harris, and Swett had also left a deep imprint on the place of the kindergarten in the nineteenth-century school bureaucracy, preferring to run these "experimental" programs directly out of the office of the superintendent through a kindergarten director whom they could select. It was an ideal arrangement, for school superintendents could continue to participate in educational reform while maintaining strict administrative control. At the same time, kindergarten directors enjoyed the special benefits of working directly with the school superintendent.[25]

By the 1890s, school superintendents charged with the incorporation of hundreds of kindergartens no longer thought of themselves as philosophers dabbling in lay educational reform. As Tyack has shown, superintendents began to identify more closely with scientific and corporate management than with outmoded ideas of school administration. These administrators felt that the educational experiments of the 1880s had placed too much power in the hands of lay reformers. By consolidating, coordinating, and integrating the smaller, separate units, school superintendents hoped to reassert their power over the kindergarten program. Specifically, they rejected the use of volunteers as practiced in Saint Louis and favored the professional superintendent, the business manager, and the full-time paid kindergarten director.[26]

The new educational elite aimed at making the kindergarten part of a socially efficient system of urban public education in a double sense. First, by joining the kindergarten to other agencies of public education—manual-training schools and vocational high schools—school superintendents hoped to achieve gains in both education and management. They believed that the child's education—from the family to employment—could be most easily guided within a single centralized system. Second, at the same time the kindergarten system could be most effectively managed as part of the public school system. In an age of business efficiency, the vertical management of education from the kindergarten to the university seemed logical, the expense justified by anticipating that the educational investment in the child would pay the real dividends of better future workers and citizens.[27]

By the mid-1890s, school superintendents were determined to eliminate the charity vestiges of free kindergartens. The neighborhood orientation of the kindergarten, once its chief strength, was now under attack. Spread throughout the city, the lines of authority and communication within the kindergarten system became confused. The continued influence of lay kindergarten associations, training schools, and parents' associations in the operation of the public kindergartens made coordination and planning difficult. Accordingly, the quality of the child's education varied widely from section to section of the city. Age and standards of admission, qualifications of teachers, and selection of curricular materials also lacked uniformity, now a hallmark of the public school system. Without a general policy for all public kindergartens in the city it was also impossible to evaluate kindergarten programs. Home visits, community meetings, and parent workshops were viewed as potentially valuable but disorganized and uneven in quality. As a result, the schoolmen believed, neither charity nor education was well served.

Superintendents outlined three steps for the reorganization of the former free kindergartens. First, the autonomy of the independent kindergarten director, unchecked for almost two decades, would be controlled. "The independent direction of the kindergarten director," one superintendent charged, was "a perpetuation of separateness." Second, school superintendents favored the elimination of the charitable work in the kindergarten program; education and social welfare, they argued, had become separate professions. Finally, school superintendents sought to bring the kindergarten into closer alignment with primary education by standardizing curriculum and upgrading teaching standards. Together the proposed changes comprised an agenda for the active transformation of the kindergartens.[28]

Curtailing the authority of the kindergarten supervisor was the priority for many school superintendents. At first some school officials seemed remarkably tolerant, even appreciative, of kindergarten supervisors. "A kindergarten is not safe in the hands of any one who has not become indoctrinated with its aims and methods," wrote Philadelphia Superintendent of Schools James MacAlister. "It can only flourish in congenial soil." Other school superintendents apparently compromised their standards to provide immediate managers for the new public kindergarten systems. For example, in Boston the position of Director of Kindergartens was tailored for Laura Fisher, Shaw's former supervisor. Fanniebelle Curtis, a former student and personal friend of Susan Blow, managed the New York public kindergartens with much of the autonomy of a private kindergarten director. In Philadelphia, public kindergartens were placed under the supervision of local school principals, though some authority remained with Constance MacKenzie, an active leader in the Sub-Primary School Society. The expedient administrative arrangements, however, made some school superintendents uneasy, a feeling heightened by the power of former kindergarten directors.[29]

The price of expediency became clear to both superintendents and kindergarten directors when the former lay reformers began to work in the bureaucratized setting of urban public education. The original function of the kindergarten director was simply outdated: "The key of the position was "to provide a bridge between the volunteer and the paid staff," as Harris had noted twenty years earlier, "in order to make it worthwhile for volunteers to join as well as to secure the development of the salaried teachers." Despite the evolution of a paid professional teaching force, the responsibilities of the kindergarten supervisor changed little at first. Training and supervision, based on the assumption of a volunteer work force, remained official duties. Mornings were devoted to classroom visits while afternoons were occupied in the "instructions in the theory and manipulation of the gifts and occupations."[30]

The contest for the administrative control of the Saint Louis public kindergarten program was particularly long and hard-fought. Edward H. Long, Harris's successor, favored the public kindergarten program but objected to its independent organization. "The kindergarten still remains a distinct organization and to most persons, there seems to be no connecting link between the instruction imparted in the kindergarten and the primary school." After the failure of an experiment in combining primary and kindergarten instruction under Blow's supervision, Long was more convinced than ever that "engrafting the kindergarten on the old stalk of the primary school" would not work. Long next proposed a joint training program for primary and kindergarten teachers. Blow frustrated this plan by refusing to change the content of the course, effectively eliminating primary teachers. After Blow's departure in 1885, Long accomplished by administrative fiat what he had failed to achieve through educational experiment. All barriers between kindergarten and primary teachers were removed from the teacher-training program and kindergarten teachers were placed under the authority of local school principals.[31]

The power and prestige of the kindergarten director were also undermined in other American cities. The Philadelphia Board of Education took steps to eliminate kindergarten directors and bring the kindergartens under the direct supervision of principals or the school superintendent. Other superintendents rejected the reformers' contention that public kindergarten programs suffered from the lack of sympathetic administration. "Large systems suffer from excessive, as small systems do from inadequate supervision," one school superintendent replied. School superintendents were also concerned about the growing expense of separate kindergarten supervision. Finally, the power of the kindergarten director challenged the very concept of expert school management. One school administrator candidly admitted, "How can I say that the kindergartens suffer without embarrassing my ego?"[32]

The struggle for control over kindergarten supervision also reflected the larger shift of power from women to men in school administration. For two decades women dominated all phases of the kindergarten movement—training, teaching, classroom instruction, and administration. Advancement in the kindergarten hierarchy—assistant, kindergartner, director, trainer, and supervisor—was largely controlled by women. In sharp contrast, administrative power in the public school was largely reserved for men. By 1890 this division was well-established, since most public schoolmen considered kindergarten work a matter of domestic science and not public education throughout the nineteenth century. Even in Saint Louis, Blow's authority as kindergarten director derived from Harris's power as superintendent. Incorporation of the kindergarten in the public school on an equal basis changed the older relationships. Female kindergartners and directors now reported to male principals and superintendents respectively, while classroom teaching became an overwhelmingly (90 percent by 1912) female occupation. Kindergartners provided little resistance to the sex-biased administrative changes; indeed, many welcomed the change. "To the extent that education is becoming solely a woman's business," Nina Vandewalker warned earlier, "to that extent is it endangered, for it is a man's business as well as a woman's."[33]

Many public kindergarten teachers welcomed the administrative changes because they feared the hegemony of kindergarten directors more than the authority of school superintendents. If bureaucratization meant a certain loss of power and ideological purity, it also marked the end of a half-century of isolation. The public school offered new career opportunities as compensation for lost ideological innocence. Moderate kindergarten leader Patty Smith Hill, for example, was critical of school superintendents but looked forward to new leadership. "School superintendents and principals are needed who have studied Froebel," she wrote. "They either honestly state their ignorance regarding Froebel and the kindergarten, and leave the kindergartner to run things her own way . . . or thinking the whole kindergarten situation rather a farce, they criticize the idea unintelligently and ruthlessly." Another public-school kindergarten teacher called for superintendents "able to unify, not uniformize the work of kindergartens, to raise standards . . . and to check and regulate the tendencies on the part of teachers to extravagant forms of experimentation." The faith of kindergartners in the expertise or sympathy of school administrators was, then, not as naive as revisionist historians have suggested. Many willingly and knowingly traded vocational experience for professional opportunity. Bureaucratization, moreover, to some kindergarten leaders was merely the fulfillment of the plans for a rationalized school system announced twenty years earlier in Saint Louis.[34]

The administrative autonomy of kindergarten directors was largely curtailed in most public school systems by 1910. When the Bureau of Education conducted a survey of kindergarten directors in that year, most responded that their job had changed from "making most of the decisions" to "no responsibility whatsoever." Without the rank of assistant superintendents, kindergarten directors never fully regained control of their programs. Paradoxically, as the number of public kindergartens continued to grow—Philadelphia (271), Boston (143), Los Angeles (137), and Pittsburgh (100), by 1910—the duties of the kindergarten director contracted. Individual classroom visits, training, and afternoon home visits were eliminated from most large urban school systems. In many public school systems, a new position, the elementary-kindergarten supervisor, replaced the kindergarten director. Other kindergarten directors simply became advisors to the boards of education. Only a vestige of the training function of kindergarten directors remained after World War I. "Although the supervisor is no longer of necessity a training teacher," one classroom teacher wrote in 1918, "she is still looked upon as the leader in the formation and conduct of study classes."[35]

A more sensitive issue was the future of the social-welfare function in the public kindergarten. Initially the charitable work of the free kindergartens had been directly transferred to the public school. In Boston and Philadelphia, for example, school boards conducted home-visit programs and mothers' classes for more than a decade after public-school adoption. In Cincinnati kindergarten philanthropy continued until 1912, when public teachers were still visiting more than two thousand homes each year; similar programs were conducted in Queens and Brooklyn (New York) until 1905. But the rationale of the programs had changed. School superintendents were less interested in extending their influence into neighborhood social concerns than in preparing children for primary instruction. One superintendent expressed his belief in the compatibility of preschool education and formal schooling in this way: "The truest kindergartner stands in a midway place between home and school, working in unison with the mother on the one hand, and with the first grade teacher on the other."[36]

School superintendents also showed an early interest in the kindergarten mothers' meetings. In New York, Fanniebelle Curtis initiated an active program of mothers' classes in the public school. In Philadelphia, dormant mothers' classes, clubs, and meetings were actually reinstated in public schools. By 1894 Constance Mackenzie reported over a dozen active public-school mothers' programs. In Los Angeles, mothers' classes expanded into parents' classes, laying the groundwork for the Parent-Teacher Association. So pleased was a Los Angeles superintendent that he wrote, "One half of the usefulness of kindergarten is lost if this close helpful sympathy between the kindergarten and the home is not kept up."[37]

The growing need for economy in public education after 1895 reinforced the desire of school superintendents to eliminate charity programs. For example, the cost of educating a kindergarten child in Massachusetts, according to historian Marvin Lazerson, rose 30 percent between 1889 and 1909. Superintendents argued that public kindergartens should not only be "socially efficient" but also "cost efficient." The special equipment, texts, rooms, and furnishings of the kindergarten program all added to the rising costs of public education. Special kindergarten programs—mothers' meetings, evening classes, and home visits—all came under close financial scrutiny. "Economical questions must have proper consideration in school administration," a Massachusetts superintendent wrote. "The cost of the kindergarten . . . is too great to warrant maintenance."[38]

One means of adjusting kindergarten costs to the shrinking public school budgets was the double session. Even without economic retrenchment, it was a likely reform because school superintendents had always doubted the educational usefulness of morning classroom teaching followed by afternoon social work. A. R. Brubacher, superintendent of schools in Schenectady, New York, spoke for other schoolmen when he called the single-session schedule "an unwarrantable expense of time and energy." By using the expensive kindergarten equipment, classroom space, and teaching hours all day, school superintendents hoped to reduce the cost of educating the kindergarten child. Harris had limited the expense of kindergarten education twenty years earlier by using volunteers. The new superintendents now simply doubled the teaching load of the teacher and eliminated the volunteer. Some favored the double session for reasons other than economy. For the public kindergarten teacher, double-session teaching was also an important step toward professionalization. "The double session promotes a general feeling on the part of the community, the teaching body and the teacher," one public kindergarten teacher summarized, "that the kindergarten is a vital, integral part of the school system and not a luxury, exceptional in its organization and privileges."[39]

But many kindergarten teachers were bitterly opposed to double-session teaching. These teachers argued that the double sessions shortchanged the child and the teacher, for afternoon kindergarten instruction was impossible when children were tired from morning play or lessons. Critics claimed that the double teaching load overtaxed the kindergarten teacher, whose teaching, unlike the primary teacher's, required inspiration. Finally, Froebelian opponents correctly charged that afternoon kindergarten lessons marked a virtual end to the home-visit program. Theirs was, however, a minority protest from the few kindergartners who continued to believe that the kindergarten had a special mission of social and educational reform.[40]

School superintendents were able to adjust even the most stubborn kindergarten teachers to the pattern of urban, bureaucratic education. Initially kindergarten teachers made home visits late in the afternoon or in the evening; but as the teaching load was gradually increased, contact with the urban family was ultimately eliminated. Under pressure from school boards, school superintendents required kindergarten teachers to cover morning and afternoon sessions, and by 1912, almost two-thirds of nine hundred public kindergarten programs were taught under the double-session plan. The Froebelian kindergartner had become a classroom teacher.[41]

New administrative guidelines also directly affected the classroom teacher. In Saint Louis during the 1870s, the kindergartner had complete classroom authority, delegating only routine matters to an assistant who called attendance, kept classroom order, participated in mothers' meetings, and aided in simple stories and games. The planning and teaching of lessons, however, was reserved for the "mature judgment" of the kindergartner. In the public kindergarten, the kindergarten teacher's classroom authority was sharply curtailed. Curriculum was now subject to the approval of a department supervisor, usually a primary educator, and to the final approval of the school principal. In Philadelphia and Boston, superintendents charged that kindergarten assistants were costly and unnecessary and were quick to point out that the primary teacher maintained control without an assistant. By 1900 most kindergarten assistants were eliminated from public-school teaching.[42]

Primary school teachers also resisted the separate status of the kindergartner and used distinctions in training as an effective weapon. The kindergarten training course varied in length from six months to two years; by contrast most primary teachers had completed a four-year normal-school course of study including practice teaching. Primary teachers also criticized the emphasis on literature and philosophy and the lack of training in child psychology. They feared that kindergartners would undermine the recent professional gains of primary teachers. Finally, primary teachers objected to the differences in salaries. While kindergartners initially received less compensation, they also worked far fewer hours in the classroom. Professional resistance to kindergartners in one school system was so great that full incorporation was delayed. "Because of the constant friction between the kindergartners and the first grade teachers," wrote Allen P. Keith, superintendent of schools in New Bedford, Massachusetts, "the kindergartens have never extended in the system." It was an extreme example of a more widespread problem, stemming from the confusion over training.[43]

Faced with overcrowding and an inadequate supply of kindergarten teachers, school superintendents initially waived state or school-board training requirements for many former free kindergartners. In Philadelphia, the kindergarten teachers of the Sub-Primary School Society, for example, became public school teachers overnight. In order to impose some order on the hurried arrangements, a few superintendents required makeshift examinations. Minimally, public kindergarten teachers were required to pass tests in spelling, penmanship, arithmetic, and English. The state of Connecticut considered all eligible women over the age of seventeen with "satisfactory testimonials of character and work" for the new public kindergarten positions. The State Board of Education, however, later acknowledged the unhappy results of low standards of admission, noting that "many incompetent and half-trained instructors have done much to destroy the confidence of the public in this system."[44]

Without state standards of certification, superintendents created their own requirements. In New York City, for example, a kindergarten certificate was granted to qualified women between the ages of eighteen and thirty-five who held a high-school diploma and had completed a two-year training program. In Philadelphia the public schools initiated training programs in which experienced kindergarten teachers were given refresher courses in psychology, history of education, school hygiene, and methods of teaching. New kindergarten teachers were required to take a two-year training course at the State Normal School.[45]

In-service training programs provided another means of upgrading kindergarten teaching. Superintendents encouraged both kindergarten and primary teachers to attend summer courses offered by colleges, universities, and normal schools. Parker's Cook County Summer School, the Martha's Vineyard Lectures, Hall's Summer School in Psychology, and the Chautauqua course all enjoyed a renewed popularity among public kindergartners and primary teachers during the 1890s. Summer training was also offered by old-school Froebelians like Eudora Hailmann in La Porte, Indiana and at the Summer School of the South in Knoxville, Tennessee. The courses were aimed primarily at correcting the deficiencies of kindergartners and introducing primary teachers to kindergarten innovations. But unlike the earlier Froebelian "summer retreats," the new programs pruned away the last vestiges of the Saint Louis curriculum: literature, philosophy, and poetry. The summer catalog of the Chicago Normal School characteristically announced that "it will aim to make the work of the school professional rather than academic in character."[46]

A more radical solution to the shortage of public kindergarten teachers was offered by the city normal school. "Nothing will maintain the kindergarten in its purity but the presence of broadly cultured and thoroughly trained kindergartners," Philadelphia Superintendent James MacAlister optimistically wrote, "and I can see no safeguard but in providing a training school of our own." The city established a kindergarten training program as part of the Girl's Normal School within a year after the opening of public kindergartens. Superintendent Maxwell urged a similar normal school in New York. However, when Chicago schoolmen proposed adding a kindergarten training department to the Chicago Normal School, the *Tribune* called the venture a "fad" and unnecessary in a city with a half-dozen private training academies. Though initially touted as a solution to the problem of teacher shortages, most city normal schools ended in failure. "It was doomed from the first," wrote a Philadelphia school official, "and accomplished nothing beyond certifying a few kindergartners to meet the immediate needs of the city."[47]

In many cities free-kindergarten training programs continued to meet the need for public-school kindergarten teachers. In this function free-kindergarten associations had taken pride and through it they hoped to continue to influence public education. The training program of the Cincinnati Kindergarten Association was, perhaps, the best example. Principal Lillian Stone early noted that the new interest in "certification" could, in fact, be turned to advantage by demonstrating the "evident lack of knowledge concerning kindergarten courses" among city normal schools, colleges, and universities. Later Stone would take a less sanguine view of the encroachments of city normal schools, though she acknowledged that they provided a "solid foundation." Stone spoke for other free kindergartners when she voiced her fears: "The danger of combining kindergarten and primary work to such an extent that the kindergarten might gradually be merged into mere primary or elementary methods" was always present.[48]

By 1900 public school superintendents had become increasingly critical of the free-kindergarten training methods, specifically noting their old-fashioned psychology and pedagogical theory. The rationale for public adoption of the kindergarten as an educational innovation was itself in peril if the quality of teacher training did not improve. Adopting the language of the superintendents, kindergarten trainer Nina Vandewalker wrote: "The realization that the school was not producing socially efficient individuals, and was, therefore, itself lacking in social efficiency was the first step in a new order of things." Kindergartens, playgrounds, and manual-training schools required more, not less, professional preparation. The flaws of kindergarten training schools, unchanged in over two decades, became even more apparent to the superintendents. Chicago Superintendent of Instruction Andrews called the private academies "extremely conservative institutions . . . bent on preserving the symbolism and mysticism" of Froebel.[49]

Not all Froebelians were satisfied with the developments in kindergarten training. Susan Blow was especially critical of the free-kindergarten training programs and of the city normal schools. Blow confided in her former student Elizabeth Harrison, now Director of the Chicago Kindergarten College, that she "was heartsick about the poor quality of kindergarten training in the country." The greatest challenge to the kindergarten movement, however, was posed by training programs influenced by child-study reforms. "This party of kindergartners has no great strength in any center except in Chicago," Blow wrote to Harris, adding: "They send their pupils to small towns and do great harm." Blow really was mourning the decline of the informal setting of kindergarten training: the Saturday morning lecture and the afternoon philosophical chat. Blow vainly declared that "no true representative of Froebel's ideas can hereafter neglect" the use of the mothers' class and the lecture hall as the means of disseminating the kindergarten.[50]

Other fears grew from educational rather than professional concerns. Trained in the principles of discipline and order as the basis of early education, elementary teachers remained suspicious of play in the classroom. They feared that the kindergarten child would be inattentive, unable to follow directions, and unprepared for the discipline of the three Rs. Any evidence of laxness became the occasion of renewed attack. One elementary teacher, Marion Carter, chastised her gullible colleagues who thought the public kindergarten would bring on an "educational millennium." To the contrary: the kindergarten made the work of the elementary teacher more difficult since primary teachers would have to contend with "the flabby kindergarten intellect of the kindergarten child." Because nonkindergarten children seemed to respond well to elementary education, primary teachers were reluctant to embrace the kindergarten. The nub of the criticism, however, was lack of preparation, discipline, and skills needed in primary education. One teacher felt that the kindergarten child was "more restless, less attentive, less interested in primary work" than the nonkindergarten child. Another elementary teacher suggested that the kindergarten child should spend a complete year in silence before entering the primary school.[51]

Despite frustrations, public-kindergarten teachers believed the benefits of bureaucratization outweighed the losses. The reforms of school superintendents were at once imposed and readily accepted by public-kindergarten teachers. Isolated from professional education for two decades, kindergartners were eager to share the special professional benefits that many public-school teachers had already earned. No longer guardians of the Romantic idea of childhood or charity visitors to the poor, public-kindergarten teachers began to view themselves as classroom specialists in the early education of the child. One former free-kindergarten advocate explained the ready acceptance of public scrutiny that "compelled the kindergartner to get outside of her work and regard it with the eye of the critic. It created a sense of uneasiness, of noble discontent, of a determination to know how far her critics were in the right." This faction of kindergartners, firmly established within the public school system, was now in a position to push for full professional status within the university community.[52]

9

Froebelians at the University (1893–1920)

To many American kindergartners, the educational meetings of the World's Columbian Exposition (1893) marked a high point in the kindergarten movement. Not since the Philadelphia Centennial Exposition of 1876 had kindergartners participated in a national celebration. In Chicago Midwestern Froebelians convened a special "kindergarten congress" presided over by William Hailmann, while other members of the movement attended the kindergarten section of the International Congress of Education. The International Kindergarten Union (1892) had also actively planned special department meetings at the World's Congress of Representative Women. The organization, in addition, helped to sponsor special exhibits and an operating kindergarten in the Children's Building.[1]

The setting of the short-lived triumph was significant, for Chicago had long been a center of kindergarten discontent. Taking time from a busy schedule of educational meetings, Blow visited the innovative kindergarten at the University of Chicago under the charge of John Dewey, at that time a young professor of education and philosophy. The day Susan Blow visited the school the instructors were working on the problem of the origins of the child's imagination. "I saw Dr. Dewey's school," she wrote to Harris; "they said it was not a fair showing, but the whole principle they were working on seemed wrong." The kindergarten pioneer objected to the amount of individual freedom granted to each child, but was not blind to the real educational excitement at the school. "In Saint Louis they are afraid to change things, so they go in the old manner," she admitted to

Harris, "but in a dead and alive way Chicago is alive—but as it seems to me going very wrong."[2]

Blow was witness to a profound change in the kindergarten movement and higher education: the beginning of training and research in early education in American universities. Under the leadership of William Rainey Harper at the University of Chicago and Nicholas Murray Butler at Columbia University, university education departments were able to draw upon a remarkable reservoir of talent in their effort to make early childhood education a university discipline. At first the reform of kindergarten training began outside universities; the Cook County Normal School, under the leadership of Colonel Francis W. Parker, provided the unlikely setting for a rehearsal of later university reforms. By 1892 Harper had appointed John Dewey to a professorship in pedagogy and philosophy at the University of Chicago, where he remained until 1904. During the same period James Earl Russell helped to transform Teachers College, Columbia University, into a center of educational reform. Both schools attracted formidable faculties. At Teachers College William Kilpatrick, John Angus MacVannel, and Edward Lee Thorndike would all help to reevaluate the kindergarten program. At Chicago John Dewey and George Herbert Mead became the critics of the Froebelian program. Catholic in their interests, Dewey and Russell encouraged educational excellence at every level—from kindergarten through graduate school.[3]

Nicholas Murray Butler, William Rainey Harper, and to a lesser extent Charles W. Eliot were typical of the new breed of college presidents who changed their minds about the place of women in the university at the turn of the century and began to court kindergarten students and teachers. Like William Torrey Harris, they began their careers with a certain sympathy for German educational reforms, but leadership in educational reform movements had migrated from the public school superintendency to the university presidency between 1870 and 1890. Unlike Harris, the new college presidents were trained in the university rather than in the philosophical circle. Harper earned his doctorate at the age of eighteen from Yale; Eliot was educated at Harvard University, where he later assumed the presidency; Butler received a Ph.D. from Columbia University and was introduced to the formal study of education by Frederick A. P. Barnard. After doctoral training the new men entered the university rather than follow public-school careers. The rapid growth of American universities in the 1890s had created professional opportunities comparable to those in public education in Saint Louis in the 1870s. Their careers had also brought the male college presidents into contact with female teachers and reformers, whom they admired as much for their adherence to traditional social roles as for their departure from educational prescription. For example, William Rainey Harper told an audience of the Association of Collegiate Alumnae in 1900: "In my opinion the greatest career in life for a woman, next to that of a mother, is that of teacher." It was a broad invitation to university life which at least to some socially conservative kindergartners was attractive. Progressive in outlook and confident of the new role the university would play in reshaping American public education, Butler, Harper, and Eliot also saw a new role for the kindergarten as a foundation for higher education.[4]

The college presidents had learned of the Froebelian movement firsthand during the peak of the popularity of free kindergartens in the 1880s. In different ways, all three had participated in local educational reform campaigns. Eliot attacked the "bad methods of instruction and wasteful methods of administration" in Massachusetts schools. Butler, active in several education movements in New York City, helped to form the Industrial Education Association in New York in 1887. The Association was an outgrowth of Emily Huntington's "Kitchen Garden" movement, an attempt to teach slum children the rudiments of domestic management by substituting miniature dishes for the Froebelian gifts and occupations. Inspired by the Haines kindergarten in New York, Huntington saw the kitchen garden as a potent instrument for tenement-house social reform. "In a moment my fancy painted my poor children in the same pretty framing, setting little tables, washing little dishes," she had written in *The Kitchen Garden* (1878). "Work had become play and the instruments of toil were playthings." By 1884, the Kitchen Garden Association had expanded beyond its limited base of support, dissolved, and reorganized as the Industrial Education Association. The new Association maintained links to popular reform but now aimed to introduce industrial education into the public school. Harper pioneered in university extension work during the same period, at times using the free kindergarten and the social settlement as educational branches of the university. In the loose-knit urban educational communities in the last decades of the nineteenth century, university presidents freely experimented in public-education reforms, and superintendents recognized that the colleges and universities would now play an increasing role in urban education.[5]

The university men were also critical of some of the consequences of the public adoption of kindergartens. Too often, the college presidents agreed, educational experimentation had been lost during the transfer of training from the private academy to the normal school. University men became critical of both institutions. Eliot and Butler abandoned the easy optimism of the arguments for free kindergartens and public adoption that they had advanced just a few years earlier. For example, speaking before an audience of the International Kindergarten Union, Eliot argued that the educational innovations of the kindergarten movement had been sacrificed in the effort to meet the increased demand for public school kindergarten teachers. But he stopped short of blaming public school officials. The Harvard president specifically outlined the contributions of German educational reform, including the kindergarten, to American higher education. He traced the university teaching assistant, the laboratory method, nature study, and motivational psychology to German pedagogical reformers. "All of this sort of teaching has been instituted since the introduction of the kindergarten into the United States," Eliot concluded."[6]

Within the university these men now stood for rational order, professionalism, and organization; but they never forgot their earlier experience within educational-reform movements. Eliot decried the "machine methods" that penetrated public, university, and graduate-school education while other college presidents railed against the "forced average pace" of American education. They believed that they understood the limits of individualism in education, but were unwilling to sacrifice the ideal of individuality that they saw in the early kindergarten movement. Though critical of the conservative nature of the kindergarten movement, Nicholas Murray Butler, in a speech before the IKU in 1899, concluded: "The greatest hope of our school system lies in this fact, that the spirit of individualism is working down from the university and up from the kindergarten."[7]

At first university officials were interested in the approach of Colonel Francis W. Parker, a teacher-trainer and educational reformer. At the Cook County Normal School, Parker helped to transform an older practice-teaching facility into a model school, a place where teachers might observe the best teaching under ideal pedagogical conditions. Though Parker's school upheld standards of excellence, it failed to provide stimulus for further educational innovations. Instead, men like Harper, Butler, and Eliot now proposed university experimental schools, a controlled setting where educational inquiry could take place. Unlike Hall's program in psychology at Clark, the experimental school would apply the inert child-study data to real pedagogical situations. The kindergarten training ideal of direct observation, implicit in Parker's school, would become explicit in the new programs at the university level.[8]

The intellectual excitement of the University of Chicago—what Parker called "the educational storm center" of the nation—also attracted John Dewey in 1893, when he was asked to head the department of philosophy and to teach in the subdepartment of pedagogy. Dewey was ready for a change. At the University of Michigan he had climbed the academic ladder from instructor in philosophy to chairman of the department. Chicago offered the opportunity to continue his reading, writing, and teaching in philosophy, while exploring his growing interest in education. For his part, Dewey was already familiar with the innovative work of Parker, a man whom he would later call, somewhat modestly, the "father of the progressive education movement." While at Michigan Dewey had also lectured at Hull House, where he became acquainted with the philanthropic work of Jane Addams. With the allurements of friends and the benefits of a wide range of educational institutions, Dewey accepted Harper's invitation as "much for the living in the city" as for the chance to build a fine academic department.[9]

At the same time Dewey was intensely interested in the stirrings of kindergarten reform in Chicago, where he was in close contact with free-kindergarten leaders. The most intimate was his relationship with the radical Froebelians of Hull House, where he remained a guest lecturer in the kindergarten training program of Alice Putnam. The reputation of the Chicago kindergartners for encouraging innovation was so great that conservatives like Blow singled them out for criticism. "There are some like Mrs. Putnam and Miss Bryan of Chicago," Blow wrote Harris, "who think every new thing true, and I suppose that there are others just like her." It was not surprising, then, that Dewey, when planning his work at the University, consulted with Anna Bryan, the reform-minded head of the kindergarten department of the Armour Institute. Out of the friendship evolved a close working relationship between the University and the Chicago Free Kindergarten Association in which kindergarten trainees served as assistants in Dewey's educational experiments. Dewey later acknowledged his "great indebtedness to Miss Bryan and her able staff, of the Free Kindergarten Association, for numberless suggestions regarding" the curriculum of the school.[10]

Dewey was able to attract Froebelians to the University when in 1897 Harper promised even "closer and more fruitful relations" with the educational agencies of the city through a series of conferences and through extension, correspondence, and lecture courses. Since pedagogy was an interest of Harper's, kindergarten and public-school teachers soon found their way to his campus. For example, the University sponsored Parker's lectures on the "science and art of teaching" in 1896 and also hosted a meeting of the Illinois Society for Child Study. Educational conferences, which included the Froebelians, were a two-way street at the University, for Harper and Dewey believed that contacts outside the University would not only upgrade the quality of public teaching but also enrich the University's commitment to education. In response to one critic, Harper wrote, "As a university we are interested above all things in pedagogy."[11]

A "Kindergarten Conference," organized by Dewey in 1897, provided the first forum at the University for discussion with the Chicago Froebelians. "The discussion of topics of vital interest from the standpoint of the different educational agencies is especially needed in this day of specialization," Nina Vandewalker later reported, "and the university and the kindergarten exchanged ideas to the interest and benefit of both." The agenda for the conference was a roster of Chicago's influential kindergarten reformers: Nina Vandewalker (University of Chicago), Anna Bryan, Flora J. Cooke (Chicago Normal School), Alice H. Putnam, and Ella F. Young (Chicago public schools). Many Froebelians believed that the conference marked an "epoch in kindergarten history in the city of Chicago."[12]

Dewey introduced the conference himself by offering some observations on Froebel's achievements and reputation as an educational pioneer. He noted that Froebel was the first to view the mind of the child as "an instrument of knowing," a sharp departure from the passive, sensation-based education of the eighteenth century. Froebel's second achievement was his understanding of the "unity of the mind," which allowed him to strike a healthy balance between learning and doing in education, intuitively recognizing that learning did not proceed in isolation. His third and final contribution was the design of the gifts and occupations that allowed the child to develop in a social environment by introducing concepts that were later modified and enriched by experience. Froebel's fatal weakness was that he did not make his educational practice conform to these principles, since he failed to discriminate between the functions of logic and those of psychology. Dewey explicitly reviewed Froebelian errors and implicitly provided an agenda for reform. He criticized Froebel's confusion of metaphysics and psychology, the "overformulated" nature of Froebelian games, and the "mechanical" use of imitation and suggestion in the kindergarten. The problem was that without an adequate psychology of childhood, Froebel was forced to rely on symbols that were derived from the logical viewpoint of the adult. He compounded the error when he attempted to make his educational system internally logical and systematic by forcing the child's play into a predetermined sequence of interest and behavior. It was a circular theory, for evidence of the child's activity was then used to prove Froebel's immutable laws of childhood, a reification of the concepts of imitation and suggestion. The purpose of the conference, Dewey concluded, was to "discover and state the principles" underlying some of the current educational controversies in order to "carry out the spirit of Froebel."[13]

The invitation of George Herbert Mead revealed Dewey's hidden agenda. Mead was at the center of a group of social psychologists at Chicago who were exploring the social origins of personality. Like Dewey, Mead had rejected Idealism and evolutionism as explanations for the formation of the self in children. He implicitly distrusted reasoning that stressed the embryonic, the racial, or the innate faculties of the child as an explanation of behavior. In fact, the Chicago sociologists reversed Romantic assumptions by searching the child's awakening social awareness for clues to understanding the development of self. Thus Mead was particularly interested in the early social, moral, and ethical behavior of children for very different reasons. Hoping for a more credible explanation than Hegelian symbolic education for the social behavior of the kindergarten child, Dewey invited Mead to participate in the conference. Speaking on "play and education," Mead argued that of the three types of human activity—play, art, and work—only play allowed an "absolute spontaneity and lack of consciousness of an end in view." Though he was indebted to the Froebelians for definitions, Mead broke new ground on the origin of the child's spontaneous interest in play. "Nowhere in the development before birth and immediately afterwards," he observed, "is an organ used simply with a view to a function that is to come later." Play, Mead continued, could be explained only by its involvement "in the entire life process," a viewpoint Mead called basic to post-Darwinian thinking. Unlike child-study advocates and kindergarten enthusiasts, Mead grounded play neither in ideal forms nor in racial vestiges, but in the child's social environment.[14]

The educational implications of Mead's talk were crucial to Dewey's evolving views on early childhood education. In a dramatic reversal of the Froebelian theory of play, Mead argued that play "depends upon the presence simply of the right stimuli to call out the spontaneous use of the new coordinations." The proper setting for early education, then, was not necessarily the kindergarten but simply "the normal environments, physical and social, of man." The real challenge of early education was neither to force coordinations as Calvin held nor to cultivate the inner child as Froebel maintained, but rather to coordinate and arrange the educational stimuli so that "they will answer to the natural growth of the child's organism." "Is the brain an empty country into which the educator can go," Mead rhetorically asked, "like the manager of a telegraph company and put wires where he will?" For Dewey the answer was becoming clear: educational theory would depend on adjustment or adaptation to the social environment.[15]

For Dewey, functional psychology provided a new set of educational hypotheses. If Mead were correct, the child's mental structures were themselves shaped by experience. The mind of the child, then, could no longer be characterized either as a Lockean circuit of associations or as a Scottish Common Sense bundle of faculties. Previous schools of psychology, the functionalists argued, had simply imposed an adult psychology upon the child. For example, faculty psychology held that the powers of the child (memory, perception, imagination, emotion, and will) were simply incomplete, or "imperfect," "dim and inadequate manifestations of adult powers." Education, then, had simply been a process of "perfecting" the immature faculties of the child. By contrast, the functionalists believed that the child was an active, dynamic being with complete interests, impulses, and activities of his own. "A child is not born with faculties to be unfolded," Dewey concluded, "but with special impulses of action to be developed through their use in preserving and perfecting life in the social and physical conditions under which it goes." What distinguished Dewey's "impulses" from Hall's "instincts" was the ability of the teacher to select the proper means for stimulating the child's mental development.[16]

Functional psychology, later called developmental psychology, was especially useful to Dewey because of its stress on the orderly sequence of the child's growth. Dewey's student Irving King later formulated the fundamental tenets of the new child psychology in his *Psychology of Child Development* (1904). Dewey and others were careful to distinguish functional psychology from the earlier metaphysical stages postulated by Froebel, Alcott, and Parker that also divided the child's growth into stages. To Romantic educators, a single metaphysical process, including an ethic, philosophy, and educational system, was required to reach the "inner child." The meaning of each stage of growth was not clear until its completion, for ultimately education was a divine process. By contrast, functional psychology made a crucial distinction between the child's development—physical, mental, and moral—and his education. Education was related to but no longer identical to development. Each stage was complete in itself and prepared the child for the next stage.[17]

Dewey's specific plans for a "laboratory school" at the University of Chicago (1895) also grew indirectly from the debate on child study versus kindergarten. Like laboratories in biology, physics, and chemistry, a "laboratory school" would "exhibit, test, verify, and criticize theoretical statements and principles" in order to add to the sum of the facts in education. "Only the scientific aim, the conduct of a laboratory, comparable to other scientific laboratories," Dewey wrote, "can furnish the reason for the maintenance by a university of an elementary school." There was a subtle but important shift in his use of the word "laboratory." For Dewey, the "laboratory school" was the "nerve" of the department of education and philosophy, a place where pedagogical principles were tested, not where facts were gathered. A department of pedagogy in the modern university, Dewey argued, must be built on the solid footing of experimental psychology, but its main purpose lay in identifying the constant changes in the educational environment.[18]

The original plan of the laboratory school, or university elementary school, excluded a kindergarten. Part of the reason was political. Harper had approved Dewey's plan only half-heartedly, because he had not entirely convinced the board of trustees of the need for a new school. In addition, Harper felt the Froebelian roots of the kindergarten would be difficult to relate to the scientific goals of the laboratory school. The set curriculum of the kindergarten did not readily lend itself to experimentation. For both reasons Dewey was reluctant to include a "kindergarten" in the laboratory school, but a deeper criticism of the organization of American education also explained Dewey's decision. Dewey believed that its arbitrary units—kindergarten, primary school, and grammar school—resulted in "isolation" and "waste."

Part of the explanation was historical accident, and Dewey used the American kindergarten movement to illustrate the larger point in his 1899 lectures at the University of Chicago. "The kindergarten movement . . . as instituted by Froebel rested on a quite different conception of the child," Dewey told an audience of future teachers. "It was carried on through voluntary agencies, philanthropy, charity, and as a private school." In a double sense, Dewey believed that the accidental organization of the school system continued to hamper the child's education. The meaningless breaks interrupted the child's development, a condition Dewey called "waste" in education. At the same time, the organization of the schools into separate units further "isolated" the child from the educational benefits of direct contact with society. Dewey explained to one group of parents and educators, "A lot of things are started in the kindergarten that do not lead anywhere."[19]

The organization and principles of the laboratory school, nevertheless, bore the deep imprint of Froebel's thought. The initial curriculum of the school was based on the child's interest in exploring social relations, what Dewey called "real wholes." Family life and household chores comprised the core of the curriculum for the kindergarten age group four to six at the laboratory school (later called the "sub-primary unit"). Socially, Dewey hoped to bridge the artificial boundaries between home and school. Psychologically, he hoped to tap the child's natural interest in the activities that surrounded him. Organizationally, he made the sub-primary unit part of the laboratory school, thereby aiming to eliminate the mischief of "isolation" and "waste" in education. Dewey, perhaps disingenuously, noted that the school was only an attempt to "carry into effect certain principles which Froebel was perhaps the first consciously to set forth."[20]

Dewey later announced that the principal objective of the sub-primary department was to "train children in cooperative and mutually helpful living." The Dewey kindergarten would accomplish such social goals, in part, through playful exercises. "The primary root of all educative activity is the instinctive, impulsive attitudes and activities of the child," Dewey explained; "accordingly numberless spontaneous activities of children . . . are capable of educational use." The curriculum of the laboratory school was planned in order to capture for the child the social life of adults *writ small*, or in Dewey's terms to "reproduce on the child's plane the typical doings and occupations of the larger, and maturer society into which he is finally to go forth." Like Harris, Hall, and Parker before him, Dewey considered himself the true American interpreter of Froebel. "So far as these statements correctly represent Froebel's educational philosophy," he concluded his statement of principles, "the School should be regarded as its exponent."[21]

Perhaps the most obvious innovation in the experimental kindergarten was the child's new freedom of movement. Dewey quickly abandoned the rigidly timed lessons of the Froebelian day with its alternating program of individual and group play. Using the "free play" program of the Santa Barbara kindergarten (Burk and Eby), he gradually increased the free time of the kindergarten child. "The first aim of the kindergartner should be to form a social atmosphere, and have her kindergarten as much a home as possible," wrote Georgia Scates, the laboratory school's kindergarten director. "In order to do this there must be freedom and as few rules as the surrounding will permit, thus throwing each child upon his own responsibility and allowing him opportunity for expressing individual traits of character." Such freedom, the progressive educators believed, would allow the child to develop "laws and rules of his own."[22]

Dewey also gave the kindergarten director a free hand in revising the curriculum. As the first step in the two-year sub-primary sequence, the kindergarten introduced the child to the larger society. The earliest lessons of the Dewey kindergarten began with those aspects of the child's social life that he understood—the home environment and the relationship to mother, father, brothers, and sisters. Gradually the child was introduced to the same relationships in other families, allowing "a little of the outside world to come creeping in." The attention of the child was then turned even more closely to the homes of other children by looking at "small homes, apartments, and large homes." Influenced by the architectural exercises of Froebel, Dewey introduced the child to the building materials, exterior decoration, interior arrangement of furniture, and living spaces. After a long winter of such activities, the kindergarten child was ready for the outdoor games, nature work, and city excursions in the spring. Dewey gave the laboratory-school kindergartners wide latitude in the choice of such activities, allowing "anything which reproduces, or runs parallel to some form of work carried on in social life."[23]

The educational materials of the laboratory-school kindergarten were also a free rendering of Froebelian equipment. The Froebelian building blocks were retained but were used as "ordinary blocks, as mediums to illustrate different phases of work." "They are adapted absolutely to the work, not the work laid out in order to bring in the gifts," wrote the kindergarten director. "This point is fundamental, as it seems to be the only way to emancipate the kindergarten." The kindergarten blocks were used in a variety of lessons, often of the children's own devising, to illustrate aspects of the social life. Froebelian materials, moreover, were not the only playthings permitted in the Dewey kindergarten. "With the gifts, when desirable, we use other material, thus satisfying sometimes an unfulfilled want," one kindergarten instructor wrote. Using larger blocks, children were now permitted to play on the floor, away from the rigid grid system of the Froebelian tables. Instructors at the laboratory-school also found many of the stylized songs and games of the Froebelian kindergarten no longer useful and substituted "old time children's games," such as pussy-in-the-corner, drop-the-handkerchief, and bean-bag races. "These traditional games of childhood seem more helpful for both social and intellectual ends," wrote director Scates, "and more appropriate to the spirit of Froebel than the so-called symbolic games, where as a rule only the teacher appreciates the idea."[24]

It was Mead's definition of play, not Froebel's, that made the laboratory-school kindergarten innovative. Dewey put it this way: "Its significance . . . means the possibility, and in many respects the necessity, of quite a radical change of kindergarten procedure." Later Dewey was even more straightforward in calling for a "complete emancipation from the necessity of following any given or prescribed system, or sequence of gifts, plays or occupations." The "social occupations" provided the critical link between the work of the sub-primary unit and that of the primary grades. Borrowing from Froebel's "occupations," Dewey redefined the substance of the classroom for an industrialized nation. Dewey now hoped to acquaint the child with activities outside an urban environment, such as farming, mining, quarrying, and the various modes of transportation. "The play reproduction of the home life passes naturally on into a more extended and serious study of the larger social occupations upon which the home is dependent," Dewey wrote. For Dewey the study of the "social occupations" provided the framework into which skills could later be introduced according to the child's own interest. "So far as the occupations, games, etc., simply perpetuate those of Froebel and his earlier disciples," Dewey later admitted, "it may be fairly said in many respects the presumption is against them—the presumption is that in the worship of the external doings discussed by Froebel we have ceased to be loyal to his principle."[25]

The Chicago years (1894–1904) made clear the fact that Dewey was not interested in alliances with the kindergarten movement. In fact, he became increasingly outspoken in his criticism of the Froebelian psychology of interest, imagination, imitation, and symbolism. The root problem was that educational practice in the Froebelian kindergarten determined child psychology—just the reverse of the relationship which Dewey proposed. He was able to cite many specific examples. Children in the Froebelian kindergarten swept "make-believe rooms with make-believe brooms" on the untested assumption that such activity stimulated the faculty of imagination. The children's preference for flat, geometric designs became the evidence for the child's interest in symbols. "We often teach insincerity, and instill sentimentalism, and foster sensationalism when we think we are teaching spiritual truths by means of symbols," Dewey later wrote of the educational practice in the kindergarten.[26]

In the preface to his *The School and Society* (1899), which later would become the manifesto of progressive early childhood education, Dewey served notice on the Froebelians that his debt had been paid. Turning upside down the kindergarten motto "Come, let us live with our children," Dewey concluded that Froebel meant "first of all, that our children shall live—not that they shall be hampered and stunted by being forced into all kinds of conditions, the most remote consideration of which is relevancy to the present life of the child." The break with Froebelians was complete. Though Dewey accepted a position in the department of philosophy and psychology at Columbia University (1905), where the university debate with the Froebelians was even more intense, he remained a bystander.[27]

At Teachers College, Columbia University, kindergarten training became an even more serious educational enterprise. Kindergarten training was not new to Teachers College. Its founders, Grace Hoadley Dodge and Nicholas Murray Butler, were both active in the popular education movements of the 1880s. In 1884 both reformers joined the Industrial Education Association, an organization that lobbied for the adoption of education reforms by the city. By 1887 the Association focused its attention on the critical shortage of teachers in the city and helped to launch the New

York College for the Training of Teachers, which changed its name to Teachers College (1892) under a new charter from the state of New York. Affiliation with Columbia University, the same year, completed the professional transformation of the school.[28]

The transformation of the Teachers College kindergarten department was marked. Initially the kindergarten program was part of five "faculties": mechanical drawing, woodworking, domestic economy, industrial arts, and kindergarten methods. As late as 1890, the department was as much committed to urban reform as to academic training. Angeline Brooks, department head, for example, remained an active member of the New York Free Kindergarten Association and helped to place Teachers College students throughout the city's free kindergartens. Frank M. McMurry, Teachers College professor of philosophy, later recalled that the department was founded on the "controlling ideas" of both the requirements of society and the nature of children. The kindergarten program, McMurry noted, grew from the belief that the elementary school had been "a less faithful servant" to society than had the kindergarten.[29]

The public adoption of the kindergartens in New York helped to change the nature of the department. Russell, now dean of Teachers College, was concerned about the rapid increase of unqualified public kindergarten teachers and supervisors. He felt that the public had been misled by the campaign for public kindergartens, which had failed to distinguish between a general acceptance of the idea of early education and an endorsement of a particular view. Russell was particularly critical of kindergarten training institutions that inadequately prepared teachers and supervisors for public school work. He charged that kindergarten training academies were distinguished mainly by poor teaching and the "intellectual immaturity" of the student body. By contrast, teacher training at the university level should aim to investigate, interpret, and apply educational methods, techniques, and principles. The implications of hasty municipal reform were clear to Russell: kindergarten training should become the province of the university department of education.[30]

The creation of the experimental Speyer School was also a critical development in the evolution of the University's kindergarten program. The school grew out of an arrangement between the University and the New York Free Kindergarten Association by which the college provided student teachers and the Association offered classroom teaching experience in the city's free kindergartens. St. Mary's Church's free kindergarten, located near the University, was the center of the Teachers College program. With the eager cooperation of the rector, Teachers College soon took over the operation of the free kindergarten to serve as a training facility. The new school, however, posed immediate problems for the College. The community showed little interest in the venture, and the "backward" children of the kindergarten program had academic difficulties at the progressive Horace Mann School, a model primary school with "good teaching under favorable circumstances." A partial solution came in 1901 when a gift of Mr. and Mrs. Speyer made possible the creation of an "experimental school" containing a kindergarten. The new facility was designed both to afford the possibility of practice teaching and to promote research and investigation.[31]

At Teachers College, Russell consciously shaped the kindergarten program to upgrade the quality of kindergarten supervision and administration. The dean believed that vocational ignorance, the discouraging expectation of small salaries, and the fear of competition from normal-school graduates discouraged college women from entering the field. Still Russell was encouraged by the recent enrollments at Teachers College. By 1901, enrollments in its kindergarten program had increased by 33 percent, of which 8 percent were college graduates and 56 percent normal-school graduates. Russell was convinced that graduates of university departments of education would "easily outstrip all competitors" once fitted for kindergarten work. In addition, salaries would rise as college-trained educators filled positions as kindergarten supervisors and administrators. He thought that the South and West would provide the greatest employment opportunities at first, but that ultimately college-trained women would fill all the new supervisory posts opened through the expansion of public kindergartens. In order to fulfill his vision of Teachers College as the great new training center for public kindergartners, Russell recognized the need to offer the University as a forum for a debate on the unresolved issues of kindergarten curriculum and training.[32]

One of Russell's first steps was to provide a revised kindergarten psychology at Columbia. Conveniently, Edward Lee Thorndike, an experimental psychologist trained under James McKeen Cattell, was already at work on the problem in the psychology department, where he offered an introductory course, "The Study of Children." The course description was revealing: "semi-metaphysical questions, such as the nature of the self, the nature of knowledge, or the supra-phenomenal relation of mind and body, are entirely eliminated." In the first class, Thorndike told future kindergarten teachers to disabuse themselves of any notion of studying the "mysterious transformations in the 'soul,' or 'personality,' or growth of 'spiritual nature.'" The psychology of early childhood under Thorndike was to be a discipline of "facts and laws." Early influenced by the work of Hall, Thorndike conceded that more information was needed on the role of play, objects, and imagination in early childhood; but he was equally convinced that new facts would not change his conception of the child's mind. "The truth is that a human life is a bundle of habits; that what we mean by knowledge is habits in sequence amongst ideas; that what we mean by capacity is the possibility of forming a certain set of habits." Under Thorndike's intellectual leadership and with Russell's assurances, kindergarten psychology was already shifting toward behaviorism at Teachers College.[33]

By 1904 Russell was convinced that the whole question of kindergarten pedagogy needed open discussion and invited kindergarten reformer Patty Smith Hill to deliver a series of lectures on the new perspectives in the kindergarten movement at Teachers College. Russell had become dissatisfied with the outdated ideas of Susan Blow, a guest lecturer at the University since 1896. Apparently Russell heard student complaints that the work of Hall, Parker, and Dewey was scarcely mentioned in her required course on the philosophy of the kindergarten. In his 1904 letter to Hill offering the appointment, Russell mentioned a "transitional period" at Teachers College and specifically noted the transfer of training courses from the Froebel League of New York. While Froebelian instructors Laura Fisher and Susan Blow would be retained, Russell was careful to add that "all sides of the kindergarten problem are to be represented here." The dean was specifically interested in Hill's "practical work" at the demonstration kindergarten and training school in Louisville. Ironically, in persuading her to come to Teachers College, the academician appealed to Hill's loyalty to the kindergarten cause rather than to the University ideal of reform. "It is a duty which you owe to the kindergarten movement in general." Hill privately dreaded the specter of public debate with Susan Blow but publicly welcomed Russell's invitation to lecture at Teachers College as a "rare opportunity" to disseminate the newer ideas of kindergarten education."[34]

Patty Smith Hill was typical of the Midwestern free kindergartners. The daughter of a Presbyterian minister and educator, Hill was raised in an atmosphere of liberal religion and education. Dr. William W. Hill, the head of the Belleville Seminary, abandoned the prescriptive "Sunday school" methods of teaching and stressed an atmosphere of self-creativity in his home. Encouraged in her education, Hill graduated from the Louisville Collegiate Institute (1887) and the following year entered a kindergarten training course under a local Froebelian, Anna Bryan. Bryan encouraged Hill to depart from the rigid Froebelian rules and experiment in the homes of the poor district of Louisville. Hill quickly became the leader of social and educational reform in the city as head of the Louisville Free Kindergarten Association (1893), which maintained a model kindergarten and free kindergartens throughout the city. Hill's experience, like that of other free kindergartners in the Midwest, grew from the unlikely union of Christian humanitarianism and an imported educational ideology.

With a university appointment at an early age, Hill was in a position to become one of the leading voices for reform of kindergarten training. A sometime student of G. Stanley Hall and Francis Parker, she first heard Dewey as a student at the Cook County Normal School. Along with Anna Bryan, she attended the first summer school of pedagogy at Clark University and subsequently led the drive for child-study reforms in the Midwestern kindergarten movement. By the late 1890s, Hill had incorporated the ideas of Hall, Parker, and Dewey in her Louisville demonstration kindergarten. In good progressive fashion, all three educators visited the school to observe their own pedagogical theories in classroom practice. Louisville, then, had been the location for a dress rehearsal for the university challenge to Froebelian kindergarten training. Russell's hunch was correct; Hill was well qualified to enter into a university debate with Susan Blow on all aspects of kindergarten pedagogy.[35]

The Blow-Hill lectures at Teachers College began as a series of ten free public talks on the kindergarten sponsored by the Froebel League, the Kindergarten Association, and Teachers College. Not surprisingly, Hill focused her attention on the weak points in Froebelian theory and practice: dictation, imitation, originality, and symbolism in the kindergarten curriculum. Blow delivered a traditional lecture course on Froebel's philosophy and kindergarten practice. For a time the two rival leaders worked out a compromise plan at Teachers College: Blow offered the survey of Froebel's philosophical principles and a traditional course in the use of gifts and occupations that she called "the concrete embodiments" of Froebel's ideas. Hill, on the other hand, gave her "Kindergarten Conference," a critical review of the Froebelian kindergarten program in the light of "recent developments in education, child study, and psychology." At first Blow and Hill were jointly responsible for the supervision of all kindergarten training at Teachers College.[36]

The rival courses spotlighted the curricular innovations of Frederic Burk, Francis Parker, and John Dewey (1895–1905). Their innovations provided the substance for Hill's lectures and defined the nature of Blow's response, creating, in effect, two separate training programs at Teachers College. In her lectures, Blow attempted to rekindle the debate over the "unresolved" philosophic issues of "unity," "freedom," and "symbolism." Her strategy was to cloud apparent psychological advances by raising philosophical complexities. Hill flatly disregarded the notion of the child's "spiritual unity," preferring Dewey's concept of social unity in education. In addition, Hill rejected the "higher forms" of symbolism, or adult analogies. Finally, Hill offered a much broader conception of freedom in the kindergarten, complaining that old-school Froebelians maintained an artificial distinction between "intellectual" and "physical" activity. For Hill, the Froebelian concept of play was only an "illusion" that provided another opportunity for instruction.[37]

Age and personality of the rival instructors not only heightened the interest in the debates but also helped the debaters to organize their strategies. One student later recalled Susan Blow as an elderly woman, "unpleasantly didactic" and with an "air of finality" about her. In contrast, the younger Hill was viewed as "simple, straightforward, open-minded, practical, generous, and not given to philosophical speculation." Blow, relying on her Saint Louis lecture style, used examples drawn from literature, art, and philosophy to unify, once again, the areas of "childhood" and "culture." Hill illustrated her points by "practical detail" and "example" in the scientific spirit of Hall and Dewey. The Blow-Hill "debates," then, pitted erudition, abstraction, and philosophy against common sense, practicality, and science.[38]

Intellectual style also reflected the professionalization and the deep generational divisions within the kindergarten movement. The intangible sense of a "burning mission" that had attracted early Froebelians was lost at Teachers College. The interest in philosophical study, which even child study had failed to snuff out, had disappeared at the professional schools. Most Teachers College students had little interest in the increasingly arcane aspects of Froebelianism. "I am finding it simply impossible to get the class at Teachers College to consider Froebel's ideal," Blow confided to her friend Fanniebelle Curtis, "because they nearly [all] have the idea that I am standing for a formal, arbitrary and unpsychological procedure." Always politically astute, Susan Blow recognized the shift in attitude and realized that she was at a distinct disadvantage within the University. At first she felt that her age was the cause of her troubles at Teachers College and briefly considered leaving the College post for the good of the movement. At the peak of the debate, she wrote to an old friend: "What we need is a young leader!" What she sensed was that the women at Teachers College had already chosen one.[39]

The kindergarten pioneer also recognized that generational differences alone did not explain her difficulties at Teachers College. Under the active leadership of Russell, the Teachers College curriculum was drifting steadily away from idealism toward pragmatism and behaviorism. In the new intellectual climate, Blow finally admitted to Harris that kindergarten training was no longer "inspiring." In the University, Blow could control neither events nor ideology. "The worst thing that ever happened [to the kindergarten movement] is the pseudo-alliance with Teachers College," she wrote to Curtis. But Blow was able to comprehend only partially the changed aspirations of the first generation of college-educated early-childhood educators. Collegiate women at the turn of the century, as historian Roberta Frankfort has shown, were no longer in pursuit of "self-culture" in professional training. Like advocates of the home-economics movement, collegiate kindergarten women now looked on their field as a professional option, a "way of insuring that traditional woman's work would take on a larger significance." Ironically, the Saint Louis kindergartner had helped to create this sense of professionalism that she now found less than "intoxicating" in the University setting.[40]

By the spring term (1905) Blow knew she had become embroiled in a University political struggle beyond her control. Formerly a capable political infighter within the kindergarten movement, she now seemed unable to judge even the most obvious intentions of her colleagues at Teachers College. "A number of other professors have looked in," she wrote to Harris in reference to her course on "Kindergarten Principles and Practices," "but I don't imagine they are much interested." Dewey, Thorndike, and MacVannel, however, were interested though Blow was never able to persuade them of the merits of her viewpoint. She was most disappointed in Dewey. "There are so many more things in heaven and earth than are dreamed of in his philosophy," she confided in Harris, "and which his native defect of imagination seems to conspire to hide from him that one wonders that he should carry influence." Blow finally dismissed Dewey as "blunt-minded." At the same time, she misjudged the politics of the kindergarten department, incorrectly assuming that Chairman MacVannel "stands firmly with us" and that she had made a "little impression" on Dean Russell. By the spring she changed her mind. Russell had "no conception whatever of the educational questions at issue in the kindergarten," she complained to Harris, "and is representing the issues between the kindergartners as mere quarrelling between women."[41]

In desperation she requested and received Harris's pledge to intercede with Russell on her behalf. In his appeal to Russell, Harris argued that the remedy of the "radicals" was worse than the disease. Hill's "reforms" would place the decision of the "educative value" of play in the hands of the individual kindergarten teacher. Harris maintained that "not more than one kindergartner out of a hundred" had any real talent for choosing the proper educational activity. The radical program, Harris believed, would substitute "ninety-nine absurdities for every one in Froebel." Hill's appeal to students was based on "the eloquence and popular manner of the reformer and not the logical essence of her ideas." The real worth of the kindergarten trainer, Harris concluded, was to explain the relationship of the kindergarten, through ideas, to the institutions of higher learning in the country.[42]

Harris vainly argued that it was a task for which Blow was uniquely qualified. Russell conceded that not all play activities carry equal educational value, but maintained that training at Teachers College allowed the individual teacher to discriminate. Even during Harris's final appeal Russell was preparing for an academic year in which the issues before the kindergarten movement would come to a head at Teachers College. "In view of the fact that no other institution is in the position to attempt to advance the kindergarten," he wrote to Hill during the same year, "our attempt next year will be unique and the opportunity it gives you is not to be lightly regarded."[43]

In response to the popularity of the lectures, John Angus MacVannel, soon to be the head of the Kindergarten Department (1906), invited Blow and Hill to return and present their viewpoints in a joint course at Teachers College. In a remarkably candid appeal to Hill, MacVannel noted that the new chairmanship "disturbed his dream . . . of doing some fairly good work . . . in the philosophical side of education." He argued that the same administrative changes favored Hill's career. He confided Russell's impression that "the work of Miss Blow is almost over." MacVannel also tipped Russell's hand in revealing his plans for making Teachers College the major kindergarten training center in the city after the "breaking up of the Froebel League." Russell himself joined the appeal, noting that Blow's "strong opposition" to Hill's reappointment would make it necessary for him to lead a "very strenuous life" in order to be fair to both sides.[44]

But by 1906, Russell's and MacVannel's conception of "fairness" included major concessions to the reform movement. Hill would have control over the Speyer School along with two assistants and would also have complete freedom in the "supervision course." "I feel deeply now in offering you this position the College is giving you a unique opportunity to equip and perfect yourself to assist in raising the standards of Kindergarten instruction in this country to a higher level than it has hitherto attained anywhere," MacVannel wrote. Together the two University men were persuasive. At the same time, the shift in power and influence could no longer be hidden. "We are not fighting a few kindergartners but a whole trend in general education," Blow wrote to a friend. The following year Hill received a regular appointment; Blow remained a visiting lecturer.[45]

The events at Teachers College reached a climax in the spring term, 1906. Hill's course was made a requirement; Blow's remained an elective.

"The struggle must go to Miss Hill," Blow accurately observed. "Radicals can get their degree without coming to me." But her travail at Teachers College did not end here, for at mid-term a group of reform-minded students threatened to leave the University if Blow's course continued. The kindergarten pioneer was justifiably outraged at the school's decision to accede to the wishes of these students. She did not blame Hill for the "stopped lecture course" but rather the "majority of the professors" who acted in a spineless manner. Blow now occupied the ethical high ground in the debate; she could tolerate intellectual criticism but not academic interference at Teachers College. "If there seems any reason to hope for good results I shall stay on," she wrote to Harris, "but if I am being used merely to draw Froebelian students with the hope of perverting them, then I shall feel that it may be my duty to withdraw." Embittered by her experience, Blow left Teachers College. But her shoddy treatment at the University continued to win her support, both personal and ideological, on the lecture circuit. Her final assessment that American universities had grown "hostile" to orthodox Froebelianism was correct.[46]

The Teachers College debate reflected professionalization but its outcome also helped to shape professional issues and choices for the next two decades. Under the departmental leadership of MacVannel, Thorndike's behaviorism became the semi-official psychology at Teachers College. "The formula on which he runs a kindergarten is stimulus-response, interaction and readjustment," Blow disdainfully wrote to Harris. "This is repeated by all his subordinates." Under Hill's later chairmanship, the Dewey approach to the kindergarten was melded with Thorndike's psychology. By 1920 Hill could report to Dean Russell that "kindergarten theory and practice have been so transformed that little remains of the original product." Hill was even more impressed by the placement record of Teachers College. She estimated that more than 150 women had met the new requirements for bachelor's or master's degrees in the program and that through its graduates the "influence of the department in reconstructing kindergarten education, has gone all over the world, reshaping education theory and practice wherever work with little children is being done." Though the claims were somewhat exaggerated, Hill had been an effective instrument of University policy which in the first decades of the century had validated the search for professional status among American kindergartners.[47]

10

Progressivism and the Kindergarten Movement (1904–1918)

No symbol of humanitarianism was more meaningful to progressives than childhood. "Its guiding faith and illusion," Herbert Croly once remarked, "are shared by the most hard-headed and practical Americans." Implicit in Croly's understanding was the view that childhood had become a national resource and that its conservation was a national priority. Most progressives believed that the great social-educational movements of the nineteenth century had been only a rehearsal for new government programs in child welfare and early childhood education. In the decade before World War I the kindergarten was added to a long list of progressive agencies and institutions aimed at saving the child—family courts, nursery schools, playgrounds, and day-care centers. There was a spirit of social optimism in each program that was imprinted deeply in conception by the Froebelian movement. "More than any other educational movement of the century, the kindergarten derived its validity," one progressive reformer noted, from the assumption that "every child may have life and may have it more abundantly, that the community may be elevated, the race improved."[1]

American kindergartners were quick to recognize their own contributions to the new climate of reform before World War I. By 1907 more than three million American children—many in private schools—had received a kindergarten education. More than 25,000 young American women had taken kindergarten training in the same period and thousands of other American mothers had been influenced by Froebelian childrearing techniques. The impact of the kindergarten movement upon public education was also substantial. By 1915, 8463 public kindergartens provided early childhood education for approximately 12 percent of the population of American children. Many kindergartners of the Progressive era correctly perceived themselves as the educational vanguard of progressive child reform. One official of the International Kindergarten Union (IKU), in fact, called the two decades before World War I the "golden age" of the kindergarten in America.[2]

In many ways the prevailing social optimism of the era seemed to be in accord with the spirit of the kindergarten movement. Americans had been forced to make a choice about the nature of man and the possibilities of reform. In choosing childhood as a national symbol of human potential, progressive child reformers were, in part, belatedly responding to the inheritance from the kindergarten movement. But the intellectual debt of progressives to Froebelians was quickly paid. Dewey, Montessori, and Freud—not Froebel—would define the issues of educational reform and change in the twentieth century. Progressive reform itself was based on assumptions of innocence not depravity, rationality not irrationality, and prevention not punishment. The choices were more difficult for kindergartners who were still locked in a nineteenth-century debate over the metaphysical nature of childhood and education. Before the modern ideologies of education could overrun Froebelianism, however, an elite group of "elder statesmen" in the IKU conducted a final, instructive debate on the implications of the "new education." Ultimately a decade of internal philosophic debate left the IKU confused, divided, and impotent. Challenged externally and internally, exhausted intellectually, the kindergarten movement virtually disappeared after World War I.[3]

Seemingly no organization better reflected the progressive ideal of childhood education than the IKU. Founded in 1892 to promote national kindergarten interests, the IKU had evolved into a sprawling, complex association by 1902. The charter-member organizations of the IKU were free-kindergarten associations whose functions had been displaced as a result of bureaucratization and professionalization. By banding together into a national organization, kindergarten leaders hoped to ensure the survival of kindergarten ideals during a period of rapid growth of public kindergartens and new training institutions. For instance, at the 1904 meeting IKU President Annie Laws noted that branch membership (largely free-kindergarten associations) had grown to more than 93 organizations. The International Kindergarten Union was now the third largest educational organization in the New World, with a membership of more than 18,000.[4]

The same process of growth also helped to transform the make-up of the

IKU. Unlike other Progressive-era associations, whose members shared a professional identity based on common training and specialties, the IKU was a simple federation of kindergarten interests. Allegiance stemmed from a vague commitment to the educational thought of Froebel. The meetings were attended by a cross section of kindergarten workers that included classroom teachers, training-school directors, and public kindergarten supervisors. Accordingly, discussion topics ranged from the Froebelian gifts and occupations to the management of large urban kindergarten systems. Public kindergarten work had dramatically increased the size and diversity of the IKU but not its strength.[5]

The fault lines within the organization were even more serious than the statistics revealed, for power was unequally distributed. The influence of public kindergartners and supervisors, university and normal-school instructors in particular, was not adequately reflected in the governance of the IKU. Statements on educational policy were controlled by a relatively small group of leaders, the first generation of American-trained kindergartners. The presidency, moreover, had always been held by a conservative kindergartner. The power structure of the IKU, then, reflected the underlying nature of the organization. Rigid and hierarchical, the IKU had none of the collegial spirit of other professional associations. The ailments of the IKU were perhaps clearest to educators outside the movement. For example, Earl Barnes, a Stanford professor of education, in 1902 warned the IKU leaders of the impending "crisis" within the union. Without a "full and candid statement" of its ideology and relation to other agencies of education, Barnes told an IKU audience, the kindergarten movement would become a "cult in and of itself" within the next decade. Not just the ideology but the very structure of the movement seemed challenged by the changes in American society.[6]

Most IKU members agreed that the success of the kindergarten in America demanded a reevaluation of its objectives and ideology. Conservative Froebelians had always been skeptical about the rapid growth of membership, for they feared the dilution of ideology that newcomers might bring. "The Rochester meeting showed me that the issue [ideology] in the kindergarten cannot be much longer postponed," Susan Blow wrote to Harris in 1904. "I am clear on the fundamental principles, but the questions which can no longer be postponed are Froebel's theory and practice of the gifts." Liberal kindergartners and public kindergarten teachers and supervisors were also concerned; they wondered whether in fact social-educational movements had outlived their usefulness. Some moderate IKU members naively hoped that the International Kindergarten Union could join other progressive educational agencies while retaining its distinctiveness.[7]

In order to calm the growing discontent, the IKU leadership agreed to vest power in a "select group" of kindergarten leaders to review the history, philosophy, and current status of the kindergarten movement. Even the terms of this group's mandate reflected the deep divisions in the IKU. Radical leaders, who had earlier broken away during the child-study fight, hoped to reshape the IKU into a national association to promote the general interests of early childhood. They saw new opportunities to form alliances with government and universities that would tie the kindergarten to the mainstream of progressive reform. Conservatives, on the other hand, hoped to limit discussion to the Froebelian gifts and occupations. All members saw the need for a broad statement of principles on the nature of the child and early education.

A new committee of the IKU was empowered in 1903 to "formulate contemporary kindergarten thought" in a written statement to the membership. In order to ensure fair representation, a preliminary panel composed of Susan Blow, Lucy Wheelock, and Patty Smith Hill was chosen to select members from the conservative, moderate, and radical factions. John Dewey and William Torrey Harris, among others, were to serve as "guides, philosophers, and friends" of the IKU committee. The final selection resulted in the formation of the Committee of Nineteen.[8]

The Committee membership also reflected the generational politics of the IKU. After Blow's defeat at Teachers College, her life had resolved into a predictable coda—she once again retreated from the role of active publicist and educator to passive theoretician. Blow was never entirely free from the alternating pattern of hope and despair, public activity and personal retreat. Still the "impulse to action," which characterized her earliest work, was clear in her initial response to the Committee. "Formulating the conservative creed of the American kindergarten," she predicted, would be her last contribution to the kindergarten movement. The new strength of progressives within the IKU was also clear from the outset. The followers of Dewey—Patty Smith Hill (Teachers College), Alice Temple (University of Chicago), and Anna Bryan (Armour Institute)—now felt that they were in a position to bring progressive educational reforms to the very citadel of Froebelian orthodoxy. Significantly, conservative members were no longer able to control the agenda of the debate. "I have been trying to formulate the conservative creed of the kindergartners," Blow wrote to Harris in 1905. "The radical party insisted that psychology be the next subject discussed." In an apparent attempt to bring peace to the Committee, the moderate Lucy Wheelock was chosen as chairman, but the important subcommittee on psychology, materials, methods, and symbolism was still dominated by progressives.[9]

The first years of the Committee's meetings (1904–1907) failed to produce any agreement. All concurred that Froebel was the "fountainhead" of the kindergarten, but they could agree on few details of educational method or theory. The nature and origin of play remained one of the most troublesome issues, and Dewey's influence was implicit in most questions before the Committee. Was play innate, instinctual, vestigial, or social? Were the child's free hours to be limited, controlled, directed, or uncontrolled? The proper relation of work and play in the kindergarten also troubled the kindergartners. Should work and play be symbolic or abstract, real or concrete? Should early education introduce the child to a world of thought or a world of industry? Without a common psychological or philosophical vocabulary, the debates became needlessly complex and hopelessly stalled. By 1907 the fiction of accommodation disappeared completely. Wheelock admitted that deep divisions still separated the groups of the Committee, noting that members failed to agree on even the most basic definitions of play, instinct, sense, image, idea, interest, and symbolism. Without common terms, discussion was meaningless and compromise impossible. Wheelock half-heartedly argued that the difference of opinion was healthy, but the mandate of the Committee defied her optimism. Ideological wrangling, in fact, was so great that the chairman retreated to the use of the first person in the preface of her reports in order to avoid misrepresenting any side. Work came to an early end when it became clear that the Committee of Nineteen would eventually publish not one but three reports.[10]

The limits were perhaps made clearest by events outside the kindergarten movement. At the peak of the IKU debate over child psychology, G. Stanley Hall invited Sigmund Freud to deliver a series of lectures at Clark University in 1909. The theories of the Viennese neurologist were little known among American psychologists and unknown to most kindergartners. Even Hall knew only that Freud had made some associations between "hysterical" behavior in adults and childhood memories. Blow was informed about the conference both by her old adversary Hall and by her neurologist James Jackson Putnam. "Just at present I am hearing a great deal about a man named Freud," Blow wrote to Harris in the summer of 1909. "Dr. Hall is crazy about him and Dr. Putnam much interested in." Putnam apparently canceled a trip to visit Blow in Cazenovia during Freud's stay; the kindergarten pioneer understood that he "should not miss Freud."[11]

Blow was also sensitive to the new challenge Freudian psychology might pose in the continuing struggle with child-study proponents. "I know the radical reformers will be looking wise and swearing by [Freud's insights]," she predicted, "and trying to make the rank and file believe that Freud has upset all the old foundations." To her credit, Blow also rose to the intellectual challenge. She wrote to Putnam, "I know I must meet this whole subject frankly and fearlessly, and I want to do so." In the intellectual excitement that followed the Clark conference, Blow wanted to read anything she could locate on Freud's new psychology of personality. "I am deeply interested in Freud and anxious to learn more about his point of view," she wrote to Putnam in 1910. With characteristic energy, Blow entered into a personal study of Freudian psychology. "There is another reason why I read these and [other] radical books," she explained to Harris. "I cannot really meet the questions in the minds of many reformers without doing so, and if I am to lecture I must know what my audiences are thinking about even if it is all wrong."[12]

Much of Blow's curiosity about Freud stemmed from an interest in the therapeutic value of psychoanalysis, for she continued to suffer from recurring depressions. At first Blow reacted with "indignation at all efforts of another person to use his consciousness to influence my subconsciousness," but she continued her reading. As Blow understood psychoanalytic theory, it was an attempt to discover the earliest (childhood) experiences that caused "a morbid or diseased state of mind." She learned that such experiences could be "suppressed and rejected by their main personality and persist at subordinate centers of association." She immediately applied Freudian psychology to her own childhood and told Putnam, "I suffered tortures in my childhood because of this ['blue Presbyterianism'] and can give you any number of instances should they interest you." Blow did not get very far with her own psychoanalysis and soon confessed to Putnam: "It is simply that I cannot believe psychoanalysis in itself is curative although I can see that it may be preliminary to cure."[13]

Blow was somewhat more optimistic about the educational implications of Freudianism and in attempting to defend the old Froebelian orthodoxy from it temporarily became a convert. For Blow, Freudian psychology was really a problem of early education. "Many, indeed most persons, are not unified, but it doesn't seem to bother them," she wrote to Putnam. "Educationally, the call seems to be what Froebel called 'unification.'" If Freud were to be helpful, it was not in psychoanalysis but in preventive measures to be taken in the kindergarten. "So far as the Freud thing casts light on childhood and education," Blow concluded, "I believe it has great value. It seems to me entirely possible for mothers to keep on terms of much greater intimacy than hitherto." Freud was put into the service of the kindergarten. "In short, I think we can all learn much from Freud as to the necessity of helping a self to unify itself early."[14]

Though she never mentioned Freud by name, Blow used Freudian psychology in her report to the Committee of Nineteen. She noted that the conservative creed had gained "indirect confirmation from an unexpected source." Blow spared the committee the details of Freud's psychology but summarized his "educational hints." Popularization of ideas came easy for Blow, who explained that children "stored up experiences, motives, and emotions" from birth onward. Some experiences were recorded in daily life (morals and social conventions) and others became unused or "suppressed" (emotions). The child was engaged in a "series of introspective and retrospective functions" that could be of use to kindergarten educators. "We spy upon the mind and discover how it acts," she concluded, "then make its spontaneous mode of procedure our criterion of educational method."[15]

Though Blow attempted to enlist Freud, she really never understood his psychology. Blow tried to fit Freud into a Hegelian dialectic by postulating an ideal self and an actual self, at war in the child from birth. The discovery of this double selfhood created "the most dramatic moment in the life of the child," a moment "fraught with danger," for the child learned to identify the two selves with good and evil and risked the possibility of a "disastrous schism in the soul." If the child attempted to hide its evil self, he could divide himself into "two mutually repellent groups." Here Freud offered the most help to the kindergartner, who might prevent such schisms "by helping the children from the beginning of life to face the experiences they instinctively hide and suppress."[16]

Blow was more successful in her attempts to persuade Putnam of the importance of Froebel's outlook than Putnam was in his efforts to persuade her of the usefulness of Freudianism. Putnam, interested in a positive approach to child psychology, believed that Freud's dominant interest in the abnormal behavior of adults rather than in the education of the normal child somewhat limited the usefulness of his psychology. Freud consistently maintained, on the other hand, that no system of early education could prevent later psychoses or personality disorders. Influenced by the lingering Victorian notion of the double nature of childhood, Putnam thought that childhood contained both "elements of happiness" and "elements of suffering." He wrote: "The dark stands for delicious, as well as alarming, and mysterious." Putnam was encouraged by Blow's report to the IKU that the "objectionable and hampering features" of one's childhood could be eliminated in early education. The Boston neurologist called the Froebelian kindergarten the "best prophylactic method at our command, applicable to all children." At times Putnam sounded like a latter-day Alcott. "The child, through very simple investigations into the results of his own acts," Putnam noted, "foreshadows that kind of self-scrutiny which psycho-analysts have learned to look on as of so much value." Blow never lost an opportunity to further the Froebelian cause. "I shall be proud to have you paraphrase any parts of my report you think worthy of restatement," she wrote to Putnam in 1912. "The one thing now most necessary is that our point of view be reflected from many minds."[17]

Privately Blow became more pessimistic about the application of Freudian psychology to the kindergarten. She now had serious misgivings. The notions of the double selfhood and the earliest sexual feelings of the child were powerful ideas that reminded her of the doctrine of innate depravity. After more reading she was convinced that Freud was only "rediscovering man's total depravity." For Blow, the greatest problem with Freud was not his rediscovery of evil but Freud's refusal to admit the deepest sources of it. Blow still had haunting memories of the angry God of her youth. Religious doctrines were always before her, and in reaction to them, she shaped her peculiarly American view of the kindergarten. Modernist thinkers like Dewey and Freud were now threatening to destroy her Froebelian armor, which protected her against an inherited Calvinism, without replacing it with a new shield of faith. To Blow, Dewey's naive optimism about the child was far less dangerous than Freud's cold silence on the question of moral responsibility in the child. "The comfortable doctrine of depravity saved man from utter despair in confronting other forms of sin and prepared the way," she wrote to Putnam, "for the struggle for victory with the armies of the Lord."[18]

The IKU met the challenge of Montessorism more openly. By 1909, the year of Freud's visit to America, the ideas of the Italian educator and physician Maria Montessori were also attracting attention among American parents and teachers. Hundreds of American women, including many kindergarten teachers, were flocking to Rome to study the system directly under its originator, while American Froebelians were debating in the IKU. One American woman returning from Rome called Montessori's words "winged messengers of light." Another member of the IKU wrote that "no more earnest, sane contribution has been made . . . since the time of Froebel and Pestalozzi." Now hopelessly deadlocked in a debate, the Committee of Nineteen could not avoid Montessorism.[19]

Two prominent members of the IKU, Elizabeth Harrison (a moderate) and Patty Smith Hill (a radical), went to Rome to hear Montessori lecture. Not surprisingly, conservatives showed little interest in the new system of education. Though she declined the opportunity to visit Montessori in Italy, Susan Blow encouraged others to study the new pedagogy. "It is always inspiring to go to the eternal city," Blow wrote to her friend Fanniebelle Curtis, "but I saw no reason to travel in order to study the doctrines of Montessori. I am inclined to think that Montessori will be a waning interest among school people. It has so obviously the Pestalozzian limits." Her remarks, in this instance, proved to be prophetic.[20]

Montessori believed that the key to early education was to provide a rich sensory environment for the child. Though she specifically denied any intellectual debt to Froebel, her didactic materials (cylinders, colored tables, geometric insets, wood frames, and buttoning frames) bore striking resemblance to the Froebelian gifts and occupations. Montessori told her American visitors that the real difference lay in the educational use of the new materials. Unlike the Froebelians, she denied the possibility of learning directly through symbols. Since sense impressions preceded mental development, the didactic apparatus was designed to provide only the basis for sensations and early associations. Henry Holmes, writing in the *Kindergarten Review*, for example, noted that the new educational apparatus answered the age-old criticism that the Froebelian gifts and occupations had "no real use."[21]

The most far-reaching difference between the Froebelian and the Montessori systems was the organization of classroom space. Like Dewey, Montessori viewed the classroom as a "learning environment," a place where the child underwent a process of self-discovery. Montessori called it "a room in which all children move about usefully, intelligently and voluntarily." The Montessori child was allowed complete freedom of access to the didactic apparatus, a sharp contrast to the rigid order of the Froebelian kindergarten with its semicircle of desks, its neat cabinets filled with gifts and occupations, and its graph-patterned tabletops for the orderly construction of perfect geometric arrangements. But some progressive kindergartners were more interested in Montessori's claims of success in preparing young children for later academic skills. Montessori, unlike Froebel, believed that the child could learn elements of reading and writing long before primary education. By constantly repeating the sounds and drawing the components of letters, the child paved the way for these skills until finally the word would burst upon his consciousness. This dramatic educational breakthrough Montessori called the "explosion into reading and writing." A majority of the IKU membership, however, remained skeptical. Though they were no longer persuaded by the Transcendental rationale of self-knowledge or the child-study rationale of environmental compensation, kindergartners were not ready to accept academic preparation as the *raison d'être* of the kindergarten.[22]

The Montessori method made little headway in the Committee of Nineteen. Moderates, liberals, and radicals could all agree that Montessori's stress on prereading and prewriting skills negated the special opportunities for learning through play and imagination in the kindergarten years. Kindergartners, moreover, received outside support for their criticism of the Montessori method. William Kilpatrick, Hill's colleague at Teachers College, ridiculed Montessori's notion that training could be transferred and called the didactic apparatus "worthless." Even the Montessori materials he found "too meager a diet for American conditions." He argued that Montessorism would appeal only to women of scientific pretensions. Moderates and liberals on the Committee were apparently persuaded that the Montessori method would only substitute "a new orthodoxy for old."[23]

The final statements of the Committee of Nineteen were cast in historical rather than strictly ideological terms. Conservatives maintained that the kindergarten movement had reached its "golden age" during the period of American expansion and vainly hoped for a return to the ideological purity and "burning zeal" of the 1870s. Moderates, on the other hand, still believed that progressive educational reforms could be absorbed into Froebelian ideology. Progressives argued that Froebelianism was already in shambles: its logical structure challenged by pragmatism, its faculty psychology refuted by functionalism, and its pastoral system of ethics outmoded in an industrialized democratic nation. The IKU debates, then, served to summarize the intellectual history of the kindergarten movement rather than to reshape the issues.[24]

Patty Smith Hill wrote for the progressives. Scientific advances, Hill contended, had already undermined the Idealist epistemology of Froebelianism. The quick pace of changes in nineteenth-century biology, geology, and chemistry negated the basic assumptions of Froebel's educational theories. Specifically, Darwinian biology and functional psychology destroyed the Froebelian notions of "self-activity," "germinal ideas," and "prepatterned" development. Consequently, the central aim of Romanticism—the development of the inner child—could withstand neither the psychological challenge of functionalism nor the philosophical challenge of pragmatism.[25]

Historically, Hill argued, the Idealist epistemology of Froebelianism belonged to pre-industrial German society. The Froebelian gifts and occupations, "baptized in German Romantic thought," made sense only in the context of a bygone rural society. The real social benefits of learning the poetic and metaphysical concepts of unity had disappeared; in a democratic industrial society, the child faced a series of real choices. Hill's debt to Dewey was clear. Progressive early childhood education, based on pragmatic philosophy and functional psychology, replaced Froebelianism because it worked well in American society. Hill had broadened the scope of the debate beyond the limits of Froebelianism, but her intellectual contribution was limited, because her ideas were derived from Dewey.[26]

Progressive leaders also came to doubt the usefulness of the IKU Committee's historical approach to ideology. In fact, Hill believed that there was "something inspiring" but also "something pathetic" about the single-minded devotion of the first generation of kindergartners. No longer was it necessary for middle-class young women to "forfeit parental approval" to work in a free kindergarten, a clear reminder of the mid-Victorian social setting of the movement, nor for daughters of the well-to-do to totally devote their lives to self-culture. Hill took some pleasure in noting that progressive kindergarten teachers identified with the professional aspirations of the classroom teacher rather than with the goals of the moral crusaders. Trained in normal schools or universities, the modern kindergarten teacher would be unwilling to subscribe to a single article of kindergarten faith. Hill also criticized the historical approach of the progressive report, for it was more useful in dispelling old ideas than in formulating a new creed.[27]

The final report of the moderates, cautiously titled "liberal conservative," substituted political for ideological concerns but differed little from the progressives' report. Moderates argued that the promise of the kindergarten lay neither in science nor in philosophy but in politics, for political isolation had done more damage to the kindergarten movement than its intellectual isolation. It was not the theory of early childhood education that seemed lacking to moderates, but rather its political application. In response to a decade of inaction, moderates called for immediate efforts to join the progressive education movement. Moderates urged more cooperative efforts not only with public schools but also with playgrounds, storytellers' leagues, and parents' associations. By joining hands with other progressive reformers, moderates naively concluded, kindergartners could become part of "the great social movement which is vivifying the school."[28]

Susan Blow was best prepared to place the debates into historical and philosophical perspective. Blow deftly attacked functional psychology while affirming Idealism. The kindergarten pioneer argued that pragmatism and functionalism reduced the child's experience to a series of unrelated and therefore meaningless experiences. By contrast, the educational aim of the kindergarten was to produce a sense of unity within the child by explaining metaphysical concepts through an ordered educational world. Blow cast her final statement in the terms of cosmic or theistic evolutionism in which God's plans for the gradual perfection of mankind were manifest in the child's natural development. The challenge of modern philosophy in early childhood education, Blow correctly observed, was part of an entirely new world order.[29]

The conservative report provided an excellent summary of Blow's own intellectual development. Polished and highly literate, the essay showed her wide reading in American philosophy from Harris's Saint Louis Hegelianism to Dewey's pragmatism. She had made intellectual forays into the psychological works of Hall, James, and most recently Freud. More often than not, Blow grasped the spirit rather than the logic of their ideas. Intellectually assertive to a fault, Blow constantly shaped others' insights to fit her compassionate concern for childhood and education. After each adventure, however, she retreated to the emotional comfort of Froebel's doctrines. Her contribution to the understanding of kindergarten theory was, nevertheless, great. In her own intellectual transformation, she stripped the German Romantic quality from Froebelianism, thus making his arcane doctrines understandable to a large audience less sophisticated than herself. "I am sure you will not misunderstand me when I say that I think the one real service I have rendered the kindergarten," she wrote to Putnam in 1912, "is to state in comprehensible, general terms the ideas, which in Froebel are rather implied and not clearly and logically stated."[30]

Blow's self-assessment was essentially correct though she could never see that in translating Froebelianism she had transformed it. Outdated by the twentieth century, Blow's later philosophical works had given final expression to a native nineteenth-century strain of Romantic educational thought that included Alcott, Peabody, and Parker. Even Patty Smith Hill charitably concluded that Blow's intellectual contributions would ultimately be judged by the yardsticks used in Van Wyck Brooks's *The Flowering of New England* rather than by the psychology of Binet, Pavlov, or Watson. Blow herself made a similar autobiographical observation in her last publication, *Educational Issues in the Kindergarten* (1908): "It is true that Froebel must be classed as a mystic and a mystic is a person who is making an inward transition from faith to philosophy by beginning to realize in the typical facts of religion a universal significance." Since her work remained derivative, however, she was finally unable to join the pantheon of the other educator-prophets of the nineteenth century.[31]

Blow's final report was respectfully greeted by an audience of American women who had been shaped by fundamentally different experiences. Appearing before the 1898 meeting, she was "received with waving handkerchiefs and enthusiastic applause." Such Victorian, feminine, social conventions were abandoned by the largely college-educated women who greeted her ten years later. One younger member recalled the context of her final remarks before the IKU. Blow was seated among the "prestigious, highly elevated figures on the platform" divided into conservatives, moderates, and radicals. The audience identified "methodologically with the radicals" but still credited the older women with the "dignity and devotion to cause" which had propelled the early kindergarten movement. Blow also later recalled the IKU debates as a generational benchmark in the kindergarten movement. "Forty years have changed the kindergarten from a consecrated vocation to a profession," she wrote her friend Kate Douglas Wiggin. But for Blow, the costs had been too high. "How to renew and perpetuate that spirit is the one problem of the Kindergarten Movement." The task was, of course, impossible, and Blow's final report to the IKU marked the beginning of the end of orthodox Froebelianism in America.[32]

The publication of the kindergarten reports (1913) also marked the end of Blow's theoretical contribution to the kindergarten movement. In rapid succession, she confronted the intellectual challenges of the twentieth century—Dewey, Montessori, and Freud. At age seventy Blow was exhausted by the intellectual struggle. "Within the past twenty-five years the series of slaughters and rebirths have been so rapid," Blow confessed, "that I am almost too tired to grapple with fresh antagonists or help a fresh reincarnation." Blow's active role as the chief American theorist of the kindergarten had come to an end.[33]

IKU members recognized that the work of the Committee of Nineteen was filled with paradox. The Committee, charged with writing one report, had produced three. The debates that were aimed at bridging ideological and generational differences served only to widen them. But most members of the IKU did not blame the Committee. The findings of the Committee had, in the end, reflected the deeper troubles of the kindergarten movement. Without a homogeneous membership committed to a single cause, the effort to create a single ideological statement was hopeless. The Committee recognized that it could no more dictate ideology than it could discipline its diverse membership. The kindergarten movement had outgrown its nineteenth-century social and intellectual framework. Blow asked rhetorically: "Is the kindergarten tottering and are its very foundations giving way?" The meaning of the reports, however, was clear. The Committee had begun by formulating kindergarten thought for the twentieth century and ended by declaring its impossibility.[34]

The outbreak of hostilities in Europe (1914), one year after the publication of their report, came as a great shock to the members of the Committee of Nineteen. Only three years earlier the Committee had sponsored a "Froebel Pilgrimage" to Germany (1911) as part of a celebration of the founding of the kindergarten. The trip was regarded both in Germany and in America as a sign of the maturity of the national movements. To the older members of the Committee it was a "spiritual journey," the fulfillment of a long career in the kindergarten movement. Conservatives, moreover, hoped that the pilgrimage would help bind the ideological wounds of the past decade and rekindle an interest in orthodox Froebelianism. War in Europe, however, forced conservatives, once again, to reassess their position. "With the war in the world turning everything topsy-turvy," wrote Almira Winchester of the Bureau of Education, "institutions and existing social conventions, formerly taken for granted, are now subjected to rigid inspection and their meanings sifted."[35]

Despite the initial shock of the war, most progressives were cautiously optimistic about its final outcome. Elizabeth Harrison, who had made the journey to Germany, became an advocate of the moderate position. Her opening speech to the incoming class of the Chicago Kindergarten College, "What Has This Great War to Teach Us?" posed the central question before Froebelians: Was the war the fault of the German militarists, an episode in the rise and fall of nations, or a moral lesson in the continuing struggle for freedom in the world? Harrison concluded that the European hostilities did not deny the ideals of kindergarten but only confirmed the need for a continuous struggle to develop an education based upon moral values. Like most Americans, Harrison believed that kindergartners could set the best example at home by demonstrating that America was the center of peace and democracy.[36]

Conservatives were far more pessimistic about the turn of events in Europe. For almost six decades orthodox Froebelians had relied on the intellectual and educational leadership of Germany. The credibility of the conservative report, in fact, rested unashamedly on the "universal significance" of German thought. Suddenly, the luster of German thought was tarnished by the actions of a military regime. Many conservatives could agree, at least in part, with the progressive journalist Randolph Bourne when he wrote, "It is the tragedy of the German spirit that German ideals (Nietzsche to Hegel) have become wedded to power in a perverse universe." Most conservative kindergartners, however, could not agree with his conclusion that Americans should accept pragmatism in order to meet "in overwhelming measure the responsibility we put ourselves under in rejecting the German."[37]

Susan Blow greeted the news of the war as a personal as well as national crisis. She attributed her deteriorating health—long periods of depression that she called "breakings-up of equilibrium"—to the recent world events. But unlike Randolph Bourne, Blow abstracted a moral rather than intellectual lesson from the war. "That many others are facing them as well as myself I know," she wrote to Putnam. "How can it be otherwise when everything we thought is challenged by the great world tragedy? And when the depths of sin revealed by that tragedy find so much like themselves in our hearts?" The war posed, for Blow, the possibility of a final Dante-like intellectual descent beneath reason, both pragmatic and idealistic, that would finally discredit the naive social optimism of the Progressive era.[38]

The immediate question raised by the war was the possibility of moral and educational reform in an irrational world. Ironically, Blow found herself in the camp of disillusioned progressive reformers. "What concerns us here is the relative ease with which the pragmatist intellectuals, with Professor Dewey at the head, have moved out their philosophy, bag and baggage, from education to war," wrote Bourne. Blow's disenchantment, however, was much deeper, for she had gone farther in her critique of progressive education. She believed that progressivism, as a theory both of childhood education and human nature, was doomed because it had failed to chart the limits of man's spiritual nature, failed to take into account man's imperfection, and failed to understand that corruption preceded reform. Not having restrained the inner evil of the child, Blow believed, progressive education had prepared the way for social and moral chaos. Suddenly the underlying meaning of Freudian psychology was clear. Once unleashed, the irrational and chaotic forces penned up in childhood and civilization would run their course. Bourne himself used Freudian similes to describe the potential irrationality in war and children when he concluded that "its [the war's] chief value is the opportunity it gives for this regression to infantile attitudes." To Blow the war was an intellectual descent prefigured in the educational schemes of Dewey, Freud, and Montessori.[39]

Blow's cynicism turned to an even deeper personal bitterness in her final years. Her periods of "instability" lengthened and her periods of depression deepened as she continued to seek help from Putnam. "Many conspiring causes are responsible for it," she wrote to Putnam and listed the "challenge of the war" along with the "contrast between my own questions and a triumphant faith." As her melancholia worsened, she attempted to relieve Putnam of responsibility. "In the end the severed knot cannot be restored by even the kindest of psychoanalysts," she wrote. "A wrong deed, illness, sorrow, mental perplexity may bring on all the morbid elements in the subconscious and upset the equilibrium of mental balance." Even in the depths of her final suffering, Blow longed for the leader who would guide her through the intellectual perplexities of the modern world. "I wish someone with clear and piercing vision might arise to show us what we ought to do," she wrote to Putnam. "The absence of such vision makes me realize as never before the greatness of the heroes of vision, faith and courage who in the past crises have seen what should be done and done it." Of course, such leadership was an impossibility; the American kindergarten pioneer died an embittered woman in New York City, March 26, 1916.[40]

To progressives in the IKU, Dewey was already supplying that intellectual leadership. His massive *Democracy and Education* (1916) contained many of the answers for which liberal kindergartners were searching. The book provided little new insight on the kindergarten but did set early childhood education into a larger democratic framework. The war itself should be viewed as an opportunity for democratic education, an idea "not adequately grasped by many Americans," Dewey wrote. "It is not enough to teach the horrors of war and to avoid everything which would stimulate international jealousy and animosity," he advised. "The emphasis must be put upon whatever binds people together in cooperative human pursuits apart from geographical limitations." Dewey believed that the war could be used to illustrate "the very idea of education as a freeing of individual capacity in a progressive growth directed to social aims."[41]

Within the IKU, progressive kindergartners like Hill and Alice Temple worked to make Dewey's lofty ideals into practical programs. Temple had come under the influence of Dewey first as a student at the University of Chicago and later as an instructor in the laboratory school. Hill remained on the faculty at Teachers College and was an original member of the Committee of Nineteen. During the long years of ideological discord in the Committee, these liberal leaders were frustrated by their inability to test Dewey's central idea of the kindergarten as a social center. While other urban progressives were waging battles against child labor, juvenile delinquency, and lack of public hygiene, liberal kindergartners had been tied to endless quarreling over educational philosophy. Led by Hill and Temple, kindergarten progressives now viewed the war as "an unparalleled opportunity to show its [the kindergarten's] efficiency in this constructive work."[42]

When America entered the European struggle in 1917, many kindergartners were inspired by the high moral purpose of Wilson's war aims. Members of the IKU in particular found a natural affinity between their objectives and the war effort. "Making the world safe for democracy" meant making the world safe for their day's children and for succeeding generations; war did not distinguish between adults and children. At the 1918 Chicago meeting of the IKU, for example, Henry Neumann of Brooklyn delivered an address on the topic "What Can the Kindergarten Do for Democracy?" Neumann looked to the immediate postwar years when the children of 1918 would be grown men and women. "A democracy is sound or unsound according as the lives of its people are sound or otherwise. The great service of the kindergarten," he concluded, "is to see that the beginnings of the better life are laid square and true."[43]

Repeatedly throughout the war years, the democratic character of the American kindergarten was contrasted to the autocratic nature of German schools. One speaker at a meeting of the IKU, in fact, implicitly compared educational and political authoritarianism when he noted that democratic kindergarten methods supplanted the "old idea of breaking the child's will" and "despotic dictation" with guided development and "informed supervision." Other speakers stressed the "Americanizing" ideals of individual initiative and teamwork implicit in the kindergarten. "That the institution has become thoroughly naturalized there can be no doubt," wrote Almira Winchester of the Bureau of Education. "No other place of education is more completely democratic and American than the kindergarten." Gradually kindergarten leaders also began to distance themselves from the German origins of the movement. Speakers at IKU meetings, for example, were quick to note that the kindergarten itself had been the victim of "the spirit of Prussianism." It was inevitable that a country which rejected the principle of individual freedom would also reject the kindergarten. An official of the Bureau of Education put the matter more bluntly when she wrote: "In Germany, the geographical birthplace of the kindergarten, little more than the outer form and the name is discoverable; the essence is missing. The kindergarten is not at home in Germany."[44]

Not all the issues before the Committee stemmed from high moral purpose. As the tide of anti-Germanism built up after the United States' entry into war with Germany, public pressure mounted for the IKU and the Bureau of Education to replace the German loan word "kindergarten" with some other term. The Bureau of Education briefly considered revising its kindergarten publications under the new titles of "children garden," "subprimary," "primary circle," or "babynest"! One official, however, called the words "clumsy and inept" and persuaded the Bureau that "no other word so aptly or euphoniously describes the thing signified" as does "kindergarten." Catherine Watkins, speaking before the 1919 convention of the IKU, put the matter more eloquently when she declared: "When we broke relations with Germany, we did not break with names but with a stern and menacing reality that threatened to destroy the most cherished ideals of humanity." This affair was one of the seamier episodes of the kindergarten story in its final years, and to the credit of kindergarten leaders both public and private they bent but did not break under public pressure.[45]

By 1918, most kindergartners were willing to join other Americans in what they believed was an authentic moral crusade. Members of the IKU thought it was their special mission to reform the decadent civilizations of Europe and soon were deeply involved in every aspect of the war effort. At first kindergarten support differed little from the work of other voluntary women's organizations. Harrison summarized the nature of women's role in the war before an audience of the National Kindergarten Association. Since women could not "go into the trenches and over the top," they must become the "line behind the line." A survey of the wartime work of the kindergarten teachers by the Bureau of Education indicated that many kindergartners were selling war savings stamps, establishing thrift kitchens, instructing in elementary hygiene, teaching English, maintaining war gardens, and making surgical dressings. The ultimate challenge of the war years to most kindergartners was not material but moral. Harrison phrased the problem in familiar evangelical terms when she wrote, "The real victories are when the image of God corrects weaknesses of the inner world."[46]

The work of translating America's war ideals into programs for children was assigned to the Committee of Nineteen, which had not gone out of existence. The IKU Executive Board initially named the old Committee to look into the work of kindergartners in war zones, but broadened its mandate in 1917 to include the "question of conserving and protecting the interests of the nation's children during the war." Members of the Committee apparently took seriously their new role as "builders of the nation's future citizens." The Committee met its first challenge during the coal shortage of the winter of 1917–1918 that threatened to close schools in various parts of the country. In a strongly worded report, the Committee urged that schools should not be closed until all "saloons, clubs and places of amusement were closed and all other means of conserving coal supplies were exhausted." Committee members were not able to eliminate the moral righteousness inherited from the early movement, but their actions did finally put an end to the ideological discord of the past decade.[47]

The immediate concerns of the war had a way of giving new currency to the outdated approaches of the kindergartners. The Committee of Nineteen recognized that their unique strength lay precisely in avoiding the professional specialization of other progressive agencies. In fact, they took special pride in their role as the protectors of the child's total interest. Winchester noted that it was often helpful if a visiting kindergartner reached a family before the "district nurse" or the "social worker," for frequently the kindergartner could best understand the complex problems facing families under war conditions. Paradoxically, Froebelians seemed effective not because they offered specialized services but precisely because they did not. The very survival of the IKU—despite two decades of attack from child-study proponents, adoption by the public schools, and professionalization—seemed to give the kindergartners a new timelessness during the moral crusades of wartime America. This role, nevertheless, was limited and would expire quickly at the end of the war.[48]

Progressives in the IKU seized the opportunity to test out Dewey's ideas when the Committee of Nineteen broadened the lines of its work after 1918 to include social welfare. Working in subcommittees on education and social cooperation, progressive kindergartners were at last able to begin "an investigation of social agencies in their vicinity dealing with child saving and welfare." To some members of the movement, the war seemed to be calling out the traditional talents of "home visiting and other phases of work for which the kindergartner is specially fitted." But the war years for the IKU were not a return to the ideals of the free-kindergarten crusade. As one delegate to the 1918 IKU convention noted, "The new note which the war is emphasizing—the note of cooperation for public service—is familiar enough to the kindergartner." Froebelians now worked with the Red Cross, the Junior Red Cross, and the Bureau of Education. The IKU also joined the Children's Bureau of the Department of Labor in a massive national campaign to weigh and measure the nation's children, aimed at "saving the lives and bettering the health of 100,000 babies." Winchester noted that the kindergartners gladly accepted the special responsibility "to protect childhood from some of the blighting influences of war conditions." Under wartime conditions, progressives were able to win battles within the IKU while losing the contest for control of the organization.[49]

The humanitarian concerns of the Committee also significantly expanded in 1918 when a subcommittee was appointed to study children in the war zones of Europe. The work was to be carried out in conjunction with the Citizen's Committee for the Conservation of the Children of America during the War and the Children's Bureau of the American Red Cross in Paris. Two kindergartners, Fanniebelle Curtis and Mary Moore Orr, spent several months visiting children of war-torn Europe in "gassed regions, in bombarded areas, and in places in the range of enemy guns." Their report eventually led to direct intervention by the IKU in Europe. A "Kindergarten Unit," which included both teachers and supplies, was dispatched to France in order to establish kindergartens during reconstruction. The unit was not another missionary kindergarten but a new expression of the international humanitarian approach to childhood education.[50]

At home the wartime victories of progressive kindergartners were less impressive. Julia Wade Abbott took stock of the progress of the kindergarten movement in a speech before the International Kindergarten Union in 1920. Abbott suggested that the IKU had faced a real world crisis in which "old beliefs and traditions were challenged and the fate of democracy hung in the balance." The efforts of kindergartners during the war were praiseworthy, but the results were not necessarily favorable to the kindergarten cause. The steady growth of kindergartens, in fact, was reversed during the years 1916–1918—the first "slippage" in the history of the movement. "In all cities the building program is behind and the schools are overflowing," Abbott warned. More alarming were the draft statistics that indicated a high rate of illiteracy among American citizens. Some professional educators had already blamed the schools, tracing to the kindergarten the lack of preparation in basic skills. Other critics pointed to the relatively low percentage of American children who received a kindergarten education. Expanding the critique, many Americans agreed that when moral standards were lacking in the schools, "anarchy and license" would soon threaten the very foundations of the country. Blow predicted this reaction, though educators ultimately reached different conclusions. "We must face the fact that conditions that have arisen as the result of the war make vigorous kindergarten efforts especially needed at this time," Abbott concluded. In the educational climate of the 1920s, the final vestiges of the Froebelian kindergarten in the IKU disappeared. But their vanishing was far from being a progressive victory. John Watson's behaviorism replaced Dewey's functionalism as the kindergarten became the bulwark of democracy against the new challenges of Bolshevism.[51]

The International Kindergarten Union survived for another decade as an inward-looking organization resisting innovation. Frustrated by its narrow definition of kindergarten education, several Froebelians had already broken away from the IKU in 1916 to form the National Council of Primary Education. Composed of both primary and kindergarten teachers, the new organization, in the spirit of Dewey, sought to extend the principles of the kindergarten upward and hoped for an even closer cooperation between the primary school and the kindergarten. Despite the exodus of other dissidents after the war, the IKU remained committed exclusively to kindergarten education. It was not until 1931 that the campaign to merge the IKU and the National Council, an idea supported belatedly by Alice Temple and Patty Smith Hill, was successful. "We have suffered by holding too closely to the name kindergartner," wrote Lucy Gage, who had joined the older reformers. "We have functioned beyond it and before it." There still were voices in the 1930s, like that of Lucy Wheelock, who urged continued concentration on the kindergarten, but the membership overwhelmingly accepted the plans for merger. With the creation of the American Association for Childhood Education, the last organizational remnant of the kindergarten movement was gone.[52]

No one mourned the passing of the International Kindergarten Union. As the chief ideological center of Froebelianism, its shortcomings had been pronounced. Here for two decades the methodological weaknesses of Froebel had been exceeded by American disciples who had become firmly entrenched. The loss to American education, however, was more than ideological. For almost a half-century, the kindergarten movement had provided a flexible structure in which American parents and educators could themselves participate in a fundamental reshaping of American attitudes toward childhood and early education. Poised between Calvin and Freud, many Americans had chosen Froebel to explain the mysterious nature of childhood in an era that could not account for evil. Not until Froebel's explanation itself became a rigid dogma did Americans finally reject it. But even in failure, the Froebelians had succeeded, for they had trained the next generation of parents and kindergarten teachers who educated the children of the Depression and ironically raised a generation some of whom in a more affluent period would return to the ideals of Romantic education.

Epilogue: The Rediscovery of Childhood (1920–1980)

The professionalization of early childhood education continued unabated throughout the 1920s. By mid-decade about 12 percent of the nation's preschoolers were enrolled in kindergartens. Many classroom teachers now subscribed to *The Journal of Childhood Education* (1924), published jointly by the International Kindergarten Union and the National Council of Primary Education and later by the Association of Childhood Education International. The 1920s also gave rise to a formidable research establishment in childhood education centered in the universities, which further legitimized the field. A list of the new centers of child study included some of the nation's most prestigious institutions of higher education: the Iowa Child Welfare Research Station, the Yale Clinic of Child Development, and the Child Welfare Institute at Teachers College, Columbia University.

At Teachers College the behaviorist theories of John B. Watson and Edward L. Thorndike existed uncomfortably alongside the child-centered education of John Dewey and William Kilpatrick. In his popular trade book, *The Psychological Care of Infant and Child* (1928), Watson made clear his contempt for the sentimentalism of nineteenth-century childhood education. He specifically warned against the "dangers of too much mother love," and urged the modern teacher to "look upon herself as a professional woman and not as sentimentalist masquerading under the name 'Mother'." Thorndike continued his experiments in the reflex-arc theory of early education, emphasizing the response side as the key to early education. Patty Smith Hill tried to reconcile the two schools in the "conduct curriculum," an innovation that was popular among Teachers College graduates, for it combined Thorndike's learning objectives ("inventory of habits") with Dewey's social goals.

By the 1930s Arnold Gesell, a psychologist who began his career as a student of G. Stanley Hall, emerged as the leading theoretician of child development. Convinced that intelligence was fixed and development predetermined, Gesell set out to discover the pattern of "normal, desirable growth" at the Yale Clinic. His normative studies of child development, based on observations of children from homes of "good or high socio-economic status," became the basis of his popular theory in which "maturation proceeds in an orderly fixed rate so long as the metabolic requirements of the infant and child are met." Widely disseminated among childhood educators, Gesell's *The Child From Five to Ten* (1946) found a receptive audience among teachers and parents searching for a comprehensible plan of the child's motor, language, personal, and social development.

By the end of the depression and World War II, the American theory of childhood education was in disarray. A much diluted form of Freudianism was beginning to reach Americans in pediatrician Benjamin Spock's *The Common Sense Book of Baby and Child Care* (1946), though most parents remained unconvinced of the formative role played by early experience. Portrayed as "disorganized and incompetent" in the popular psychoanalytic literature of the 1950s, the American child was often left unstimulated in the cradle and overstimulated in the kindergarten. One European commentator, in fact, called the American "wait and hurry up" approach the great "American question."

The way beyond Gesell and Spock lay outside of the increasingly monastic world of childhood education. The launching of a sputnik by the Russians (1957), well ahead of the American space effort, was the event that prompted a reconsideration of American early education. Some critics used the occasion once again to attack child-centered education as "too permissive." There was also surprisingly widespread agreement that American education, beginning in the preschool years, was to blame for the national humiliation. Amidst the anxieties of life in cold-war America, it was not uncommon to hear parents now complain that the kindergarten was no longer "rich enough in intellectual stimulation." The shift toward preparation in the kindergarten for later academic skills, foreshadowed in the "reading readiness" programs of the 1920s, was accelerated.

The easing of cold-war tensions, and the widening gap between the educational opportunities for the children of the rich and poor in America raised new questions in the late 1960s. "Our old norms are shaken. Our old theories no longer hold up," wrote one early childhood educator. Caught between outdated theories and their sense of the need to "intervene," educators began to search for a new rationale, method, and content of early education. Three "rediscoveries" of the 1960s were critical. First, educators rediscovered the theories of the Swiss psychologist Jean Piaget. Second, American parents returned to the methods of Maria Montessori. Third, social reformers and government officials rediscovered American poverty and posited early education as a remedy.

The theories of Piaget seemed relevant in the 1960s to the concerns of early educators. In the tradition of Dewey, Piaget postulated a dialogue between the child's cognitive structures, internal rules for processing information, and the external world. His distinctions between imitation (the child accommodating to the external world) and play (the child assimilating new information into the existing frameworks) were especially useful in the classroom. American theorists were quick to recognize the originality of Piaget's contribution. The social psychologist Erik Erikson noted that the "playing child advances forward to new stages of mastery" through play, and J. S. Bruner emphasized the possibilities of educational intervention through child's play. Not since the popularity of Froebelian gifts and occupations had play assumed so crucial a role in childhood education.

While Froebel remained forgotten, the new departures in theory and parental anxieties prepared for the remarkable revival of Montessorism in the 1960s. One psychologist noted the similarity between Piaget's psychology and Montessori's psychology, both of which were based on "unusually astute observations of young children." Once out of step with the American psychological community, Montessorism now seemed part of a new "Zeitgeist" that reversed the assumptions about the unimportance of early experience, fixed intelligence, and predetermined behavior. A more radical Benjamin Spock found social explanations for the rebirth, which he attributed to the nervousness of middle-class parents whose baby-boom children were now competing for admission to good colleges.

The spirit of reform quickly spilled over into a bewildering array of educational experiments: deschool, free school, and open school. The most utopian of the schemes, in the tradition of the Transcendentalists, sought to reconstruct an ethically perfect world that would prepare for a better order of things in the future. Other schools, some modeled after the work of the English educator A. S. Neill, took on a decidedly anarchic character. "How can happiness be bestowed?" Neill asked in his popular *Summerhill: A Radical Approach to Child Rearing* (1960). "My own answer is: Abolish authority. Let the child be himself. Don't push him around. Don't teach him. Don't lecture him. Don't elevate him. Don't force him to do anything." His was precisely the kind of chaotic voice that conservative Froebelians like Susan Blow had feared at the turn of the century. More reasoned minds of the 1960s, like that of the developmental psychologist Lawrence Kohlberg, feared that Romantic education, in its most exaggerated form, would lead inevitably to the abandonment of an explicit concern for early education, a position that repelled the majority of Americans.

At the same time the federal government was attempting to expand the opportunity for early education to a greater number of American children. President Lyndon Johnson, in fact, made Project Headstart, an experiment in compensatory education for the children of the poor, a major policy initiative of his War on Poverty. "For the preschool years we will help needy children become aware of the excitement of learning," the president declared in his "Great Society" State of the Union message (1965). The summer before, more than 555,000 poor children had already crowded into 2500 Child Development Centers in depressed rural and urban areas. The educational impact of Project Headstart has been debated by politicians, sociologists, and psychologists ever since. The symbolism of the program, however, perhaps always outweighed its measurable results, for not since the Progressive era had early childhood education been made a national sign of reaffirmation.

By 1980 Headstart no longer made headlines though the program continued to enroll 400,000 preschool children annually. Headstart enrollments, however, represent only a small part of preprimary education in the 1980s. The Census Bureau estimates that by the mid-1980s more than 5.5 million children will be served annually by regular public preschools and many more will attend private programs. As a litmus test of the national commitment to early education, however, Headstart continues to be closely monitored by social scientists, educators, and historians. Revisionist historians, in particular, have been concerned by the trend in the 1970s to expand preschool opportunities while simultaneously cutting back on programs aimed at relieving poverty, unemployment, and discrimination. Historian Marvin Lazerson, for example, has gloomily compared the loss of vitality in the kindergarten and Headstart programs when pedagogical reform becomes a surrogate for social reform. The election of Ronald Reagan to the presidency in 1980 set into motion a revolution in the federal role in education which threatens to reverse the recent commitment to early childhood education. If politics is an accurate guide to more fundamental changes in American attitudes toward child training, the election may also well mark the end of the most recent cycle of Romantic education in American life.

Notes

CHAPTER 1 (PP. 1–17)

1. Francis Wayland, *The Elements of Moral Science* (Cambridge: Harvard University Press, 1963), pp. 292–294.

2. Heman Humphrey, *Domestic Education* (Amherst: I. S. and C. Adams, 1840), p. 22.

3. Crispus (Anonymous), "On the Education of Children" *The Panoplist, and Missionary Magazine* 10(September 1814):393–403, quoted in Philip J. Greven, comp., *Child Rearing Concepts, 1628–1861: Historical Sources* (Itasca, Ill.: F. E. Peacock, 1973), p. 99. See also Greven, *The Protestant Temperament: Patterns of Child Rearing . . . Religious Experience and the Self in Early America* (New York: Alfred A. Knopf, 1977).

4. Samuel Willard, *Boston Sermons,* August 31, 1679, quoted in Edmund S. Morgan, *The Puritan Family: Religion and Domestic Relations in Seventeenth Century New England* (New York: Harper and Row, 1944; Harper Torchbook ed., 1966), p. 90.

5. John Robinson, "Of Children and Their Education" (1628), quoted in Greven, *Child Rearing Concepts*, (n. 3 above), p. 14.

6. Morgan (n. 4 above), pp. 98–100. See also Lawrence A. Cremin, *American Education: The Colonial Experience, 1607–1783* (New York: Harper and Row, 1970), p. 156.

7. Daniel H. Calhoun, *The Intelligence of a People* (Princeton: Princeton University Press, 1973), pp. 138–139, 142–144. Cremin (n. 6 above), pp. 277–278. Isaac Watts, *The Improvement of the Mind* (1751), quoted in Wilson Smith, *Theories of Education in Early America, 1655–1819* (Indianapolis: Bobbs-Merrill, 1973), pp. 100–112.

8. John Locke, *Some Thoughts Concerning Children*, quoted in Greven (n. 3 above), p. 20. James L. Axtell, *The Educational Writings of John Locke: A Critical Edition with Introduction and Notes* (London: Cambridge University Press, 1968), p. 58.

9. Lyman Beecher, "Future Punishment of Infants Not a Doctrine of Calvinism," *Spirit of the Pilgrims* 1(January 1828):42–52. See also Bernard Wishy, *The Child and the Republic: The Dawn of Modern American Child Nurture* (Philadelphia: University of Pennsylvania Press, 1968), p. 17.

10. D. H. Meyer, *The Instructed Conscience: The Shaping of the American National Ethic* (Philadelphia: University of Pennsylvania Press, 1972), p. 391.

11. Wayland (n. 1 above), p. 42.

12. Lord Kames (Henry Home), *Loose Hints Upon Education, Chiefly Concerning the Culture of the Heart* (1781), quoted in Smith (n. 7 above), p. 131. See also Daniel Walker Howe, *The Unitarian Conscience: Harvard Moral Philosophy, 1805–1861* (Cambridge: Harvard University Press, 1970), p. 38.

13. Howard Miller, *The Revolutionary College: American Presbyterian Higher Education, 1797–1837* (New York: New York University Press, 1976), p. 175.

14. Kames (n. 12 above), pp. 128–131. Louisa Hoare, *Hints for the Improvement of Early Education and Nursery Discipline* (New York: Wiley and Long, 1835), p. 11. John Witherspoon, *Letters on Education* (1775), quoted in Smith (n. 7 above), p. 195. Wayland (n. 1 above), p. 288.

15. Wayland (n. 1 above), pp. 292–293. Meyer (n. 10 above), pp. 40–43. See also Anne Louise Kuhn, *The Mother's Role in Childhood Education: New England Concepts, 1830–1860* (New Haven: Yale University Press, 1947), passim.

16. Ann Douglas, *The Feminization of American Culture* (New York: Avon Books, 1977), pp. 55–87. Ruth H. Bloch, "American Feminine Ideals in Transition: The Rise of the Moral Mother, 1785–1815," *Feminist Studies* 4(February 1978):100–126. Kuhn (n. 15 above), passim. See also Carl Degler, *At Odds: Woman and the Family in America from the Revolution to the Present* (New York: Oxford University Press, 1980), pp. 66–85.

17. Lydia Maria Child, *The Mother's Book* (Baltimore: C. Carter, 1831), p. 54. Theodore Dwight, *The Father's Book: Or Suggestions for the Government and Instruction of Young Children, On Principles Appropriate to a Christian Country* (Springfield: G. and C. Merriam, 1835), p. 97.

18. Horace Bushnell, *Work and Play* (New York: C. Scribner, 1804), quoted in Douglas (n. 16 above), p. 161. See also Barbara M. Cross, *Horace Bushnell: Minister to a Changing America* (Chicago: University of Chicago Press, 1958).

19. Bushnell (n. 18 above), pp. 2, 14, 20, 161.

20. See Cross (n. 18 above), Chapter 5, "The Security of Christian Nurture," pp. 52–72.

21. See Odell Shepard, *Pedlar's Progress: The Life of Bronson Alcott* (Boston: Little, Brown and Co., 1937).

22. Charles Strickland, "A Transcendentalist Father: The Child Rearing Practices of Bronson Alcott," *Perspectives in American History* 3(1969):17.

23. See Elizabeth Palmer Peabody, *Record of a School: Exemplifying the General Principles of Spiritual Culture*, 2nd ed. (Boston: Russell, Shattuck and Co., 1836). See also Shepard (n. 21 above), p. 121.

24. "Observations on Infant Schools," *American Journal of Education* 4(January/February 1829):17.

25. Ibid., p. 8. Amos Bronson Alcott, "Observations on the Principles of Infant Instruction," in *Essays on Education, 1830–1832* (Gainesville, Florida: Scholars Facsimiles and Reprints, 1960), p. 4. See also Carl F. Kaestle and Maris Vinovskis, *Education and Social Change in Nineteenth-Century Massachusetts* (Cambridge: Cambridge University Press, 1980), pp. 46–71.

26. Alcott (n. 25 above), p. 8.

27. Peabody (n. 23 above), pp. 1–2.

28. A detailed account of Peabody's role in the early history of the kindergarten is given in Ruth M. Baylor, *Elizabeth Peabody: Kindergarten Pioneer* (Philadelphia: University of Pennsylvania Press, 1965). See also Roberta Frankfort's biographical sketch of Peabody in *Collegiate Women: Domesticity and Career in Turn-of-the-Century America* (New York: New York University Press, 1977), p. 6.

29. Amos Bronson Alcott, *Conversations with Children on the Gospels Conducted and Edited by A. Bronson Alcott* (Boston: James Monroe and Co., 1836–1837). Peabody (n. 23 above), pp. 7–8. Dorothy McCuskey, *Bronson Alcott, Teacher* (New York: Macmillan, 1940), pp. 34–35.

30. *Christian Examiner* 19(November 1835):270, quoted in Frankfort (n. 27 above), p. 7. Elizabeth Palmer Peabody, *Reminiscences of Rev. William Ellery Channing, D.D.* (Boston: Roberts Bros., 1880), pp. 356–357.

31. Peabody (n. 23 above), p. xii. Alcott (n. 29 above), p. iv. Excellent accounts of the spirited debate over the Temple School are given in Cremin (n. 6 above) and in Anne C. Rose, *Transcendentalism as a Social Movement, 1830–1850* (New Haven: Yale University Press, 1981).

32. Peabody, *Record of a School* (Boston: Roberts Bros., 1874), preface (cf. n. 23 above). Alcott, "Report of the School Committee of Concord for the Year Ending April 2, 1860," in *Essays on Education, 1830–1862* (n. 25 above), p. 297.

CHAPTER 2 (PP. 19–28)

1. *Autobiography of Friedrich Froebel*, trans. and ed. Emilie Michaelis and H. Keatley Moore (Syracuse, N.Y.: C. W. Bardeen, 1908), p. 3. Friedrich Froebel, "Letter to the Duke of Meiningen" (1827), in *Friedrich Froebel: A Selection from His Writings*, ed. Irene Lilley (Cambridge: Cambridge University Press, 1967), pp. 31–39. Denton J. Snider, *The Life of Friedrich Froebel: Founder of the Kindergarten* (Chicago: Sigma Publishing Co., 1900), p. 2.

2. *Autobiography* (n. 1 above), p. 55. "Letter to the Duke of Meiningen" (n. 1 above), pp. 36–38. Snider (n. 1 above), pp. 95, 111, 115. Henry Barnard, ed., *Papers on Froebel's Kindergarten* (Hartford: Office of Barnard's Journal of American Education, 1881), pp. 49–55.

3. Froebel, *The Education of Man,* trans. William N. Hailmann (New York: D. Appleton and Co., 1899), p. 2. See also "Letter to the Duke of Meiningen" (n. 1 above), p. 36.

4. Froebel, *Pedagogics of the Kindergarten* (New York: D. Appleton and Co., 1895), p. 146.

5. *Autobiography* (n. 1 above), p. 11. *The Education of Man* (n. 3 above, 1897 edition), pp. 121–122.

6. Froebel, "The Small Child," in *Friedrich Froebel*, ed. Lilley (n. 1 above), pp. 79–80.

7. Froebel to Arnswald, December 9, 1847, in *Froebel Letters with Explanatory Notes and Additional Matter,* ed. Arnold H. Heinemann (Boston: Lee and Shepard, 1893), p. 90. *Pedagogics* (n. 4 above), p. 6.

8. *Froebel's Letters on the Kindergarten*, ed. Emilie Michaelis and H. Keatley Moore (London: Swan Sonnenschein and Co., 1891), p. 63.

9. *Pedagogics* (n. 4 above), p. 17.

10. Froebel, "The Education of Man: In Childhood," in *Friedrich Froebel*, ed. Lilley (n. 1 above), pp. 81–96.

11. Dominick Cavallo, "The Politics of Latency: Kindergarten Pedagogy, 1830–1930," in Barbara Finkelstein, ed., *Regulated Children, Liberated Children* (New York: Psychohistory Press, 1979), p. 166. *The Education of Man* (n. 3 above), pp. 41–42.

12. *Pedagogics* (n. 4 above), pp. 13, 14, 34, 57. Cavallo (n. 11 above), p. 167.

13. *Pedagogics* (n. 4 above), pp. 261–262.

14. *Pedagogics* (n. 4 above), pp. 261–262.

15. *Froebel's Letters on the Kindergarten* (n. 8. above), pp. 64, 158–159.

16. Ibid., p. 59. *Froebel Letters*, ed. Heinemann (n. 7 above), p. 164.

17. *Froebel Letters*, ed. Heinemann (n. 7 above), pp. 31–40. *Froebel's Letters on the Kindergarten* (n. 8 above), p. 228.

18. Froebel, "General Education Unions," in *Froebel Letters* (n. 7 above), p. 43. David Allmendinger, "Mount Holyoke Students Encounter the Need for Life-Planning, 1839–1850," *History of Education Quarterly* 19 (Spring 1979):41.

19. *The Education of Man* (n. 3 above), quoted in John Kraus, "The Kindergarten (Its Use and Abuse) in America," National Education Association (NEA), *Addresses and Proceedings* (1877):194. *Froebel's Letters on the Kindergarten* (n. 8 above), p. 140.

20. *The Education of Man* (n. 3 above), p. 195.

21. Ibid., p. 194. See also *Froebel Letters* (n. 7 above), pp. 110–111. *Froebel's Letters on the Kindergarten* (n. 8 above), p. 306. Adolph E. Zucker, ed., *Forty-Eighters: Political Refugees of the German Revolution of 1848* (New York: Columbia University Press, 1950), p. 295. Carl Wittke, *Refugees of Revolution: The German Forty-Eighters in America* (Philadelphia: University of Pennsylvania Press, 1952), pp. 72, 179.

Chapter 3 (pp. 29–44)

1. "The Kindergartens of Germany," *The Christian Examiner*, 5th ser., 17(November 1859):313–314.

2. Nina C. Vandewalker, *The Kindergarten in American Education* (New York: Macmillan Co., 1908), p. 13. Elizabeth Jenkins, "How the Kindergarten Found Its Way to America," *Wisconsin Journal of History* 19(September 1930):48–62. Elizabeth Jenkins, "Froebel's Disciples in America," *American-German Review* 3(March 1937):15–18 and 4(September 1938):54. Edward W. Hocker, "The First American Kindergarten Teacher," *American-German Review* 8(February 1942):36. William Nicholas Hailmann, *Kindergarten Culture in the Family and Kindergarten: A Complete Sketch of Froebel's System of Early Education Adapted to American Institutions* (New York: Wilson, Hinkle and Co., 1873), p. 116.

3. Carl Schurz to Adolf Meyer, April 19, 1852, quoted in *Intimate Letters of Carl Schurz, 1841–1869*, ed. and trans. Joseph Schafer (Madison: State Historical Society of Wisconsin, 1928), pp. 108–109. *Notable American Women 1607–1950: A Biographical Dictionary*, 3 vols. (Cambridge: Harvard University Press, 1971), 3:242–243 (Schurz). Jenkins, "How" (n. 2 above), pp. 53–54.

4. Carl Schurz to Margarethe Schurz, July 8, 1867, quoted in *Intimate Letters* (n. 3 above), pp. 382–383.

5. Bertha Meyer, *Aids to Family Government: Or, From the Cradle to the School, According to Froebel* (New York: M. L. Holbrook and Co., 1879), p. 9.

6. Bertha Maria von Marenholtz-Bülow, *The New Education by Work According to Froebel's Method*, trans. Mrs. Horace Mann (Camden, N.J.: Philotechnic Institute, 1876).

7. Bertha Maria von Marenholtz-Bülow, *Reminiscences of Froebel*, trans. Mrs. Horace Mann (Boston: Lee and Shepard, 1877).

8. Caroline D. Aborn, "Matilda Kriege," in Committee of Nineteen (IKU), *Pioneers of the Kindergarten in America*, pp. 91–97. Mary J. Garland, "Madame Matilda H. Kriege," *Kindergarten Review* 4(December 1894):343–347.

9. Aborn (n. 8 above), pp. 93–94. Henry Barnard, ed., *Papers on Froebel's Kindergarten* (Hartford: Office of Barnard's American Journal of Education, 1881), p. 560.

10. Maria Kraus-Boelte, "Experience of a Kindergartner," *Kindergarten Messenger* (January–March, 1875), pp. 34–49. Anna Harvey, "Maria Kraus-Boelte," in Committee of 19 (n. 8 above). *Notable American Women* 2:346–348 (n. 3 above) (Kraus-Boelte). See also Rachel L. Rogers, "Professor John Kraus and Maria Kraus-Boelte and Their United Work," *Kindergarten News* 7 (September 1896):2–3.

11. Kraus-Boelte (n. 10 above), pp. 40–41.

12. Ibid., p. 45.

13. Elizabeth Palmer Peabody, *Lectures in the Training School for Kindergartners* (Boston: D. C. Heath and Co., 1886), p. 22. Peabody, "A Plea for Froebel's Kindergarten as the First Grade of Primary Education," in *The Identification of the Artisan and the Artist* (Boston: Adams and Co., Lee and Shepard, 1889), pp. 42–48.

14. Kraus-Boelte (n. 10 above), pp. 46, 52.

15. Anna C. Lowell to Elizabeth Palmer Peabody, November 22, 1870, quoted in Ruth M. Baylor, *Elizabeth Peabody: Kindergarten Pioneer* (Philadelphia: University of Pennsylvania Press, 1965), p. 98.

16. Peabody, *Lectures* (n. 13 above), p. 13. Maria Kraus-Boelte, *The Kindergarten and the Mission of Woman: My Experience as a Trainer of Kindergarten Teachers in This Country* (New York: E. Steiger, 1877), p. 25.

17. Peabody, *Lectures* (n. 13 above), p. 23. Mary Tyler Mann, "Preface" in Mary Tyler Mann and Elizabeth Peabody," *Moral Culture of Infancy and Kindergarten Guide* (Boston: T. O. H. P. Burnham, 1863), p. vi.

18. Kraus-Boelte (n. 10 above), pp. 43–44.

19. *Kindergarten Messenger* (May 1873):24 and (November 1873):9.

20. Barnard, ed. (n. 9 above), p. 560. See Elizabeth Peabody, "Kindergarten Culture," U.S. Bureau of Education, *Report 1870*, p. 359.

21. Bertha Maria von Marenholtz-Bülow, *The Child: Its Nature and Relations: An Elucidation of Froebel's Principles of Education*, trans. Matilda Kriege (New York: E. Steiger, 1872), p. 1. William Leach, *True Love and Perfect Union: The Feminist Reform of Sex and Society* (New York: Basic Books, 1980), p. 86.

22. John Kraus to Maria Kraus-Boelte, July 1871, published in Kraus-Boelte (n. 10 above), p. 55.

23. Kraus-Boelte (n. 10 above), p. 57. Baylor (n. 15 above), pp. 131–132.

24. Joseph Payne, *A Visit to German Schools* (London: Henry S. King and Co., 1876), p. 105.

25. John Kraus and Maria Kraus-Boelte, "Characteristics of Froebel's Method, Kindergarten Training," National Education Association, *Addresses and Proceedings* (1876):214.

26. Kraus and Kraus-Boelte (n. 25 above), p. 214.

27. Catherine Beecher, *Woman's Position as Mother and Educator with Views in Opposition to Woman Suffrage* (Philadelphia and Boston:Geo. Maclean, 1872), pp. 88–89.

28. Barnard, ed. (n. 9 above), p. 558.

29. Payne (n. 24 above), p. 105.

30. Kraus and Kraus-Boelte (n. 25 above), p. 215. Elizabeth Peabody, *Kindergarten Messenger* (June 1874).

31. Kraus-Boelte (n. 16 above), pp. 4–5.

32. Peabody (n. 13 above), pp. 19, 85–86. Kraus and Kraus-Boelte (n. 25 above), p. 214.

33. Kraus-Boelte (n. 16 above), p. 10.

34. Barnard, ed. (n. 9 above), p. 557.

35. Kraus-Boelte (n. 16 above), pp. 5–6.

36. Matilda Kriege, *Kindergarten Messenger* (December 1873):10–14. Kraus-Boelte (n. 16 above), pp. 5–6.

37. Marenholtz-Bülow (n. 6 above), p. 32. Mary Mann, "Preface" to the preceding.

CHAPTER 4 (PP. 45–63)

1. The most recent treatment of the Saint Louis public kindergartens is Selwyn K. Troen, "Operation Headstart: The Beginnings of the Public School Kindergarten Movement," *Missouri Historical Review* (January 1972):211–229, which was later republished as a chapter in his *The Public and the Schools: Shaping the Saint Louis School System, 1838–1920* (Columbia: University of Missouri Press, 1975).

2. *Journal of Speculative Philosophy* 1:1 (1867) quoted in Lawrence A. Cremin, *The Transformation of the School: Progressivism in American Education, 1876–1957* (New York: Vintage Books, 1964), p. 16.

3. William Torrey Harris, *The Theory of American Education* (Syracuse: C. W. Bardeen, 1893), p. 31.

4. The standard biography is Kurt Friedrich Leidecker, *Yankee Teacher: The Life of William Torrey Harris* (New York: Philosophical Library, 1946). Quotations from Harris, "How I Was Educated," *Forum* (August 1886):557–558, reprinted as *The How I Was Educated Papers* (New York: D. Appleton and Co., 1888).

5. Leidecker (n. 4 above), p. 357. William Torrey Harris and Franklin Benjamin Sanborn, *Bronson Alcott: His Life and Philosophy* (Boston: Roberts Brothers, 1893), pp. 549, 596.

6. Harris, "How I Was Educated" (n. 4 above), p. 558.

7. Harris and Sanborn (n. 5 above), pp. 611–612. For an interesting description of the Saint Louis Hegelians see Denton J. Snider, *The Saint Louis Movement in Philosophy, Literature, Education, Psychology, with Chapters of Autobiography* (Saint Louis: Sigma Publishing Co., 1920), pp. 5–15, 24–35.

8. Elizabeth Peabody to Harris, August 25, 1870, William Torrey Harris Papers, Missouri Historical Society (MHS), Saint Louis, Mo.

9. Harris, in Saint Louis Board of Education, *Twenty-Fifth Annual Report of the Board of*

Directors of the Saint Louis Public Schools for the Year Ending August 1, 1979, p. 220. (Cited hereafter as Saint Louis Annual Report, various appropriate dates.)

10. Leidecker (n. 4 above), p. 183.

11. Harris, Saint Louis Annual Report 1870–1871, pp. 79–81. Annual Report 1872–1873, p. 81. Annual Report 1876, p. 79. (See n. 9 above.) See also Troen (n. 1 above), p. 213.

12. Harris, Saint Louis Annual Report 1879 (see n. 9 above), p. 218. Troen (n. 1 above), p. 215. See also Karl Rosenkranz, *Pedagogics as a System*, trans. Anna C. Brackett (Saint Louis: R. C. Studely Co., 1872), reprinted from *Journal of Speculative Philosophy* 6(October 1872):290–312. For background see Harold B. Dunkel, "W. T. Harris and Hegelianism in American Education," *School Review* (February 1973):233–246.

13. Rosenkranz (n. 12 above), pp. 78–79.

14. Harris, Saint Louis Annual Report 1871–1872 (see n. 9 above), p. 80. Rosenkranz (n. 12 above), p. 141.

15. Peabody to Harris, March 28, 1871 (see n. 8 above). William Leach, *True Love and Perfect Union* (New York: Basic Books, 1980) p. 134.

16. Felix Coste, "Report of the President," in Saint Louis Annual Report 1870, p. 9. Harris, Saint Louis Annual Report 1871, pp. 9–10. (See n. 9 above.)

17. See Dorothy Ross's biographical sketch of Susan Elizabeth Blow in *Notable American Women 1607–1950* (3 vols., Cambridge: Harvard University Press, 1971). The richest biographical source for Susan Blow is her correspondence with Harris located in the William Torrey Harris Papers, Missouri Historical Society (MHS). See especially the long autobiographical letter, Blow to Harris, July 9, 1892. The most complete biographical work is Margaret Hilliker, "Life and Work of Susan Elizabeth Blow" (unpublished manuscript, Harris-Stowe State College Library, Saint Louis, 1953).

18. Blow to Harris, July 9, 1892 (see n. 17 above). Henry Blow to Minerva Blow, March 19, 1858, Blow Family Papers, Missouri Historical Society.

19. Blow to Harris, July 9, 1892 (see n. 17 above).

20. Snider (n. 7 above), p. 295. Blow to Harris, July 9, 1892 (see n. 17 above).

21. Blow, "The Service of Dr. Harris to the Kindergarten," International Kindergarten Union (IKU), *Proceedings of the Seventeenth Annual Meeting* (1910):127–128, reprinted in *Kindergarten Review* 20(June 1910):589–603.

22. Blow to Harris, July 9, 1892 (see n. 17 above). Leach (n. 15 above), p. 169.

23. Blow to Harris, November 14, 1872 (see n. 17 above).

24. John Kraus and Maria Kraus-Boelte, "Characteristics of Froebel's Method," *Kindergarten Training*, National Education Association, *Addresses and Proceedings* (1871):212–213.

25. Ibid., p. 214.

26. Elizabeth Harrison to a Friend, February 1883, published in Harrison, *Sketches Along Life's Road* (Boston: Stratford Co., 1930), p. 88.

27. Blow to Harris, November 14, 1872 (see n. 17 above).

28. Blow to Harris, November 10, 1873 (see n. 17 above).

29. Francis Berg, "Report of the Assistant Superintendent for German Instruction," Saint Louis Annual Report 1868 (see n. 9 above), pp. 80–81. Leidecker (n. 4 above), pp. 273–275. Snider (n. 7 above), pp. 21–22, 138, 217.

30. Harris, Saint Louis Annual Report 1874 (see n. 9 above), p. 96. Saint Louis Public Schools, *Official Proceedings* 2:34–35 (1876–1877).

31. Blow, "Report of the Director of the Des Peres Kindergarten," Saint Louis Annual Report 1874 (see n. 9 above), pp. 196, 198–199.

32. Harris, Saint Louis Annual Report 1876 (see n. 9 above), pp. 95–96.

33. Harris, Saint Louis Annual Report 1879 (see n. 9 above), pp. 206–211.

34. Harris, *Psychologic Foundations of Education: An Attempt to Show the Genesis of the Higher Faculties of the Mind* (New York: D. Appleton and Co., 1898), pp. 281–283.

35. Harris, Saint Louis Annual Report 1876 (see n. 9 above), pp. 92, 95–96. See also Harris, "Preface," Friedrich Froebel, *The Mottoes and Commentaries of Friedrich Froebel's Mother Play*, trans. Susan Blow (New York: D. Appleton and Co., 1895). "The Pedagogical Creed of William Torrey Harris," in Ossiah Lang, ed., *Educational Creeds of the Nineteenth Century* (New York: E. L. Kellogg, 1898), p. 40. Leach (n. 15 above), p. 208.

36. Harris, "Preface" (n. 35 above), p. xii. Harris, Saint Louis Annual Report 1876, pp. 96–112. Annual Report 1879, pp. 200–206. (See n. 9 above.)
37. Harris, Saint Louis Annual Report 1879 (see n. 9 above), p. 217.
38. Harris, "Preface" (n. 35 above), p. xiv.
39. Peabody to Harris, October 28, 1879 (see n. 8 above).
40. Harris, Saint Louis Annual Report 1879 (see n. 9 above), p. 79.
41. Peabody to Harris, August 25, 1870 (see n. 8 above). Harris, Saint Louis Annual Report 1879, p. 222.
42. Harris, Saint Louis Annual Report 1876 (see n. 9 above), pp. 85. 89–90.
43. Blow to Harris, December 3, 1876 (see n. 17 above).
44. Hilliker (n. 17 above), p. 49.
45. Harris, Saint Louis Annual Report 1875–1876 (see n. 9 above), p. 84. Saint Louis Public Schools, *Official Proceedings* 2:372, 396, 417; 3:123, 425, 447 (1876–1877, 1878–1879).
46. Snider (n. 7 above), pp. 321–323. See also Blow to Harris, December 4, 1882 (see n. 17 above).
47. Harrison (n. 26 above), pp. 62–63. Snider (n. 7 above), p. 296
48. Harrison (n. 26 above), p. 61.
49. Blow (n. 21 above), p. 139.
50. Snider (n. 7 above). Harrison (n. 26 above), pp. 63–64.
51. Harrison (n. 26 above), p. 64. William A. Leach, *True Love and Perfect Union* (New York: Basic Books, 1980), p. 21.

CHAPTER 5 (PP. 65–83)

1. Lawrence A. Cremin, *American Education: The National Experience, 1783–1876* (New York: Harper and Row, 1980), p. 333. William A. Leach, *True Love and Perfect Union* (New York: Basic Books, 1980), p. 17.
2. Nina C. Vandewalker, *The Kindergarten in American Education* (New York: Macmillan Co., 1908), pp. 7–8, 38–43. "Education in the Centennial Exhibition," *New England Journal of Education* 1(March 13, 1875):126.
3. William Torrey Harris, "Reflections on the Educational Significance of the Centennial Exposition," *Twenty-Second Annual Report of the Saint Louis Board of Education 1876*, pp. 174–179.
4. Edgar B. Wesley, *NEA: The First Hundred Years* (New York: Harper and Brothers, 1957), pp. 156–164. See Paul H. Mattingly, *The Classless Professional American Schoolmen in the Nineteenth Century* (New York: New York University Press, 1975).
5. National Education Association (NEA), *Addresses and Proceedings* 1872:141–148.
6. Ibid., 1873:230–237.
7. James J. Shea, *It's All in the Game* (New York: G. P. Putnam, 1960), pp. 17–31. "Milton Bradley," *Kindergarten Review* 23(September 1911):63.
8. David Wallace Adams and Victor Edmonds, "Making Your Move: The Educational Significance of the American Board Game, 1832 to 1904," *History of Education Quarterly* (Winter 1977):359–383. Milton Bradley Co., *Milton Bradley, a Successful Man* (Springfield, Mass.: Milton Bradley Co., 1910). Shea (n. 7 above), pp. 78–87.
9. Edward Wiebe, *The Paradise of Childhood*, quarter century ed. (Springfield, Mass.: Milton Bradley Co.,1896). Ruth Baylor, *Elizabeth Peabody: Kindergarten Pioneer* (Philadelphia: University of Pennsylvania Press, 1965), pp. 94, 102.
10. Milton Bradley, "A Reminiscence of Miss Peabody," *Kindergarten News* 4(February 1894):39–40. Milton Bradley, "Editor's Preface" in Wiebe (n. 9 above), p. 5. Shea (n. 7 above), p. 11.
11. Bernard Mergen, "The Discovery of Children's Play," *American Quarterly* 27(October 1975):399. Inez McClintock and Marshall McClintock, *Toys in America* (Washington: Public Affairs Press, 1961). Foster Rhea Dulles, *America Learns to Play: A History of Popular Recreation, 1607–1904* (New York: D. Appleton-Century Co., 1940).

12. Charles Porterfield Krauth, *Popular Amusements* (Winchester, Va.: n.p., 1851), p. 2. Marvin R. Vincent, *Amusement, a Force in Christian Training* (Troy, N.Y.: William H. Young, 1867), p. 14. James L. Corning, *The Christian Law of Amusement* (Buffalo: Phinney and Co., 1859), p. 31.

13. *Family Pastime; or, Homes Made Happy: A Collection of Games for the Social Circle* (New York: Bunce and Brother, 1855), p. 3. Frank Bellew, *The Art of Amusing, Being a Collection of Grateful Arts, Merry Games, Odd Tricks, Curious Puzzles, and Charades* (New York: Carleton, 1866), pp. 2–3.

14. *Descriptive List of Kinder Garten Gifts Manufactured by Milton Bradley and Co.* (Springfield, Mass.: Milton Bradley Co., 1876), contained in Philadelphia International Exhibition, *Centennial Pamphlets*, Van Pelt Library, University of Pennsylvania, Philadelphia, Pa. Ernst Steiger, *Educational Directory for 1878* (New York: E. Steiger, 1878).

15. Steiger, *Der Kindergarten in Amerika* (New York: E. Steiger, 1872). Steiger, "A Few Words to Parents," Philadelphia International Exhibition, *Centennial Pamphlets.* (See n. 14 above.)

16. "American Periodical Literature," pamphlet (n.p., n.d.), John D. Rockefeller Library, Brown University, Providence, R.I.

17. Milton Bradley Co., *Catalogue of Bradley's Kindergarten and School Supplies* (Boston: Milton Bradley Co., n.d.). Steiger, *Educational Directory for 1878* (n. 14 above).

18. "Letter to the Boston Meeting of Kindergartners," *New England Journal of Education* 4(May 13, 1876):153.

19. *Kindergarten Messenger* (1873–1877). Elizabeth Peabody, "Our Reason for Being," *Kindergarten Messenger* (May 1873).

20. *New England Journal of Education* 2(July 10, 1875):16. Vandewalker (n. 2 above), pp. 31–33.

21. See Vandewalker's "Ruth Burritt, the Centennial Kindergartner, 1832–1921," in Committee of Nineteen, International Kindergarten Union, *Pioneers of the Kindergarten in America* (New York: Century Club, 1924), pp. 134–145.

22. *Frank Leslie's Illustrated Historical Register of the Centennial Exposition*, ed. Frank H. Norton (New York: Frank Leslie's Publishing House, 1877), p. 118. Arnold Gesell, "Looking Backward: To a Demonstration Kindergarten, 1876," *Childhood Education* 10(January 1934):171–172.

23. *Philadelphia Ledger*, 1876, quoted in Committee of Nineteen (see n. 21 above), pp. 138–139.

24. Frank Lloyd Wright, *An Autobiography: Frank Lloyd Wright* (London, New York, Toronto: Longmans, Green and Co., 1932), p. 11. Grant Manson, "Wright in the Nursery," *Architectural Review* 113(June 1953):349–350.

25. Wright (n. 24 above), p. 11.

26. Nora Archibald Smith, *The Kindergarten in a Nutshell: A Handbook for the Home* (Philadelphia: Curtis Publishing Co., 1899).

27. John Kraus, "The Kindergarten (Its Use and Abuse) in America," National Education Association, *Addresses and Proceedings* (1877):186–206.

28. *New England Journal of Education* 4(September 30, 1876):138; (August 19, 1876):69.

29. "A Model American Kindergarten" and "American Kindergarten and Normal School," Philadelphia International Exhibition, *Centennial Pamphlets*. (See n. 14 above.)

30. *New England Journal of Education* (July 10, 1875):16.

31. See n. 29 above.

32. See n. 29 above.

33. Kraus (n. 27 above).

34. "Letter to the Boston Meeting of Kindergartners," *New England Journal of Education* 4(May 20, 1876; June 3, 1876).

35. Harris (n. 3 above).

36. Harris, "Kindergarten Americanized," *New England Journal of Education* 5(January 11, 1877):18–19.

37. Harris, "The Relations of the Kindergarten to the School," National Education Associa-

tion, *Addresses and Proceedings* (1879):142–163. Harris, "The Theory of American Education," National Education Association, *Addresses and Proceedings* (1871):177–191.

38. Peabody to Harris, January 19, 1877, Harris Papers, Missouri Historical Society. Peabody, "The Americanizing of Froebel's Kindergarten," *Kindergarten Messenger* (January-February 1877).

39. Peabody, "Last Words on the Centennial Kindergarten," *New England Journal of Education* 4(December 23, 1876):285. U.S. Centennial Commission, International Exhibition, 1876, *Reports and Awards*, 9 vols., ed. Francis A. Walker (Philadelphia: Lippincott and Co., 1877–1878; Washington, D.C.: Government Printing Office, 1880).

CHAPTER 6 (PP. 85–105)

1. Jacob A. Riis, "The Children of the Poor," in *Jacob Riis Revisited: Poverty and the Slum in Another Era*, ed. Francesco Cordasco (New York: Doubleday Anchor Books, 1960), p. 60.

2. See: Marvin Lazerson, *Origins of the Urban School: Public Education in Massachusetts, 1870–1915* (Cambridge: Harvard University Press, 1971). Lazerson, "The Historical Antecedents of Early Childhood Education," in National Society for the Study of Education (NSSE), *Seventy-First Yearbook* (1972) (Bloomington, Ill.: Public School Publishing Co., 1972).

3. U.S. Bureau of Education, *Report 1887–1888*, p. 824. Nina C. Vandewalker, *The Kindergarten in American Education* (New York: Macmillan Co., 1908), p. 76.

4. Felix Adler, "Free Kindergarten and Workingman's School," in *Papers on Froebel's Kindergarten*, ed. Henry Barnard (Hartford: Office of Barnard's American Journal of Education, 1881), pp. 687–691. Adler, "A New Experiment in Education," *Princeton Review* 11(March 1883):143–157.

5. Howard B. Radest, *Toward Common Ground: The Story of the Ethical Societies in the United States* (New York: Frederick Ungar, 1969), pp. 42–44, 96–97.

6. Adler, *An Ethical Philosophy of Life Presented in Its Main Outlines* (New York: D. Appleton and Co., 1918). Robert H. Beck, "Progressive Education and American Progressivism: Felix Adler," *Teachers College Record* 60(November 1958):77–89.

7. "Principal's Report: The Free Kindergarten," *Ethical Society Report* (1881):9–11. See also William Torrey Harris, "The Educational Value of Manual Training," National Education Association (NEA), *Addresses and Proceedings* (1889):417–423. Susan Blow to Harris, September 6, 1887, and October 15, 1897, Harris Papers, Missouri Historical Society.

8. Cincinnati Kindergarten Association (CKA), *Annual Report* (1890):27.

9. CKA, *Annual Report* (1888/1889):6.

10. Thomas Haskell, *The Emergence of Professional Social Science* (Urbana: University of Illinois Press, 1977), pp. 103, 141–143.

11. William A. Leach, *True Love and Perfect Union* (New York: Basic Books, 1980), p. 315. William Torrey Harris, Emily Talbot, and Henry Barnard, "Kindergarten System," *Journal of Social Science* 12(September 1980):8–10. See also Merle Curti, "William T. Harris, the Conservator, 1835–1908," Chapter 9 in Curti's *The Social Ideas of American Educators* (New York and Chicago: Charles Scribner's Sons, 1935).

12. Haskell (n. 10 above), pp. 136–138.

13. Robert H. Bremner, "Scientific Philanthropy, 1873–93," *Social Service Review* 30(June 1956):168. See also Bremner, *American Philanthropy* (Chicago: University of Chicago Press, 1960).

14. Mary Mann, "The Kindergarten and Homes," *American Journal of Education* 30(1880):125–133, reprinted in *Papers on Froebel's Kindergarten*, ed. Barnard (n. 4 above), pp. 654–664. See Jacob Riis, "The Problem of the Children," in Cordasco, ed. (n. 1 above), p. 129.

15. Charles Loring Brace, *The Dangerous Classes of New York, and Twenty Years' Work among Them* (New York: Wynkoop and Hallenbeck, 1872). See also David J. Rothman, *The Discovery of the Asylum: Social Order and Disorder in the New Republic* (Boston: Little, Brown and Co., 1971).

16. Anna Hallowell, "The Care and Saving of Neglected Children," *Journal of Social Science* (September 1880):122. John N. Foster, "Ten Years of Child-Saving Work in Michigan," National Conference of Charities and Correction (NCCC), *Proceedings* (1884):132–142.

17. In NCCC *Proceedings* (n. 16 above), see: Sarah B. Cooper, "The Kindergarten as a Character Builder" (1885):222–228. Kate Douglas Wiggin, "The Relation of the Kindergarten to Social Reform" (1888):247–261, reprinted in Wiggin, ed., *The Kindergarten* (New York: Harper and Brothers, 1893). John H. Finley's "The Child Problem in Cities" (1891):124–135, summarizes child reform for the preceding twenty years. Hallowell, "The Care and Saving of Neglected Children" (n. 16 above), p. 123.

18. *Encyclopedia of Social Reform*, 1897 ed., s.v. "Poverty," pp. 1073–1074. W. Alexander Johnson, "Minutes and Discussion," NCCC *Proceedings* 16(1889):227.

19. Finley (n. 17 above), p. 127. Sarah Cooper to Harriet Cooper, September 14, 1889, Julius A. Skilton Papers, Department of Manuscripts and University Archives, Cornell University, Ithaca, N.Y.

20. *Notable American Women 1607–1650*, 3 vols. (Cambridge: Harvard University Press, 1971), 1:380–382 (Cooper).

21. Sarah Cooper to Robert G. Ingersoll, August 11, 1877; and December 23, 1878: Robert G. Ingersoll Papers, Illinois Historical Society, Chicago (microfilm).

22. Sarah B. Cooper, "The Kindergarten as Bible Class Work," *Fourth Annual Report of the Golden Gate Kindergarten Association* (1883), p. 11, Sarah Cooper Papers, Department of Manuscripts and University Archives, Cornell University, Ithaca, N.Y.

23. James B. Roberts to Sarah Cooper, June 29, 1881, and Sarah Cooper to James B. Roberts, June 30, 1881, Cooper Papers (n. 22 above).

24. A list of formal charges against Cooper is contained in the Cooper correspondence for November 1881, Cooper Papers (n. 22 above). Kate Douglas Wiggin gives an account of the trial in her *My Garden of Memory: An Autobiography* (Boston and New York: Houghton Mifflin Co., 1923), pp. 129–130.

25. Cooper to Ingersoll, April 29, 1879, Ingersoll Papers (n. 21 above). Cooper (n. 22 above), p. 8.

26. Amalie Hofer, "The Social Settlement and the Kindergarten," National Education Association, *Addresses and Proceedings* (1895):518; also printed in *Kindergarten Magazine* 8(September 1895):47–59.

27. For portraits of "free kindergartners" see the following articles in *Notable American Women* (n. 20 above): Anna E. Bryan, Sarah Brown Ingersoll Cooper, Anna Hallowell, Patty Smith Hill, Alice Harvey Whiting Putnam, and Kate Douglas Smith Wiggin. See also Wiggin (n. 24 above), pp. 100–126. "Miss Harrison and the Chicago Kindergarten College," *Kindergarten Magazine* (June 1893):739.

28. Clifford S. Griffin, "Religious Benevolence as Social Control, 1815–1860," in David B. Davis, ed., *Ante-Bellum Reform* (New York: Harper and Row, 1967). See also Timothy L. Smith, *Revivalism and Social Reform in Mid-Nineteenth Century America* (New York: Abingdon Press, 1957).

29. Vandewalker (n. 3 above), p. 61.

30. "City Charities for Neglected Children," *American Journal of Education* 30(1880):829–832. Emma Marwedel, "Free Kindergarten Work in California," in Bernard, ed. (n. 4 above), pp. 665–772. Riis (n. 1 above), p. 114.

31. Fanny L. Johnson, "History of the Kindergarten Movement in Boston," *Kindergarten Review* 12(April 1902):478. *New York Times*, December 6, 1878, pp. 4–6.

32. Sarah Cooper to Phoebe Apperson Hearst, June 3, 1890, Hearst Papers, Bancroft Library, University of California, Berkeley, California.

33. *Fourth Annual Report of the Jackson Street Kindergarten Association* (1883):10–11, Sarah Cooper Papers (see n. 22 above). *Sixteenth Annual Report of the Golden Gate Kindergarten Association* (1895):20, Cooper Papers (see n. 22 above). Susan Blow, "The History of the Kindergarten in the United States," *Outlook* 55(April 1897):936. Cincinnati Kindergarten Association, *Annual Report* (1890/1891):6–7.

34. *Report of the Chicago Froebel Kindergarten Association* (1885):8, Chicago Historical Society, Chicago.

35. "Public and Private Kindergartens," U.S. Bureau of Education, *Report 1897–98* 2:2537–2579. "Statistics of Public Kindergartens," U.S. Bureau of Education, *Report 1898–99* 2:2257–2262. Amalie Hofer, quoted in Vandewalker (n. 3 above), p. 74.

36. Louisville Free Kindergarten Association, *Report for 1894–95*, p. 8, Library, School of Education, Harvard University, Cambridge, Massachusetts. Cincinnati Kindergarten Association, *Annual Report* (1880):8.

37. Harris et al. (n. 11 above), pp. 8–10. Hamilton W. Mabie, "The Free Kindergarten," *Harper's Magazine* 111(October 1905):654.

38. Mabie (n. 37 above), pp. 649–657. Frank B. Vrooman, "Child Life and the Kindergarten," *Arena* 13(1895):292–302. Richard Watson Gilder, "The Kindergarten: An Uplifting Social Influence in the Home and District," National Education Association, *Addresses and Proceedings* (1903):391.

39. Free Kindergarten lesson plan, typescript in Patty Smith Hill Papers, Filson Club, Louisville, Kentucky.

40. Mabie (n. 37 above), p. 655. Gilder (n. 38 above), p. 391.

41. Cincinnati Kindergarten Association, *Annual Report* (1885):21.

42. CKA, *Annual Report* (1884):28; (1885):21; (1887):19. Constance MacKenzie, "Free Kindergartens," National Conference of Charities and Correction, *Proceedings* (1886):48–53. Riis (n. 1 above), pp. 174–187. Gilder (n. 38 above), pp. 388–394.

43. Gilder (n. 38 above), p. 390. Wilhelmina T. Caldwell, "Mothers' Meetings among the Poor," *Kindergarten News* 5(October 1895):283. Helen L. Duncklee, "The Kindergartner and Her Mothers' Meetings," *Kindergarten Review* 10(September 1899):12–15. Elizabeth Harrison, "The Scope and Results of Mothers' Meetings," National Education Association, *Addresses and Proceedings* (1903):400–405. Cincinnati Kindergarten Association, *Annual Report* (1892/1893):9.

44. John P. Gavit, comp., *Bibliography of College, Social, and University Settlements* (Cambridge, Mass.: Cooperative Press, 1897), p. 26. Caroline F. Brown, "Elizabeth Peabody House," *Kindergarten Review* 12(October 1901):63–64.

45. See for background Allen F. Davis, *Spearheads for Reform: The Social Settlements and the Progressive Movement, 1890–1914* (New York: Oxford University Press, 1967). Robert A. Woods and Albert J. Kennedy, *The Settlement Horizon: A National Estimate* (New York: Russell Sage Foundation, 1922), p. 131. See also Vandewalker (n. 3 above), p. 63. Woods and Kennedy, eds., *Handbook of Settlements* (New York: Charities Publication Committee, 1911).

46. Gavit (n. 44 above), p. 26. "Settlements and Settlement Kindergartens in New York City," *Kindergarten Magazine and Pedagogical Digest* (May 1907):610. Jane Addams, *Twenty Years at Hull-House, with Autobiographical Notes* (New York: Macmillan Co., 1910; reprint edition, New York: New American Library, 1960). *Hull House Bulletin* (October 1896):127–128.

47. Addams, *Twenty Years at Hull-House* (n. 46 above), p. 83. Elizabeth Manson, "The Ideals of a Kindergarten Settlement," *Kindergarten Review* 19(November 1908):136–144.

48. The contrast is clear in Addams's essay, "The Subjective Necessity for Social Settlements" (1892), read at a conference of the Ethical Culture Society in Plymouth, Massachusetts in 1892 and printed as Chapter 6 of Addams, *Twenty Years at Hull-House*. See also Addams, "A New Impulse to an Old Gospel," *Forum* 14(November 1892):345–358. Addams, *Democracy and Social Ethics* (New York: Macmillan Co., 1902), p. 180.

49. Addams, *Twenty Years at Hull-House* (n. 46 above), p. 86. Hofer (n. 26 above), in *Kindergarten Magazine* 8(September 1895):47–59.

CHAPTER 7 (PP. 107–129)

1. G. Stanley Hall, "The Contents of Children's Minds," *Princeton Review* 11(May 1883):249–272; reprinted in *Pedagogical Seminary* 1 (June 1891):139–173 and in Hall's popular collection of essays, *Aspects of Child Life in Education*, ed. Theodate L. Smith (Boston: Ginn and Co., 1907), pp. 1–52. Dorothy Ross, *G. Stanley Hall: The Psychologist as Prophet*

(Chicago: University of Chicago Press, 1972), p. 122. Hall, "Child Study as a Basis for Psychology and Psychological Teaching," National Education Association (NEA), *Addresses and Proceedings* (1893):173–179.

2. For a discussion of natural education see *Health, Growth, and Heredity: G. Stanley Hall on Natural Education*, eds. Charles E. Strickland and Charles Burgess (New York: Teachers College Press, Columbia University, 1965), and Dominick Cavallo, *Muscles and Morals: Organized Playgrounds and Urban Reform, 1880–1920* (Philadelphia: University of Pennsylvania Press, 1981), pp. 53, 55–65.

3. Hall, "The Contents of Children's Minds," *Pedagogical Seminary* 1(June 1891):139–173.

4. Hall, *Life and Confessions of a Psychologist* (New York and London: D. Appleton and Co., 1924), pp. 42, 149, 200.

5. Ibid., pp. 132, 497. Ross (n. 1 above), pp. 45, 56, 106.

6. Thomas Haskell, *The Emergence of Professional Social Science* (Urbana: University of Illinois Press, 1977), pp. 141–143. See Harris's annotations in Emily Talbot, ed., *Papers on Infant Development* (Boston: Tolman and White, 1882), pp. 5–6, in his personal copy in the John D. Rockefeller Library, Brown University, Providence, Rhode Island.

7. John Fiske, *The Meaning of Infancy* (Boston: Houghton Mifflin Co., 1909), which contains reprints of Fiske's earlier essays on childhood: "The Meaning of Infancy" from *Excursions of an Evolutionist* and "The Part Played by Infancy in the Evolution of Man" from *A Century of Science.*

8. Wayne Dennis, "Historical Beginnings of Child Psychology," *Psychological Bulletin* 46(May 1949):224–235.

9. Hall, "Introduction" in Wilhelm Preyer, *The Mental Development of the Child*, trans. H. W. Brown (New York: D. Appleton and Co., 1893), p. xxv. Harris's comments appear as marginal annotations in his personal copy of Preyer's book in the John D. Rockefeller Library, Brown University, Providence, Rhode Island.

10. For a more complete study of "recapitulation" see: Charles E. Strickland, "The Child and the Race: The Doctrines of Recapitulation and Culture Epochs in the Rise of the Child-Centered Ideal in American Educational Thought, 1875–1900" (Ph.D. dissertation, University of Wisconsin, 1963). Ross (n. 1 above), pp. 129–131. Wilbur H. Dutton, "The Child-Study Movement in America from Its Origin (1880) to the Organization of the Progressive Education Association (1920)" (Ph.D. dissertation, Stanford University, 1945). Sara Wiltse, "A Preliminary Sketch of the History of Child Study in America," *Pedagogical Seminary* 3(October 1895):182–212. Cavallo (n. 2 above), pp. 55–60.

11. *Pedagogical Seminary* 1(January 1891). "The Plan and Purpose of the Illinois Society for Child-Study," Illinois Society for Child-Study, *Transactions*, vol. 1, no. 2(1895):5–9.

12. Ross (n. 1 above), pp. 281–282. Wiltse (n. 10 above), pp. 189–212.

13. Hall, "Child Study and Its Relation to Education," reprinted in Strickland and Burgess, eds. (n. 2 above), pp. 78–79.

14. Hall, "Kindergarten Syllabus," *Topical Syllabi, Clark University, 1894–99*, Archives, Clark University, Worcester, Massachusetts (hereafter CUA) and Patty Smith Hill's personal copy, Patty Smith Hill Papers, Filson Club, Louisville, Kentucky.

15. William H. Burnham, "Child Study as the Basis of Pedagogy," NEA, *Addresses and Proceedings* (1893):719. Hall, "Psychological Education," *American Journal of Insanity* 52(1896):228–229.

16. Hall, "Child Study in Summer Schools: President G. Stanley Hall," University of the State of New York, *Regents Bulletin*, no. 28(July 1894):333–336, contained in Hall, *Collected Works*, vol. 4, CUA.

17. See E. W. Scripture, "Methods of Laboratory Mind Study," U.S. Bureau of Education, *Report 1892–1893*:378–382, and Abraham Aaron Roback, "The Psychological Laboratory Comes to America," in his *History of American Psychology* (New York: Library Publishers, 1952). Unsigned letter (G. Stanley Hall?), February 17, 1892; Charles McMurry to Louis N. Wilson, February 7, 1893; Earl Barnes to Louis N. Wilson, February 17, 1893: Clark University Summer School Papers, 1892–1893, CUA.

18. "Summer School of Psychology, Biology, Pedagogy, and Anthropology" (1896), in bound volume *Summer School Circulars*, CUA.

19. Patty Smith Hill to Hall, March 21, 1895, Hall Papers, CUA. Register (1894), Clark University Summer School Papers, 1892–1898, CUA.

20. Blow to Harris, June 21, 1896, William Torrey Harris Papers, Missouri Historical Society (MHS), Saint Louis, Missouri.

21. Haskell (n. 6 above), pp. 141–143.

22. Blow to Harris, January 31, 1893, Harris Papers, MHS.

23. Susan E. Blow, *Symbolic Education: A Commentary on Froebel's "Mother Play"* (New York: D. Appleton and Co., 1894), pp. 35, 53, 116, 127, 182. Blow to Harris, October 16, 1891; September 20, 1891; January 12, 1895; March 3, 1896, and May 17, 1896: Harris Papers, MHS. James Jackson Putnam, *James Jackson Putnam and Psychoanalysis*, ed. Nathan G. Hale, Jr. (Cambridge: Harvard University Press, 1971), pp. 20–21, 49–51.

24. Blow to Harris, July 2, 1894; September 9, 1894; June 21, 1896; June 12, 1896; July 29, 1896: Harris Papers, MHS.

25. William Torrey Harris, "The Old Psychology versus the New," in A. Tolman Smith, "The Psychological Revival," U.S. Bureau of Education, *Report 1893–1894* 1:433–437.

26. Harris, *Psychologic Foundations of Education* (New York: D. Appleton and Co., 1898), pp. 3–5.

27. "The Cazenovia Conference," *Kindergarten News* 4(September 1894):215.

28. Harris, *Psychologic Foundations* (n. 26 above), pp. 112–115.

29. "The Cazenovia Conference" (n. 27 above), p. 215. Blow to Harris, September 9, 1894, Harris Papers, MHS.

30. Blow to Harris, July 29, 1896, Harris Papers, MHS.

31. Blow to Harris, June 12, 1896, Harris Papers, MHS.

32. Blow to Harris, April 19, 1896; October 15, 1897: Harris Papers, MHS.

33. Blow to Harris, June 21, 1896, Harris Papers, MHS.

34. Patty Smith Hill, Address to the International Kindergarten Union (IKU), 1897, typescript, Patty Smith Hill Papers, Filson Club, Louisville, Kentucky. "Report of the Child Study Committee," International Kindergarten Union, *Proceedings* (1896).

35. Caroline T. Haven, "Changes in Kindergarten Material," *Kindergarten Review* 9(March 1899):412.

36. Sara E. Wiltse, "Child Study Up to Date," NEA, *Addresses and Proceedings* (1897):837–843. "Department of Kindergarten Education," NEA, *Addresses and Proceedings*(1897):584–613. Hall, "Psychological Education" (n. 15 above), pp. 228–229.

37. Louis N. Wilson, comp., "List of Degrees Granted at Clark University and Clark College, 1899–1920," in *Publications of the Clark University Library*, vol. 6, no. 3 (December 1920), CUA. Frederic Burk, "From Fundamental to Accessory in the Development of the Nervous System and of Movements," *Pedagogical Seminary* 6(October 1898):5–64. Frederick Eby, "The Reconstruction of the Kindergarten," *Pedagogical Seminary* 7(July 1900):229–286.

38. Burk, "The Kindergarten Child Physically," NEA, *Addresses and Proceedings* (1899):570–574.

39. Frederic Burk and Caroline Frear Burk, *A Study of the Kindergarten Problem in the Public Kindergartens of Santa Barbara, California, for the Year 1898–9* (San Francisco: Whitaker and Ray Co., 1899), pp. 16–21, 45, 56, 80.

40. Susan E. Blow, *Educational Issues in the Kindergarten* (New York: D. Appleton and Co., 1908), pp. 161, 162.

41. Ibid., pp. 167–168.

42. Blow to Harris, August 6, 1891; August 29, 1891; September 20, 1891; October 16, 1891; February 6, 1891; November 11, 1891: Harris Papers, MHS.

43. Blow to Harris, January 31, 1893, Harris Papers, MHS. Harris, "Editor's Preface" to Blow, *Symbolic Education* (n. 23 above), p. xii.

44. Hall, "Some Defects in the Kindergarten in America," *Forum* 28(January 1900):579–591. Blow to Harris, August 5, 1899, Harris Papers, MHS.

45. Hall (n. 44 above), pp. 579–591.

46. Hall's final comments on the child-study and kindergarten movements are contained in "The Pedagogy of the Kindergarten," Chapter 6 in Hall, *Educational Problems*, 2 vols. (New York and London: D. Appleton and Co., 1911). Blow's position is contained in *Educational Issues in the Kindergarten* (n. 40 above).

47. Hugo Münsterberg, "Psychology and Education," *Educational Review* 16(September 1898):105–132.

48. Nicholas Murray Butler, "Editorial," *Educational Review* 12(November 1896):411–413. William James, *Talks to Teachers on Psychology: And to Students on Some of Life's Ideals* (New York: Henry Holt and Co., 1899). See also Edward Lee Thorndike, *Notes on Child Study* (New York: Macmillan Co., 1901).

49. John Dewey, "The Kindergarten and Child Study," NEA, *Addresses and Proceedings* (1897):585–586. Dewey, "Criticisms Wise and Otherwise on Modern Child Study," NEA, *Addresses and Proceedings* (1897):867–868.

50. Dewey, "Play and Imagination in Relation to Early Education," in "The School of Psychology Held in Chicago during April, 1899," *Kindergarten Review* 9(May 1899):603. See also: Dewey, "Results of Child Study Applied to Education," Illinois Society for Child Study, *Transactions* 1(January 1895):18–19. Dewey, "Interpretation of the Culture Epoch Theory," National Herbart Society, *Second Yearbook* (1896):89–95.

51. "The School of Psychology Held in Chicago during April 1899," *Kindergarten Magazine* (May and June 1899):636–642.

52. "The School of Psychology" (n. 51 above), 636–642.

Chapter 8 (pp. 131–50)

1. Jacob Riis, "The Children of the Poor," in *Jacob Riis Revisited*, ed. Francesco Cordasco (New York: Doubleday Anchor Books, 1960), p. 114.

2. U.S. Bureau of Education, *Report 1898–99*, vol. 2, p. 2257. Nina C. Vandewalker, *The Kindergarten in American Education* (New York: Macmillan Co., 1908), pp. 56–58, 66. Providence Free Kindergarten Association, *Records 1894–1912* (see entry for April 16, 1896), Rhode Island Historical Society, Providence, Rhode Island.

3. Sarah Cooper to Harriet Skilton, July 21, 1890; October 25, 1893: Julius A. Skilton Papers, Cornell University Archives. Vandewalker (n. 2 above), pp. 184–187. Cincinnati Kindergarten Association, *Report* (1887), p. 7.

4. "New York Kindergarten Association," *Kindergarten Review* 17(April 1907):461–471. "Editorial Notes," *Kindergarten Magazine* (September 1892). *New York Times*, March 13, 1895; March 15, 1895; March 17, 1895.

5. Cincinnati Kindergarten Association, *Report* (1890/1891), p. 11. *Notable American Women, 1607–1950* (3 vols., Cambridge: Harvard University Press, 1971) 2:122–123. Susan Blow to Fanniebelle Curtis, undated, Association for Childhood Education International (ACEI) Archives, Washington, D.C. Stella Wood, "The Kindergartner as a Business Woman," *Kindergarten Review* 22(September 1911):16–19.

6. "New York Kindergarten Association" (n. 4 above), pp. 461–471. Cincinnati Kindergarten Association, *Report* (1887), p. 15.

7. David B. Tyack, *The One Best System: A History of American Urban Education* (Cambridge: Harvard University Press, 1974), pp. 133, 139.

8. Hamilton W. Mabie, "The Free Kindergarten," *Harper's Magazine* 111(October 1905):649–657. Frank B. Vrooman, "Child Life and the Kindergarten," *Arena* 13(1895):292–302.

9. Joseph Mayer Rice, *The Public School System in the United States* (New York: Century Co., 1893; reprint ed., New York: Arno Press), p. 99.

10. Ibid., p. 168.

11. Sarah Cooper to Phoebe Hearst, April 4, 1893, Phoebe Apperson Hearst Papers, Bancroft Library, University of California, Berkeley, California.

12. Chicago Education Commission, *Report of the Education Commission of the City of Chicago by the Mayor, Honorable Carter H. Harrison* (Chicago: R. R. Donnelley and Sons Co., 1898), pp. xii–xiii. George H. Counts, *School and Society in Chicago* (New York: Harcourt, Brace and Co., 1928), p. 38. Tyack (n. 7 above), p. 131.

13. Chicago Education Commission, *Report* (n. 12 above), sec. 4, art. 5, pp. 95–96.

14. Report of Elizabeth Harrison in Chicago Education Commission, *Report* (n. 12 above), pp. 192–193.

15. "The Cleveland Plan," Cleveland Board of Education, *Fifty-Eighth Report* (1894):89, 91; *Fifty-Ninth Report* (1895):66, 68.

16. Chicago Education Commission, *Report* (n. 12 above), pp. 192–193. U.S. Bureau of Education, *Bulletin* (1914) (Washington, D.C.: Government Printing Office, 1914), p. 100.

17. School Committee of Boston, *Annual Report* (1897):18–22; (1888):13. Fanny L. Johnson, "History of the Kindergarten Movement in Boston," *Kindergarten Review* 12(April 1902):478. Philadelphia Superintendent of Public Schools, *Annual Report* (1888):80. U.S. Bureau of Education, *Bulletin* (1926), no. 13, p. 13. See also Constance MacKenzie, *Free and Public Kindergartens in Philadelphia* (Philadelphia: n.p., 1899).

18. *History of the Chicago Public School Kindergartens*, pamphlet, National College of Education Archives, Evanston, Illinois.

19. Louise Schofield, *Kindergarten Legislation,* U.S. Bureau of Education, *Bulletin* (1916), no. 45; (1917), pp. 21–31.

20. National Kindergarten Association, *Report* (1909–1911):3–5, 27–28.

21. Nina Vandewalker, "Five Years of Progress," U.S. Bureau of Education, *Report 1913,* 1:147–156.

22. National Kindergarten Association, *Report* (1913):1, 7.

23. Lillian M. Clark, "Kindergarten Legislation in California," NEA, *Addresses and Proceedings* (1915):632–637. U.S. Bureau of Education, *Bulletin* (1916), no. 45, pp. 21–27. Mrs. H. N. Powell, "What the California Congress of Mothers Has Done for Kindergarten Legislation," NEA, *Addresses and Proceedings* (1915):631.

24. On the role of public school superintendent see Tyack (n. 7 above), p. 129. Philadelphia Superintendent of Public Schools, *Annual Report* (1888):80.

25. Carl Lester Byerly, "Contributions of William Torrey Harris to Public School Administration" (Ph.D. dissertation, University of Chicago, 1946), pp. 38–63. William Torrey Harris, "The Kindergarten in the Public School System," *Journal of Education* 30(December 1881):625–642.

26. Tyack (n. 7 above), pp. 134–136. Harris, "City School Supervision," *Educational Review* 3(February 1892):167–172.

27. Tyack (n. 7 above), p. 134.

28. See Marvin Lazerson, *Origins of the Urban School* (Cambridge: Harvard University Press, 1971). "Why Should the Kindergarten Be Municipalized?" *Kindergarten Magazine* 9(March 1897):507.

29. Philadelphia Superintendent of Public Schools, *Annual Report* (1888):90. MacKenzie (n. 17 above), pp. 24, 30.

30. Almira M. Winchester, *Kindergarten Supervision in City Schools*, U.S. Bureau of Education, *Bulletin* (1918), no. 38, p. 8.

31. Saint Louis Board of Education, *Annual Report* (1879–1880):155–157. Blow to Mrs. Henry Hitchcock, April 15, 1890, Saint Louis Public Library. U.S. Bureau of Education, *Bulletin* (1926), no. 38, p. 34.

32. Winchester (n. 30 above), p. 45.

33. Tyack (n. 7 above), p. 59. Vandewalker, "The Curriculum and Methods of the Kindergarten Training School," *Kindergarten Review* 13(June 1903):643.

34. Patty Smith Hill, "Some Conservative and Progressive Phases of Kindergarten Education," National Society for the Systematic Study of Education (NSSE), *Sixth Yearbook* (1907), pt. 2:83 (Bloomington, Ill.: Public School Publishing Co., 1907).

35. Winchester (n. 30 above), pp. 8, 9, 24, 30, 46.
36. Los Angeles Board of Education, *Annual Report* (1898–1899):106. Fanniebelle Curtis, "Report of the Kindergartens: Boroughs of Brooklyn and Queens," New York City Superintendent of Schools, *Eighth Annual Report* (1906):305–306. Julia S. Bothwell, "Kindergartens," *Cincinnati Public Schools Annual Report* (1911–1912):77–81. MacKenzie (n. 17 above), pp. 10, 36.
37. Los Angeles Board of Education, *Annual Report* (1898–1899):106. MacKenzie (n. 17 above), pp. 10, 36. Fanniebelle Curtis, "Mothers' Meetings in Public School Kindergartens," *Kindergarten Magazine* 12(November 1899):161.
38. Lazerson (n. 28 above), pp. 130, 133.
39. *Kindergartens in the United States: Statistics and Present Problems*, in U.S. Bureau of Education, *Bulletin* (1914), p. 99. Luella Palmer, *Adjustment between Kindergarten and First Grade*, U.S. Bureau of Education, *Bulletin* (1915), no. 24, p. 25. Chicago Board of Education, *Forty-Eighth Annual Report* (1902):64.
40. MacKenzie (n. 17 above), p. 25.
41. MacKenzie (n. 17 above), pp. 25, 32. Chicago Board of Education (n. 39 above), pp. 63–64. Colorado Superintendent of Instruction, *Tenth Annual Report* (1896):406. *Kindergartens in the United States* (see n. 39 above), pp. 19–53. Palmer (n. 39 above), p. 22.
42. Joanna A. Hannah, *The Relation of the Director and Assistant in the Kindergarten*, U.S. Bureau of Education, *Bulletin* (1914), no. 6, pp. 120–121.
43. *Kindergartens in the United States* (n. 39 above), p. 101.
44. Connecticut Board of Education, *Annual Report* (1890):388–389.
45. *Kindergarten Review* 13(April 1903):519. Philadelphia Superintendent of Public Schools, *Annual Report* (1888):87. See also Willard S. Elsbree, *The American Teacher: Evolution of a Profession in a Democracy* (New York: American Book Co., 1939).
46. See Benjamin W. Frazier, *History of Professional Education of Teachers in the United States*, U.S. Bureau of Education, *Bulletin* (1933), no. 5, pt. 1.
47. Philadelphia Superintendent of Public Schools, *Annual Report* (1888):87.
48. Cincinnati Kindergarten Association, *Report* (1914/1915).
49. Nina C. Vandewalker, *The Standardizing of Kindergarten Training*, U.S. Bureau of Education, *Bulletin* (1914), no. 6, pp. 114–118. Vandewalker (n. 33 above), p. 644.
50. Blow to Elizabeth Harrison, May 16, 1893, National College of Education Archives, Evanston, Ill. Blow to Harris, September 15, 1899, Harris Papers, MHS.
51. MacKenzie (n. 17 above), p. 32. Marion Hamilton Carter, "The Kindergarten Child—After the Kindergarten," *Atlantic Monthly* 83(March 1899):358–366. *Kindergartens in the United States* (n. 39 above), p. 98.
52. MacKenzie (n. 17 above), p. 13.

Chapter 9 (pp. 151–70)

1. Selim H. Peabody, "The Educational Exhibit at the Columbian Exposition," National Education Association (NEA), *Addresses and Proceedings* (1894):60–66. John Eaton, "The Exhibit of Education at the Columbia Exposition," NEA, *Addresses and Proceedings* (1894):515–526. Susan Blow to William T. Harris, June 28, 1893, Harris Papers, Missouri Historical Society (MHS), Saint Louis, Missouri.
2. Blow to Harris, June 13, 1893; June 28, 1893: Harris Papers, MHS.
3. See Richard J. Storr, *Harper's University: The Beginnings* (Chicago: University of Chicago Press, 1966). Richard Whittemore, *Nicholas Murray Butler and Public Education, 1862–1911* (New York: Teachers College Press, Columbia University, 1970), pp. 28–38.
4. Whittemore (n. 3 above), pp. 16–27. Hugh Hawkins, *Between Harvard and America: The Educational Leadership of Charles W. Eliot* (New York: Oxford University Press, 1972). Roberta Frankfort, *Collegiate Women* (New York: New York University Press, 1977), p. 90.
5. Hawkins (n. 4 above), pp. 224–262. Lawrence A. Cremin, David A. Shannon, and Mary E. Townsend, *A History of Teachers College, Columbia University* (New York: Columbia Uni-

versity Press, 1954), pp. 12–14. See also Ellen Condliffe Lagemann, *A Generation of Women: Education in the Lives of Progressive Reformers* (Cambridge: Harvard University Press, 1979). Emily Huntington, *The Kitchen Garden* (New York: Trow Printing Co., 1878), p. 9, quoted in Whittemore (n. 3 above).

6. Nicholas Murray Butler, "Some Criticisms of the Kindergarten," *Educational Review* 18(1899):291. Charles W. Eliot, "The Improvements which the Kindergarten Has Suggested in Higher Departments of Instruction," *Kindergarten Review* 12(June 1902):592. Minnie H. Glidden, "Kindergarten Methods in Higher Education," *Education* 18(October 1897):83–94.

7. David B. Tyack, *The One Best System* (Cambridge: Harvard University Press, 1974), pp. 124–140. Butler, "The Meaning of Infancy and Education," *Kindergarten Review* 10(October 1899):459–466.

8. George W. Luckey, *The Professional Training of Secondary Teachers in the United States* (New York: Macmillan Co., 1903), pp. 116, 125–127, 150.

9. George Dykhuizen, *The Life and Mind of John Dewey* (Carbondale: Southern Illinois University Press, 1973), pp. 1–3, 83. John Dewey to William Rainey Harper, February 15, 1894, The President's Papers, University of Chicago Archives (hereafter UCA), Chicago.

10. Robert L. McCaul, "Dewey's Chicago," *School Review* 67(Summer 1959):258–280. McCaul, "Dewey and the University of Chicago," *School and Society* 39(March 1961):152–157. Blow to Harris, September 15, 1893, Harris Papers, MHS. John Dewey, "Froebel's Educational Principles," *Elementary School Record* 5(June 1900):fn., 149–150.

11. Storr (n. 3 above), pp. 94, 96, 134. McCaul, "Dewey's Chicago" (n. 10 above), pp. 258–280. Dewey to Flora Cooke, November 18, 1896; March 4, 1897: Flora Cooke Papers, Chicago Historical Society, Chicago.

12. "The Kindergarten Conference," *University Record* 2(May 1897):49–53.

13. Dewey, "Some Points in Froebel's Psychology," reported in "The Kindergarten Conference" (n. 12 above), pp. 49–53.

14. Dewey, "George Herbert Mead as I Knew Him," *University of Chicago Record* 17(1931):173–177. George Herbert Mead, "The Relation of Play to Education," *University Record* 1(May 1896):141–145. See also Mead, "The Child and His Environment," Illinois Society for Child Study, *Transactions* 3(April 1898):1–11.

15. Mead, "The Relation of Play to Education" (n. 14 above), p. 145.

16. Dewey, *Moral Principles in Education* (Boston: Houghton Mifflin Co., 1909), p. 13.

17. Irving King, *The Psychology of Child Development, with an Introduction by John Dewey* (Chicago: University of Chicago Press, 1904), pp. 215, 244.

18. Dewey, "Plan of the Organization of the University Primary School," in *John Dewey: The Early Works, 1882–1898*, ed. Jo Ann Boydston (Carbondale: Southern Illinois University Press, 1967–1972), vol. 5, pp. 224–241. Dewey to Harper, December 5, 1897; December 6, 1897: President's Papers, UCA.

19. Dewey to Harper, December 9, 1896, President's Papers, UCA. Dewey, *The School and Society* (Chicago: University of Chicago Press, 1899; reprint edition, Chicago: University of Chicago Press, 1971), pp. 65, 75. Dewey, *Lectures in the Philosophy of Education, 1899,* pp. 162–163.

20. Dykhuizen, (n. 9 above), p. 95. Dewey, *The School and Society* (n. 19 above), pp. 67, 75. Dewey, *Lectures in the Philosophy of Education* (n. 19 above), pp. 162–163.

21. Dewey, "Froebel's Educational Principles" (n. 10 above), pp. 143–144. See also Dewey, *The School and Society* (n. 19 above), pp. 116–131.

22. See Frederic Burk and Caroline Frear Burk, *A Study of the Kindergarten Problem* (San Francisco: Whitaker and Ray Co., 1899). Georgia P. Scates, "The Subprimary (Kindergarten) Department," *Elementary School Record* 1(June 1900):129.

23. Dewey, "Froebel's Educational Principles" (n. 10 above), p. 143.

24. Scates (n. 22 above), pp. 137–139.

25. Dewey, "Froebel's Educational Principles" (n. 10 above), pp. 144–145. Dewey, *The School and Society* (n. 19 above), pp. 132–138.

26. Dewey, *The School and Society* (n. 19 above), p. 124.

27. Ibid., p. 60. Cremin et al. (n. 5 above), pp. 12–13.

28. Cremin, *The Transformation of the School: Progressivism in American Education, 1876–1957* (New York: Alfred A. Knopf, 1961), p. 24.
29. Frank M. McMurry, "Controlling Ideas in Curriculum of Kindergarten and Elementary School," *Teachers College Record* 3(November 1902):305–321.
30. James Russell, "The Function of the University in the Training of Teachers," *Teachers College Record* 1(January 1900):10.
31. Russell, "The Purpose of the Speyer School," *Teachers College Record* 3(November 1902):261–265. Jesse D. Burks, "History of the Speyer School," *Teachers College Record* 3(November 1902):266–272. Charlotte M. Jammer, "Patty Smith Hill and the Reform of the American Kindergarten" (Ed.D. progress report, Columbia University, 1960), pp. 136–139.
32. Russell, "The Organization and Administration of Teachers College," *Teachers College Record* 1(January 1900):49–50. Teachers College, Columbia University, *Dean's Report* (1901).
33. E. L. Thorndike, "Notes on Psychology for Kindergartners," *Teachers College Record* 4(1903):377–408.
34. Russell to Hill, November 10, 1904, Patty Smith Hill Papers, Filson Club, Louisville, Kentucky.
35. Jammer (n. 31 above). See also Beulah Amidou, "Forty Years in Kindergarten: An Interview with Patty Smith Hill," *Survey Graphic* 7(September 1927):506–509, 523.
36. Russell, *Founding Teachers College: Reminiscences of the Dean Emeritus* (New York: Teachers College Press, Columbia University, 1937), pp. 61–62. Russell, "The Kindergarten Outlook," *Teachers College Record* (November 1904):407–411. Blow to Harris, April 19, 1898; April 3, 1905: Harris Papers, MHS.
37. Jammer (n. 31 above), p. 104. See also Teachers College, Columbia University, *Announcements* (1902–1918), Teachers College Library, Columbia University, New York.
38. Jammer (n. 31 above), pp. 114–116. Blow, *Educational Issues in the Kindergarten* (New York: D. Appleton and Co., 1903), pp. 2–7, 150–153, 226–230, 281.
39. See Isle Forrest, "Patty Smith Hill: A Biographical Account by One of Her Students," MS 105, Teachers College Library. Blow to Fanniebelle Curtis, June 15, 1908, and undated, Association for Childhood Education International (ACEI) Archives, Washington, D.C. See also Blow to Harris, March 2, 1906; April 30, 1905: Harris Papers, MHS.
40. Blow to Curtis, undated (1906?), ACEI Archives, Washington, D.C. Frankfort (n. 4 above), pp. 104–110.
41. Blow to Harris, March 27, 1905; April 30, 1905: Harris Papers, MHS.
42. Blow to Harris, May 5, 1905, Harris Papers, MHS, which also contain a typescript of Harris's comments to James Russell dated May 1, 1905.
43. Russell to Hill, February 2, 1905, Patty Smith Hill Papers, Filson Club, Louisville, Kentucky.
44. John Angus MacVannel to Patty Smith Hill, January 2, 1906, Patty Smith Hill Papers, Filson Club, Louisville, Kentucky. Blow to Curtis, undated (1906?), ACEI Archives, Washington, D.C.
45. MacVannel to Hill, January 2, 1906, Patty Smith Hill Papers, Filson Club, Louisville, Kentucky. Blow to Curtis, undated (n. 44 above).
46. Blow to Curtis, February 13, 1906, ACEI Archives, Washington, D.C. See also Blow to Harris, June 24, 1909, Harris Papers, MHS. Nina Vandewalker, *The Kindergarten in American Education* (New York: Macmillan Co., 1908), p. 201.
47. "Department of Lower Primary (Kindergarten-Primary) Education," MS report to Dean Russell from Patty Smith Hill, Patty Smith Hill Papers, Filson Club, Louisville, Kentucky.

Chapter 10 (pp. 171–91)

1. Herbert Croly, *The Promise of American Life* (New York: E. P. Dutton and Co., 1963), p. 401. Ida Van Stone, "Introduction," National Society for the [Scientific] Study of Education (NSSE), *Sixth Yearbook* (1907), pt. 2:9 (Bloomington, Ill.: Public School Publishing Co., 1907).

2. Nina C. Vandewalker, "Some Conservative and Progressive Phases of Kindergarten Education," NSSE, *Sixth Yearbook* (1907), pt. 2:115. "Statistics of Public Kindergartens," U.S. Bureau of Education, *Report 1907*, p. 115. Vandewalker, "Five Years of Kindergarten Progress," U.S. Bureau of Education, *Report 1911*, vol. 1, pp. 146–156.

3. See Nathan G. Hale, *Freud and the Americans: The Beginnings of Psychoanalysis in America, 1876–1917* (New York: Oxford University Press, 1971).

4. Vandewalker, *The Kindergarten in American Education* (New York: Macmillan Co., 1908), pp. 129–136. Caroline T. Haven, "The International Kindergarten Union—Why It Was Organized," IKU, *Proceedings of the Fifteenth Annual Meeting* (1908):115–119.

5. Evelyn Weber, *The Kindergarten: Its Encounter with Educational Thought in America* (New York: Teachers College Press, Columbia University, 1969), p. 67.

6. Comments of Earl Barnes in "Home Discipline," Round Table Discussion, IKU, *Proceedings* (1902):40–50.

7. Susan Blow to William T. Harris, May 16, 1904, William Torrey Harris Papers, Missouri Historical Society (MHS). "Report of the Committee of Nineteen (Materials and Methods)," IKU, *Proceedings* (1905):32–36.

8. Blow to Harris, April 1903; February 19, 1904: Harris Papers, MHS.

9. Blow to Harris, February 1, 1905, Harris Papers, MHS. Alice Temple, "Materials and Methods (Appendix)," IKU, *Proceedings* (1905):98–101.

10. Patty Smith Hill, "Materials and Methods (Appendix)," IKU, *Proceedings* (1905):71–80. See also Charlotte M. Jammer, "Patty Smith Hill and the Reform of the American Kindergarten" (Ed.D. progress report, Columbia University, 1960). Lucy Wheelock, "Report of the Committee of Nineteen," IKU, *Proceedings* (1908):45–49.

11. Blow to Harris, August 21, 1909, Harris Papers, MHS. Blow to James Jackson Putnam, November 14, 1909, James Jackson Putnam Papers, The Francis A. Countway Library of Medicine, Boston, Massachusetts. See also James Jackson Putnam, *James Jackson Putnam and Psychoanalysis* (Cambridge: Harvard University Press, 1971).

12. Blow to Harris, October 19, 1909, Harris Papers, MHS. Blow to Putnam, March 11, 1910, Putnam Papers (see n. 11 above).

13. Blow to Putnam, November 14, 1909; November 24, 1909; June 10, 1909: Putnam Papers (see n. 11 above).

14. Blow to Putnam, November 14, 1909, Putnam Papers (see n. 11 above).

15. "Conservative Report," IKU, *Proceedings* (1910):116–123, later republished as Susan Blow, "First Report," in *The Kindergarten: Reports of the Committee of Nineteen on the Theory and Practice of the Kindergarten* (New York: Houghton Mifflin, 1913), pp. 68, 91–92.

16. Blow, *First Report*, pp. 81–82.

17. Putnam, "On Freud's Psycho-Analytic Method and Its Evolution," in Putnam, ed., *Addresses on Psycho-Analysis* (London, Vienna, and New York: International Psychoanalytical Press, 1921), p. 110. Putnam, "Services to Be Expected from the Psycho-Analytic Movement in the Prevention of Insanity," in Putnam, ed., *Addresses on Psycho-Analysis*, pp. fn. 202, 295. Blow to Putnam, August 21, 1912, Putnam Papers (see n. 11 above).

18. Blow to Putnam, June 26, 1910, Putnam Papers (see n. 11 above).

19. Weber (n. 5 above), p. 74. Elizabeth Florence Ward, "The Montessori Method," *Kindergarten Review* (November 1912):143. See also her *The Montessori Method and the American School* (New York: Macmillan Co., 1913).

20. Weber (n. 5 above), p. 74. See also Elizabeth Harrison, *The Montessori Method and the Kindergarten*, U.S. Bureau of Education, *Bulletin* (1914), no. 28 (Washington, D.C.: Government Printing Office, 1914). Blow to Fanniebelle Curtis, August 13, 1912 and December 28, 1912, Association for Child Education International (ACEI), Archives.

21. "Aspects of the First Three Gifts and Some Montessori Materials," *Kindergarten Review* 23(September 1912):73–79. Henry W. Holmes, "Promising Points in the Montessori System, *Kindergarten Review* (April 1913):481–486.

22. Weber (n. 5 above), pp. 75–76.

23. William H. Kilpatrick, "Montessori and Froebel," *Kindergarten Review* 23(April 1913):491–496. See also Earl Barnes, "Comparison of Froebelian and Montessori Methods and Principles," *Kindergarten Review* (April 1913):487–490.

24. See *The Kindergarten: Reports of the Committee of Nineteen* (n. 15 above),
25. "Views of the Liberal Kindergartners of the Committee of Nineteen," IKU, *Proceedings* (1910):123–132, republished as the "Second Report," in *The Kindergarten* (n. 15 above), pp. 231–294.
26. "Second Report," pp. 231–294.
27. Beulah Amidou, "Forty Years in the Kindergarten: An Interview with Patty Smith Hill," *Survey Graphic* (September 1927):506–509.
28. "Liberal Conservative Report," IKU, *Proceedings* (1910):132–137, republished as the "Third Report," in *The Kindergarten* (n. 15 above), pp. 295–301.
29. Blow, "First Report" (n. 15 above), pp. 1–230.
30. Blow to Putnam, August 21, 1912, Putnam Papers (see n. 11 above).
31. Blow, *Educational Issues in the Kindergarten* (New York: D. Appleton and Co., 1908), pp. 146, 150–189; "Author's Preface," p. xiii. Patty Smith Hill, "Susan Blow: The Woman," typescript, Patty Smith Hill Papers, Filson Club, Louisville, Kentucky.
32. Agnes Snyder, *Dauntless Women in Childhood Education, 1836–1931* (Washington, D.C.: Association for Childhood Education International, 1972), pp. 63–65, 70. Blow to Kate Douglas Wiggin, undated, ACEI Archives. See also Blow (n. 31 above), p. 6.
33. Blow to Harris, March 3, 1908, Harris Papers, MHS. Blow to Curtis, October 9, 1908, ACEI Archives. Blow to Putnam, April 10, 1914, Putnam Papers (see n. 11 above).
34. Blow, "Author's Preface" (n. 31 above), pp. xi–xiv.
35. IKU, *Proceedings* (1912):77. Almira Winchester, *Kindergarten Education*, U.S. Bureau of Education, *Bulletin* (1918), no. 49, p. 3.
36. Elizabeth Harrison, "What Has This Great War to Teach Us?" typescript of an address delivered to the Chicago Kindergarten College, September 15, 1914, National College of Education Archives, Evanston, Illinois.
37. Randolph S. Bourne, *War and the Intellectuals, Collected Essays 1915–1919*, edited with an introduction by Carl Resek (New York: Harper and Row, 1964), pp. 48–52.
38. Blow to Putnam, October 20, 1915, Putnam Papers (see n. 11 above).
39. Bourne (n. 37 above), pp. 56, 74.
40. Blow to Putnam, October 15, 1915; January 7, 1916; February 3, 1916: Putnam Papers (see n. 11 above). Obituary notice for Susan Blow by James J. Putnam, *Boston Transcript*, March 28, 1916.
41. John Dewey, *Democracy and Education: An Introduction to the Philosophy of Education* (New York: Macmillan Co., 1916; reprint ed., New York: Free Press, 1966), pp. 98–99.
42. IKU, *Proceedings* (1919):90.
43. Henry Neumann, "What Can the Kindergarten Do for Democracy?" IKU, *Proceedings* (1918):129–137.
44. Ibid. Winchester (n. 35 above), p. 7.
45. Alice Temple and Catherine R. Watkins, "Is It Advisable to Change the Name of the Kindergarten?" IKU, *Proceedings* (1919):148–159.
46. Elizabeth Harrison, "Women's Role in the War," speech delivered before the National Kindergarten Association, March 19, 1918, typescript in the National College of Education Archives.
47. "Report of the Committee of Nineteen," IKU, *Proceedings* (1918):81–84; (1919):78–80.
48. Winchester (n. 35 above), p. 6.
49. Report of the Committee of Nineteen," IKU, *Proceedings* (1919). Winchester (n. 35 above).
50. IKU, *Proceedings* (1917):129–131. Rachel Clark Neumann, *Two Years in the Kindergarten Unit in France, 1919–1921* (privately published), ACEI Archives.
51. Julia Wade Abbott, "The Kindergarten Situation Today," IKU, *Proceedings* (1920):127–132.
52. Snyder (n. 32 above), pp. 345–352, 365.

A Note on Manuscript Sources

The search for manuscript material relating to the kindergarten movement in America confirmed two of my earliest suspicions. First, the movement attracted a diverse following, hence the records would be found in a wide variety of depositories. Second, the kindergarten movement was national in scope, hence the records would be scattered over a wide geographic area. A lengthy bibliographic essay that discusses this material and gives fuller documentation can be found in Michael S. Shapiro, "Froebel in America: A Social and Intellectual History of the Kindergarten Movement, 1848–1918" (Ph.D. dissertation, Brown University, 1980); copies are available at the John D. Rockefeller Library, Brown University, Providence, Rhode Island, or through University Microfilms, Ann Arbor, Michigan. In conducting research for this book, I have visited or used the following archives and libraries:

Jane Addams Memorial Collection and the Hull House Association Papers, Hull House, Chicago.

Blow Family Papers, Missouri Historical Society, Saint Louis.

Susan Blow Manuscript Essays and Lectures, Carol McDonald Rare Book Room, Saint Louis Public Library.

Chicago Institute Records, Special Collections, University of Chicago.

Chicago Women's Club Records, Chicago Historical Society.

Cincinnati Free Kindergarten Association Records, Cincinnati Historical Society.

Clark University Summer School Papers, Clark University Archives, Worcester, Massachusetts.

Flora Cooke Papers, Chicago Historical Society.

Sarah Ingersoll Cooper Papers, Cornell University Archives, Ithaca, New York.

Mary Crane Nursery League Papers, Manuscript Section, Chicago Circle Library, University of Illinois.

Ethical Humanist Society Papers, Manuscript Section, Chicago Circle Library, University of Illinois.

Grand Rapids Kindergarten Training School Records, Michigan Historical Collections, University of Michigan, Ann Arbor.

G. Stanley Hall Papers, Clark University Archives, Worcester, Massachusetts.

William Torrey Harris Papers, Missouri Historical Society, Saint Louis.

William Torrey Harris Personal Library, John D. Rockefeller Library, Brown University, Providence, Rhode Island.

Elizabeth Harrison Papers, National College of Education Archives, Evanston, Illinois.

Phoebe Apperson Hearst Papers, Bancroft Library, University of California, Berkeley.

Patty Smith Hill Collection, Teachers College Library, Columbia University.

Patty Smith Hill Papers, Filson Club, Louisville, Kentucky.

Maria Kraus-Boelte Papers, Library of Congress.

Benjamin P. Mann Collection, Antioch College Library, Yellow Springs, Ohio.

National Congress of Parents and Teachers Papers, Manuscript Section, Chicago Circle Library, University of Illinois.

New England Women's Club Records, Arthur and Elizabeth Schlesinger Library on the History of Women in America, Cambridge, Massachusetts.

Francis W. Parker Papers, Special Collections, University of Chicago.

Elizabeth Palmer Peabody Papers, Arthur and Elizabeth Schlesinger Library on the History of Women in America.

President's Papers, Special Collections, University of Chicago.

Providence Free Kindergarten Association Papers, Rhode Island Historical Society.

James Jackson Putnam Papers, Francis A. Countway Library of Medicine.

Pauline Agassiz Shaw Papers, Arthur and Elizabeth Schlesinger Library on the History of Women in America.

Julius A. Skilton Papers, Cornell University Archives, Ithaca, New York.

Robert L. Straker Collection, Antioch College Library, Yellow Springs, Ohio.

William Howard Taft Family Papers, Library of Congress.

Lucy Wheelock Letters, Wheelock College Library, Boston, Massachusetts.

Index